Pursuing Consciousness

Other books by Peter Ralston
- *The Book of Not Knowing*
- *Zen Body-Being*
- *Ancient Wisdom, New Spirit*
- *Reflections of Being*
- *The Art of Effortless Power*
- *The Principles of Effortless Power*

Pursuing Consciousness

The Book of Enlightenment and Transformation

Peter Ralston

author of *The Book of Not Knowing*

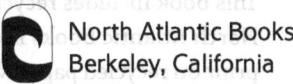

North Atlantic Books
Berkeley, California

TABLE OF CONTENTS

Introduction x

About Reading This Book xiii
   That Book xiii
   This Book xv

PART ONE: What Are We Dealing With?

CHAPTER ONE: Consciousness and Change 3
   Pursuing Self-Improvement 5
   Transformation versus Enlightenment 8
   Why Are We Motivated to Change? 12
   Four Unnoticed Traps 14
      Overlooked Trap #1: Positivity 14
      Overlooked Trap #2: Pretending 16
      Overlooked Trap #3: Confusion about
         "Being Ourselves" 18
      Overlooked Trap #4: Models Aren't True 20
   Confronting the Reality of Our Task 22

CHAPTER TWO: Self-Transformation 27
   What Is a Self? 27
   Confusing Self-Improvement with Transformation 30
   Manipulating Ourselves versus Changing Ourselves . . . 32
   How Transformation Relates to Consciousness
      and Enlightenment 35
   Bliss Is Not the Truth 39
   Grounding Our Pursuit 41

CHAPTER THREE: What Is and Isn't Enlightenment 43
   Clarifying Enlightenment—sort of 43
   The Challenge of the "Object"-ive Mind 46
   Being Trapped within Experience 50

Why Becoming Conscious Doesn't Always Create
  Change 54
Enlightenment and the Human Condition 58
The Absolute Is Beyond Distinctions 61

PART TWO: Getting Down to Work

CHAPTER FOUR: Setting the Stage for Transformation . 67
Letting Go Rather Than Attaining 67
Why Ideals Become Objectives for Transformation 73
Penetrating Your Core Experience..................... 75
Creating a Transformation Objective.................. 77
Clarifying Your Objective by Being Specific 82
Four Principles to Help Design an Objective 85
Divide and Conquer................................... 88

CHAPTER FIVE: Freeing Self from Object-Identity 91
The Usefulness of Feedback in Pursuing Consciousness.. 91
Becoming a Cloud—A Mental Exercise 92
Using Transformation to Pursue Consciousness 95
You Already Don't Exist 98

CHAPTER SIX: Mechanisms of Experience 104
Approaching Change................................. 104
Unseen Layers of Our Emotions 106
The Evolution of Emotion 108
The Sequence of Encounter 112
It's All about You 115
How the Self-Identity Creates "Perception" 119

CHAPTER SEVEN: Transforming Your Emotions 125
Emotional Dominance Revisited 125
Learning to Relate to Emotions Differently 127
Experiencing the Source of Your Emotions 130

Table of Contents

The Negative Building Blocks of Self-Identity 135
Relating to the Negative Building Blocks 142
Freedom from Emotions 144
Transcending Your "Real Self" 147

CHAPTER EIGHT: Predictable Pitfalls 150
Some Immediate Obstacles 150
Manipulation versus Communication 153
    Pre-Manipulation Communication 157
    Suppressing Internal States Anchors Them to Self... 162
Cheese Chasing 165
Orgy versus Attainment 168
Confronting the Reality of Change 172
More Misconceptions and Traps 174
    Madness Is Not Enlightenment 174
    An Acid Trip Is Not Enlightenment 175
    Don't Act Out or Suppress 175
    Avoid Dramatizing Discoveries 176
    Stay on Track 177

CHAPTER NINE: Transcending Your Life Story 179
Living as a Story 179
Experience Always Degrades into Concept 184
Life Story as Context 188
Giving Up Your Life Story 193

CHAPTER TEN: Breaking Free of Assumptions 199
The Closed Loop of Self-Referencing Perception 199
Revealing What's Invisible 203
How the Self Is, Is That the Self Is 206
It's a Problem of Identity 214

CHAPTER ELEVEN: Transforming 219
Dropping Preconceptions 219

Learning to Enjoy Suffering (or at least get through it) 221
Putting Away Childish Things 229
Creating a Practice 233
    Practicing Contemplation and Consciousness........ 233
    A Transformation Practice 236
The "Do It Now" Principle 243
Summary Review...................................... 245

PART THREE: The Absolute and Beyond

CHAPTER TWELVE: Enlightenment: Some Nothing from Which to Come................................ 249
The Opening Power of Enlightenment 249
The Need for Openness and Not-Knowing 256
The Koan of Now 259
The Overlay of Perception 265
The Siren of Experience 270

CHAPTER THIRTEEN: Approaching Absolutes 274
Absolute Mischief 274
Challenges of Understanding the Absolute........... 280
Life and Death 283
Completing Enlightenment........................... 287

CHAPTER FOURTEEN: Persisting and Maturing........ 290
Responsibility and Balance 290
    Responsibility 290
    Balance.. 293
    Balancing between Mind and Consciousness 296
The Principle of Joining 299
The Truth Transcends Negative and Positive 304
Intense Contemplation and Life...................... 307
Ask Consciousness 311
In Conclusion 314

INTRODUCTION

In the Introduction to *The Book of Not Knowing*, I shared a description of my first enlightenment experience. I hoped to inspire people, but also wanted to indicate that I was writing from a direct-consciousness of the subject matter and not a belief system, as it is never my intention to disseminate opinions or fantasies. That book is a meticulous discourse on the nature of the human condition, crafted with the lofty goal of revealing the foundations of the self and challenging them as unreal, often detrimental, and largely unnecessary.

Over the years I've encountered many sincere people who want to pursue a much deeper consciousness of themselves, life, and the nature of reality. It is a worthy yet extremely difficult undertaking because, as we saw in the six hundred pages of *Not Knowing*, there's not only a lot to tackle, but the dynamics and design loops inherent in a self make it very slippery to confront. Our cognizant minds are not designed to grasp the truth of our unrecognized foundations, nor the absolute nature of *anything*. As any Zen master would happily avoid explaining to you, intellect alone is insufficient for understanding the truth of these matters.

Limiting your investigation to intellectual understanding doesn't increase consciousness, nor does it allow you to confront overlooked assumptions and beliefs. While sustained contemplation will take any study deeper, during a few years with my consciousness apprentices I've noticed that the most fruitful efforts are simultaneously grounded in the pursuit of self-transformation. *The Book of Not Knowing* was designed to guide readers to an understanding of the nature of self, which is the foundation of this work. Here I present the possibility of transforming that self while also pursuing enlightenment.

These two efforts to pursue consciousness are quite different but complementary. While enlightenment work is often limited solely to contemplation and direct-consciousness, transformation work is itself a useful tool that helps ground your pursuit in your actual experience of self and life. While challenging you to the core, it also provides feedback and an ongoing "reality check" about your level of understanding, helping you recognize areas of unconsciousness that won't be noticed through intellect, and possibly not even through contemplation alone.

This book begins by clarifying enlightenment and transformation, and then guides you in creating a "transformation objective" to use as a tool to help ground and deepen your consciousness work. By revealing the core and design of your current experience, the transformative work will help you address the very source of persistent unwanted reactions and internal struggles. You'll learn to make new distinctions in your emotions and perceptions, as well as recognize how much your life story determines your self-identity. All along the way, I will alert you to hidden obstacles both large and small, and help you to avoid or overcome them. And, of course, I will bang on the subject of enlightenment and Absolute Consciousness far more than is reasonable.

This book will speak to those who've had an enlightenment experience or two, as well as to those who haven't. I've come into contact with quite a few people who've had some sort of direct experience but still don't know what to do with it or what it "means." There is a lot of misinformation and misunderstanding about these matters, and very little straightforward communication for those who've had some degree of enlightenment and wish to proceed. I want to help clarify what I can, while countering the huge mountain of nonsense that comes with the territory, even among the sincerely committed.

Introduction

It should be noted that this form of communication assumes the reader already trusts that the author is genuine and coming from a direct conscious experience of the subjects discussed. If this is the case, the book can be helpful in your own work. If not, it may come off as presumptuous opinions, which will not be useful at all. Best to approach with openness, and see what you can find. Without trust, the way the book zig-zags between subjects and seemingly repeats basic communications may be disconcerting. You might get whiplash moving from the pragmatic to the existential and back again, but it is deliberate and I hope the ride is exhilarating. The goal is nothing less than to grasp the reality of *you* and the nature of existence. Have fun!

ABOUT READING THIS BOOK

That Book

Strangely enough, it turns out that one of the drawbacks of *The Book of Not Knowing* is that it was too well written. I don't mean that it's a work of literature, but that sometimes the text makes the subject matter seem deceptively simple. Although the depth and nature of the communication are quite challenging to grasp, the way it's laid out is a clear-cut progression that is almost too easy to follow. Rather than grappling with the implications of what's being said, readers tend to slide over the material too easily, thinking they understand the communication because they understand the text. This is a mistake.

I'm not saying this is a flaw in the reader (or the author), just a commonly overlooked impediment to comprehending anything one reads, but particularly this kind of communication, which often, of necessity, skirts the limits of human understanding. Of course, if you haven't read *Not Knowing* I highly recommend that you do before tackling this book. A large part of what I communicate here stands on that material, so reading it first may save you a great deal of confusion. But not all—you are, in fact, *supposed* to be a bit perplexed.

Understanding something previously unclear can be a source of great pleasure, but feeling good is not the same as learning. In fact, people often learn best when they're feeling challenged and uncomfortable. Anyone who looks back fondly on an effective teacher will probably also recall that the fondness only came later, after their distress subsided. In that case, the fear may have been an aversion to disappointing someone whose opinion you respect; in this case, what you struggle with may be self-disappointment.

About Reading This Book

With something like that in mind, thirty years ago I made a change in the way I worked with my apprentices. Instead of just lecturing, dialoging with them, and having them engage in personal introspection, I challenged them to teach the material themselves. This new demand had startling results.

Previously, when asked if something was understood, they'd generally give an affirmative, but that changed overnight. Knowing they would have to facilitate others in a live interactive workshop—where participants were likely to challenge their assertions, require proof or convincing, and ask who-knows-what kinds of questions—made them realize that they weren't experientially taking in all they could. Now when asked whether they understood, they suddenly weren't so sure and were eager to delve more thoroughly into the subject matter to try to work out a more genuine experiential understanding for themselves. Not surprisingly, several went on to become excellent teachers, both in consciousness work and in their chosen fields. They had learned how to learn.

Simply because an understandable thought, association, or concept arises, stimulated by and in reference to the words you hear or read, that doesn't mean you've grasped or experienced what is intended. In consciousness work especially, you must recognize that your initial comprehension still needs investigation, contemplation, and experiential confirmation. Factoring in any self's natural resistance, it's a safe bet that whatever comes to mind upon a first reading is incorrect, or at least superficial. What you come away with is unlikely to be a conscious *experience* of the material, and so it will not have the power to help you change in any significant way.

*Always be suspicious
of the news you want to hear.*
—Francis Everitt, physicist

This Book

Some communications just cannot be grasped until certain breakthroughs have already occurred. Since becoming conscious of one truth allows you to hear and begin taking in another, there is frequent overlap, and repetition is necessary in my work to accommodate shifting levels of comprehension. As always, my goal in writing this book is not to entertain, or even to be immediately intelligible, but instead to invite the reader to make an experiential shift in consciousness.

If you want to be in accord with that purpose, don't approach this book as conventional "information" and read through it trying to intellectually grasp what's said, agreeing or disagreeing with it. Your interpretation of the text may be correct, but that's still not a direct experience of the truth of the matter, only a concept of something said. To understand the truth for yourself, you need to do the work for yourself. Keep in mind that it is not just the material but your participation that will lead to a personal transformation or an increase in consciousness.

The first trap people fall into with such writing is trying to discriminate between what's true and false by using their own beliefs as a guide. In listening for what's genuine, it's very important to look past your own beliefs, and refrain from listening with the intent to confirm or reject. Relating what's said to your beliefs prevents you from being able to listen for authenticity and truth. In the end, no matter what others say, you're the one who needs to become conscious or transform, but you have to do this independently, apart from anything you believe. The truth can only be found in what's true.

Know that I don't expect or even want you to believe me. Throughout the book, I will continually invite you to directly experience for yourself whatever is true, and attempt to offer candid

About Reading This Book

communications on enlightenment and direct-consciousness to assist you. Beyond supporting you in deepening your own consciousness, I also want to alert you to the many pitfalls and obstacles that can stand in the way of your progress.

Admittedly, this will not be easy reading. I recommend you go slowly and pause frequently to contemplate. Every now and then you'll hit a point being made, and get it! You may think this is because it's the only point made in the section, but there will probably be many other missed communications throughout. After having experienced a point here and there, you should develop a deeper understanding and ideally a better platform from which to reread the material and grasp some of the experiences that you missed previously. I know you can do it. Your courage is evident just in the attempt to tackle this book. Along with openness and honesty you have all you need in order to get the most out of these communications.

PART ONE

What Are We Dealing With?

CHAPTER ONE

Consciousness and Change

1:1   Most people have some idea about unusual depths of understanding. We've all seen images of wise old men dispensing advice from mountaintops, read historical accounts of saints and sages possessed of great compassion and wisdom, or heard stories about the sudden radical intelligence or insight achieved by philosophers, monks, and other solitary types. We consider such accounts to be entertaining—possibly true, or maybe not at all—but it rarely occurs to us that this kind of fabled wisdom and "higher" consciousness is something we can pursue for ourselves.

1:2   You picked up a book with "enlightenment" in the title, but you're likely aware that, in our culture, such a possibility is usually placed into the "mystical" category of rare and highly unlikely human phenomena. Maybe you hold it that way yourself. With little grounded information available, it's difficult to discern what enlightenment really is, or whether it's anything more than a fantasy. That doesn't stop people from offering opinions about it, however, and there's a lot of talk out there that is misleading or confusing. Whether or not it's clear to you yet, enlightenment is simply a deep personal consciousness of one's true nature or the true nature of absolute reality. Since it doesn't occur as an aspect of rational thinking, it doesn't lend itself well to explanation. Although I'll ask you to challenge everything you've ever heard about it, I also want you to consider that enlightenment is a real possibility for you.

WHAT ARE WE DEALING WITH?

> *Most people, in fact, will not take the trouble*
> *in finding out the truth,*
> *but are much more inclined to accept the first story they hear.*
> —Thucydides

1:3   There are a great many opportunities today in the broad domain called "personal growth" as well as an abundance of information. Self-improvement is now a mainstream value, but what comes to mind when you consider such an endeavor? Going to the gym? Taking up yoga? Learning meditation? Perhaps undergoing a rigorous multi-step program to change the way you think or interact? All of these undertakings might be considered a form of transformation, some personal change toward improvement. But most of what they propose is adding to the self as it is, or perhaps altering some behavior. The matter of real transformation, in which the subject is you and the goal is a complete change, is hardly ever considered.

1:4   There is a lot of misunderstanding about both transformation and enlightenment. What are they? Are they the same thing, or are they both just smoke and mirrors? Is there a relationship between the two? Such questions seem to be reasonable and yet are almost never asked. I became more acutely aware of this confusion while watching my students struggle to get past so much hearsay and common misunderstandings.

1:5   One student came to me after having his first enlightenment experience—what Zen people call *kensho*, or "first glimpse." Weeks had passed since then, and he was troubled. He told me that this breakthrough in consciousness meant the world to him, and that he now understood much more about what I was communicating in ways that he just couldn't have before. He asserted that he was clear about his true nature, what he really is, but was confused.

1:6 When I asked him why, he told me that he still experienced being the same self he's always been. Why didn't it go away? Why was he still stuck with so many of the same patterns and programs that had plagued him prior to his enlightenment? He acknowledged that he had a new relationship to all that because of his new consciousness, but asked: "Since those patterns and programs are not me, why do they remain?"

1:7 Good question. I told him that the self is a stronger force than people imagine, and breaking free requires a much deeper degree of consciousness. Besides, there are simple "mechanical" reasons for much of one's self to remain—but that's another story. I also told him not to confuse enlightenment with transformation. Few people understand this distinction, but clarifying the matter makes an enormous difference in attempting either one.

I wanted to try to live in accord with the promptings which came from my true self. Why is that so difficult?
—Hermann Hesse

Pursuing Self-Improvement

1:8 You might aspire to become enlightened in order to bring about a personal transformation and become free and happy. The painful reality of this perspective is that it is founded on false assumptions. Although there is a relationship that can be made between enlightenment and transformation, the goal of each is different, and so are the motives to pursue one or the other. You don't attain enlightenment by pursuing personal change, and you won't transform yourself simply by having a few enlightenment experiences. To grasp why this is so demands a new understanding about self, reality, and the nature of the practices we undertake to achieve such ends.

1:9   In order to make genuine personal growth possible, we need to work through what is and what isn't transformation. Just so, in order to pursue a personal and deep understanding or "consciousness" about who and what we really are, we're served greatly by clarifying what is and isn't enlightenment. If we don't know what our goal is, as well as what it is not, how can we go about accomplishing it, or avoid pursuing an unproductive course?

1:10   Many belief systems, human growth techniques, practices, and methods claim to lead to a deeper understanding of ourselves and the nature of life. The fields of spiritual belief and personal growth abound with a variety of possibilities. Since the goal of all these organized efforts is to accomplish something not yet known or attained by the practitioner, he or she is necessarily restricted to ideas, images, fantasies, or beliefs about the reality and nature of the goal. Because of this, there is a great deal of misunderstanding, often even by the teachers of those chosen paths.

1:11   Some of these misunderstandings are inevitable simply because of the nature of the subject matter and the limitations inherent in our minds. But some misconceptions can be cleared up, and such clarity is necessary if we're going to seriously engage in any practice attempting to pursue grasping our true nature or fundamentally changing the way we are.

1:12   As is often the case, much of this confusion can be found in what I call the "overlooked obvious." We tend to make many assumptions about life and reality that go unchallenged, and our certainty stands in the way of grasping what's right in front of us. We need to rethink the obvious.

> *The most profound insights arise*
> *from questioning the overlooked obvious.*

1:13   Although confusion reigns in regard to this subject, when we speak of *enlightenment* we are generally referring to a domain of increased consciousness, "awakening" to an indisputable truth about the nature of something. Such enlightenment is charged with producing profound changes in the person having it, or "transforming" them in some good way, so it's fairly obvious how the two have become confused. *Transformation,* which is defined as "a thorough or dramatic change," is a term we might use to indicate significant personal growth or improvement.

1:14   There are overlooked principles involved in the pursuit of both enlightenment and self-transformation that are difficult to grasp. Only a direct conscious encounter—which is often paradoxical and beyond our shared experiences—can reveal what's true about the foundational realities behind these pursuits. Although we might try, it's not possible for one person to convey a direct-consciousness to another, but someone who has become conscious of what's true in these matters can inform others about possibilities that remain hidden from view. In this way, we can more easily avoid unproductive practices and be pointed in directions we never would have thought to look, and so engage in a deeper contemplation of these topics.

WHAT ARE WE DEALING WITH?

1:15 Although pretty much everyone desires to improve either themselves or their circumstances, only a few have the idea of pursuing a significant personal transformation. These few have come to understand that simply trying to "polish up" the self as is, or trying to manage life to fit their needs and desires, ultimately just doesn't work to bring about any major change in themselves.

1:16 Your *self-identity*—what you experience *as* your self—is the source of both your personal perspectives and strategies for life management. Your individual collection of motivational impulses—needs, fears, and characteristic behaviors, including how you relate to your self, others, and life—I call your *self-agenda*. Without radically changing this self-identity and its agenda, you can't transform either your self or your life.

1:17 Still, there are only a few people who would want to pursue such an all-encompassing project. Perhaps this is because what they really want is merely to end some form of suffering or dissatisfaction in their lives. Transformation can indeed change how we experience suffering, but there's an even more compelling reason to engage in a process of complete personal transformation: It can assist you in discovering your *true nature*, as well as the absolute truth of reality. How this is so is a bit of a story, and the focus for this book.

Transformation versus Enlightenment

1:18 One of the most common misconceptions people have in the domains of personal growth and "consciousness" work involves a confounding of enlightenment with transformation—which is the same as confusing "is" with "change." In other words, people think that enlightenment is about changing a person, or at least changing their experience; and they might also assume that transforming someone is basically the same thing as enlightening them. This mistake permeates most "spiritual" practices.

1:19 Rather than being committed to facilitating adherents in personally becoming conscious of whatever is true, the methods aimed at "improving" a person are most often restricted to the adoption of a belief system. Adding some artificial structure to the self is a move in the opposite direction of increasing consciousness. It also allows misunderstandings to go unquestioned and errors to go unnoticed. Following a set of beliefs does not reveal the truth in any way, but there are valid reasons for confusing the search for the truth with an attempt at transformation.

1:20 As a search for Absolute truth, enlightenment stands on the possibility that someone could grasp the deepest nature of existence. This demands an openness to something beyond one's current experience and could easily be seen as changing one's experience, and perhaps even fundamentally changing the "person" having the enlightenment. Anyone who entertains the notion of contemplation or achieving enlightenment is already open to change since they have created for themselves the idea that they can discover something about reality that is not already known. This in turn leads to the idea that changing something fundamental about oneself is possible—and may even be necessary—in order to become enlightened.

1:21 The first thing to consider regarding enlightenment, however, is that we're not trying to change anything. We're trying to grasp what *is*—existentially. When it comes to attaining enlightenment, no change is necessary. The truth is *already* the truth and so change is irrelevant. Becoming directly conscious of the nature of self or reality may be seen as a change in consciousness, but that doesn't mean anything changes. This is why it is often referred to as "awakening." Enlightenment is not transformation. It is becoming directly conscious of the Absolute truth. Such an increase in consciousness can be said to be "transformative" because it does tend to change aspects of the person, but that's a side effect that this awakened consciousness has on the mind.

1:22 Although the central element of any enlightenment is an increase in one's consciousness, this isn't simply becoming aware of some new experience or idea, or having an unusual perception, as is often imagined to be the case. It is directly encountering for oneself the true nature of something, usually oneself. Such an increased consciousness creates a new possibility in which to "revisit," as it were, what was previously seen as "known" but only assumed to be true.

1:23 Through the resulting openness, all experience is seen in a new light. The mind is exposed to possibilities previously inconceivable. Apparently random aspects of the self-experience—such as long-held beliefs, ingrained personal convictions and outlooks, foundation perspectives that fuel certain characteristic behaviors—are all open to change, because they are now seen differently and are often revealed to be unnecessary and ineffective. The scope of such scrutiny depends on the depth of the enlightenment. Still, this is not a function of the enlightenment itself but of what one's mind does with it.

1:24 Grasping what's true about your own mind and experience—not the Absolute truth of enlightenment, but the truth about why you experience what you do, and why your mind works the way it does—is not transformation either and does not require change.

Obviously, comprehending your make-up doesn't demand that anything change because it's already your make-up. Increasing consciousness about anything isn't about transforming because you're not trying to change anything—you're simply attempting to understand what is already true.

1:25 Grasping the true nature of what's there doesn't change what's there. Conversely, if you change or transform what's there, that doesn't mean you have in any way grasped the true nature of what's there. Perhaps you imagine that you need to transform yourself into someone who can then grasp the truth. But this postulates that the truth is separate from you and unattainable until you build the ladder of a transformed self to reach it—or some such metaphor. Yet the truth is already the truth. You don't need to change a thing.

1:26 Transformation, on the other hand, *is* change.

> trans·for·ma·tion: *a complete change, usually into something with an improved appearance or usefulness.* (Trans = *to go beyond;* formation = *the action of forming, or process of being formed.*)

The very word means "to change the form of." It does *not* mean to understand the form or to know the truth. *Change* and *form* are the operative words here. Whatever "form" our self-experience currently enjoys or suffers, this is the subject matter for transformation. Our personal goal might be to make an improvement, and the more we understand the self-mind, the more capable we are of changing it. Yet understanding alone does not change the thing we understand.

Why Are We Motivated to Change?

1:27   The most common draw to attempt transformation will likely be suffering of some kind, often in the form of ineffective or painful social relations, or self-disappointment. When this is the case, people will be responsive to any promise that claims to lift them out of their suffering. Some sort of pain or dissatisfaction may be the motive to attempt change, but such a motive is actually secondary to the matter of transformation itself.

1:28   Another reason to pursue or at least fantasize about transforming might be the desire to perfect your self-image. At first, you may not see this motive as linked to suffering because trying to accomplish a positive self-image appears as a good and hopeful possibility. Yet if you look more closely, you see that the desire for a better self-image (how you see yourself and want to be seen by others) or a better experience *of* and *for* yourself overall arises from the assessment that whatever you have now isn't good enough. That in itself is a form of suffering.

1:29   While it may not be obvious at first glance, your motive for attempting transformation is likely to be based on suffering. Cultural assumptions and beliefs provide an array of standards from which to assess your place in the community, so any ideal image of transformation is bound to be based on both cultural and personal values about what it is to be an acceptable or lovable or worthy person. These can vary yet are always based on wanting to experience yourself in a way that you feel you do not now, which means you suffer with the belief that your current experience is inadequate.

1:30   The main selling point of almost every spiritual practice or personal-growth endeavor is the promise to free you of your suffering or deficiencies and give you something better. These usually provide limited success at best. There's more detail on why this is so in *The Book of Not Knowing* (unfolding throughout Parts I–IV), but basically such work is done on a level too superficial to make lasting change possible. I don't intend to address these dynamics again but instead will focus on what stands in the way of progressing beyond them. Our task here is to somehow recognize and transcend these barriers even while we're stuck right in the middle of the dynamics that created them.

1:31   Understanding what runs us or holds us back is our first step toward finding a way to get free from these drives and barriers. This may be difficult but not impossible. Contemplation and honest investigation into our personal experience are necessary whether we desire change or simply want to recognize what's there—the unseen core that shapes our personality and personal agenda. In fact, much hinges on an honest investigation of oneself, but we need to go beyond what's true for us personally. It is important to realize that we all share cultural assumptions and human design parameters that force us down roads of dissatisfaction as well as entice us to engage in fruitless efforts to resolve this distress. Even our motives for desiring change must come under scrutiny.

1:32   Understanding all this takes deliberate, usually long-term effort, but the final outcome isn't the only reason to take on such investigation. Simply making the shift to investigating the foundations of our experience already makes a big difference *in* our experience. When we contemplate something, we have immediately changed our relationship and perspective to the matter, and this indeed changes our experience of it. This simple act opens the door for transcending whatever we contemplate, instantly creating the possibility of understanding the matter rather than just suffering its effects.

Four Unnoticed Traps

1:33 Even at the very beginning of your investigations, you're bound to run into some traps that you may not think to watch out for. Most of these are built into the collective fabric of cultural assumptions, fashioned from people's past attempts to solve the challenges of the human condition. At the forefront of these overlooked dangers are a few that call for immediate attention, such as pursuing the promise of a positive experience, pretending to be something you're not, and struggling with being yourself in a social context.

Overlooked Trap #1: Positivity

1:34 Although life can be painful, and everyone feels bad from time to time, many belief systems claim to offer relief. Usually this involves a method to transform or grow as an individual that implicitly promises to improve your experience in a positive direction.

1:35 There are all kinds of such practices—adopting positive thinking, meditation to calm the mind, believing in a higher self, pursuing ideals, adopting special diets, emotional release therapies, body-mind practices, and so on. Although there may be many benefits to be had by engaging in a particular practice, the promise to change your experience from negative to positive is fundamentally misleading.

1:36   Embracing the positive and eliminating the negative certainly sounds like a good idea. So what's wrong with this picture? There is a reason why such a pursuit is attractive, but following this path isn't going to provide any real or deeply transformative change. Why not? For the same reason it sounds so appealing: as humans we *already* work hard to avoid the negative and obtain the positive. In a nutshell, that's the entire purpose of a self!

1:37   Generally, all "transformative" or personal-growth practices are "sold" on this already occurring motivation. Adding a few atypical but acceptable ideas on how to go about it—such as believing in a new cosmology or fantasy, following a new set of rules, embracing an interesting philosophy, blaming some newly imagined cause, adopting formulas to govern our actions, joining a like-minded community, or any number of processes—might provide something positive to do or help us feel better about ourselves and more hopeful about the future, but they're not going to transform anything. This is because such attempts don't change the fundamental nature of our experience; all they do is add to it.

1:38   Pursuing a practice that is basically a different way of doing the same thing we're already doing isn't going to change what we're doing. Dressing up our primal motivation and self-agenda in "spiritual clothes" or a new set of beliefs doesn't change who we're "being." It only makes it look a bit different. Seriously engaging in some sort of transformative practice obviously requires that we fundamentally experience self, and so life, differently from how we've been experiencing them.

Overlooked Trap #2: Pretending

1:39 We work hard to build a life, accomplish goals, and overcome hardships. Yet transformation and enlightenment are rarely given anywhere close to that same amount of attention and commitment. When it comes to the pursuit of personal transformation, we tend to look for the easy answer, the "way to be" or "thing to do" that will resolve all our problems. This is a simplistic approach to a complex affair. While it might be appealing, an easy "microwavable" method will likely fail to accomplish transforming something that is multidimensional and multifaceted.

1:40 Commonly, practices aimed at some kind of transformative attainment contain rules and goals that we're instructed to follow and accomplish—often presented as if adopting a recommended recipe or formula will produce a "better" person. Frequently the goal is to obtain attributes that are seen as a personal improvement or an indication of transformation. For example, we might attempt to be more peaceful, calm, and kind, or perhaps to appear more assertive; maybe we believe that taking on a practice such as sitting up straight and breathing a certain way will help us attain a better state or greater understanding. Because it is a "promising" activity with a specific goal in mind, we can easily confuse adopting a ritual or taking up a practice with transforming our *selves*.

1:41 These goals and methods are always external to us; otherwise we wouldn't aspire to adopt them. They're not something we realized on our own, but something communicated to us or imagined by us. Because of this, their application tends to be rather subjective and can easily be misunderstood. Yet even if we correctly understand what we're told or decide to accomplish, it's still something we're adopting artificially. Since this is the case, what do we end up doing? Even if we try as hard as we can to be how we think we should be, or do all the things that are recommended by some practice, inevitably we end up pretending.

1:42 What else can we call it? We adopt some attribute or characteristic that doesn't arise naturally and pretend that it is true for us. I'm not proposing that the programmed characteristics that arise automatically are any more true, and obviously we consider them to be less beneficial since, after all, we're trying to replace them. Yet our adopted characteristic runs the risk of being inauthentic in the sense that it doesn't arise from or represent our unaltered experience of ourselves. Although it may arise from a genuine desire to have it become true of us, and ideally it is more beneficial than what we think is true for us now, it's still a "pretended" characteristic.

1:43 What's wrong with pretending to be some way we're not? Everyone seems to do it, at least occasionally. Perhaps we think that if we pretend hard enough, it'll come true, like when your mom said if you keep making that silly face it might just stay that way. Of course, your mom was simply trying to manipulate your behavior. Just so, the fact that we're pretending already acknowledges we don't think those qualities are true of us or reflective of ourselves. The danger is falling into the trap of thinking we're changing when we're only superficially acting out a role. If such characteristics are indeed desirable or indicative of transformation, the goal should be to experience those qualities naturally without having to pretend.

1:44 Transformation occurs when the new "form" of self—our characteristic perspectives, feelings, behavior, and so on—arises naturally and as a reflection of simply *being* ourselves. This is quite different from making ourselves think, feel, and act in ways that we hope and assume represent transformation. Here lies an important distinction. If we don't recognize the difference, we could easily fall into the trap of being "spiritual pretenders" rather than seeking to truly transform.

Overlooked Trap #3: Confusion about "Being Ourselves"

1:45 We've all heard and used phrases such as "just be yourself" or "be true to yourself," as well as "I wasn't myself" or "that wasn't like me." Obviously we have collectively made a distinction between something we call "being ourselves" and not doing so. This distinction clearly isn't about "being" in any existential sense, but about our behavior, what we express. So, are we being ourselves when we do what we feel like doing?

1:46 Although this may be overly simplistic, there is a difference between behavior that is consistent with our familiar internal states (what we identify as our internal "self") and behaving in ways that are not expressive of or consistent with this well-known "internal person." In this way, we could postulate that acting consistently with our every impulse or internal reaction is indicative of "being ourselves."

1:47 Few would suggest, however, that we should act out our every impulse. As a matter of fact, civilization is founded on *not* acting on every impulse. This usually shows up as a conflict between what we might want to do in the moment and the social consequences of doing so. We find reward from our social structure for behaving in ways consistent with social norms, and we experience consequences, both subtle and gross, for failing to do so.

1:48   We seem to struggle between behaving in the service of our individual ends, and behaving in ways that are socially acceptable to the community in which we live. We are social animals who care about how we're seen by others. We fear being rejected or suffering other negative consequences relative to our behavior and expressions. Still, from time to time we might act inconsistently with our desired self-image—maybe we behave in a cowardly way when we think we should be heroic, knowing that a display of courage would put us in a better light socially—and so in this way feel like we aren't being true to ourselves. This feeling does not relate to our overall existential survival, however, but to our social survival as tied to our desired self-image. If some physical danger or a more important core social concern arises, we might behave to protect this more "existential" aspect instead of protecting our social self-image. When we feel as though we're not living up to our socially constructed persona, conflict arises between one self-aspect and another, challenging our sense of integrity and self-consistency.

Falsehood is invariably the child of fear in one form or another.
—Aleister Crowley

1:49   It seems that the struggle involved in "being ourselves" comes from the fact that we're frequently called to suppress or modify our behavior to fit social demands. In relationship to others, we have many personal fears or ambitions that are not acceptable to express. We also have many impulses that we must override in order to survive socially. Consistent with the demands of this situation, we may have a desire to just "be ourselves" in contrast to being the one we feel is required of us by social conventions.

1:50   Of course, this is not really being ourselves or failing to be ourselves. We are being our "selves" all the time. How much we selfishly act out our self-agenda versus how much we cater to social demands and uphold a social self-image is a decision that already represents our best guess at doing what's in our own self-interest. This boundary will shift from time to time as situations internal and external put pressure on us. At any given moment we'll lean toward one side or the other—depending on our assessment of the net effect of doing so—constantly trying to reconcile our internal impulses with our social needs. Further, our way of relating to this shift characterizes us by showing the steadiness or whimsical nature of our "character."

1:51   So the matter of pretense once again comes to the fore. We may struggle to discern between the times when our pretending is a conscious affectation or insincere manipulation of others, and times when we're pretending in an earnest attempt to become a better person. Our central goal and purpose is self-survival, however, regardless of any subset of this commitment, such as what we might call "being ourselves" or failing to do so. Our drives and emotions, impulses and reactions all feed us the motivation to behave in characteristic ways. In the end, all this activity is a complex set of manipulations designed to manage our lives and relations so that we can fulfill our needs. Any real transformation demands changing these deep-seated motivating factors.

Overlooked Trap #4: Models Aren't True

1:52   Another trap or temptation that often occurs within even sincere transformational approaches is attempting to outline a "schematic" to express the reality of the self or universe, trying to provide an immediate understanding of what needs to

Consciousness and Change

be accomplished and the steps required to achieve it. This often consists of some form of hierarchical distinctions that supposedly indicate levels of consciousness or spiritual attainment, or perhaps steps to personal growth, or some other "ladder of attainment," often presented as diagrams, allegories, imagery, graphs, charts, or what have you. In Consciousness (enlightenment) work, they are *always* wrong.

1:53   In certain circumstances, it may be advantageous to create a conceptual model to help us understand something abstract or difficult to grasp. An example I've used before is the model of a molecule. In order to sort out the differences between molecular structures, it can be useful to place various colored balls on sticks to represent a particular molecule. In this way we can see relations and compare differences, and understand something hard to discern in a more direct fashion. This might assist in making certain distinctions that can act as a springboard from which to go on, but it doesn't and will never accurately represent what's considered to be true about molecules. Trying to accurately and experientially conceive the accepted theory of the reality of molecular structure is quite difficult, but we'd have to admit that it's likely much closer to the truth than the stick-and-ball models.

1:54   Even when a model is useful, we need to stay in touch with the fact that the model is not the experience or the fact—"the map is not the territory." When it comes to enlightenment, however, this distinction is even more critical and ignoring it more perilous. Using a model should be entertained only briefly and abandoned soon. Truth does not fit into any schematic or hierarchy. It does not match any representation, since by definition something represented isn't the thing itself and the Absolute truth cannot be represented. The true nature of reality can only be grasped directly, not via intellect or even experience, and so no model will ever be able to express it.

1:55 Embarking on any organized pursuit to become more conscious or to transform will be accompanied by ideas and beliefs about where we should go and how we're going to get there. This naturally lends itself to being organized into ladders or schematics and models. These kinds of inventions should not be taken too seriously or as actually true. They must exist only as temporary aids for the mind and not become held as something real, and certainly not as a way to the absolute. They should be recognized as stepping stones or tools, nothing more. We might use a trampoline to help propel us into the air, providing a different experience, but we'll never learn to fly from this.

Confronting the Reality of Our Task

1:56 One possibility in the pursuit of changing oneself, and actually the most probable outcome, is that no change occurs. Even if we adopt a practice that lets us imagine our efforts are leading to some change, the reality is that no fundamental change will likely take place. When we "observe from a distance" the effect of most so-called spiritual or growth practices we can notice that people rarely change. Usually the biggest change is simply the adoption of a belief system and practice, but the individual remains pretty much the same. This might lead us to despair if our goal is transformation.

1:57 With so many obstacles arising when merely considering this matter, we might feel like just forgetting about the whole thing. Perhaps instead we'll just hope that continuing down the road we're on will turn out well as we struggle to attain our needs and avoid our fears. Yet it doesn't take a lot of wisdom and observation to grasp that this hasn't worked so far to reconcile or transform anything, and will not work in the future. There are "design flaws" hindering our efforts to resolve our inner disquiet or attain self-imagined ideals (explored in detail in *The Book of Not Knowing*). In short, we suffer from the illusion that our present course of action will somehow put an end to our discontent or make life work out as we desire. If either enlightenment or transformation is our goal, we are ill-advised to carry on being driven solely by our self-agendas.

1:58 Seeing reality from our current perspective, our only option appears to be accepting whatever is experienced as if it is an accurate reflection of what's so. This is how we already live, though, and we still have a nagging sense that there's something else to grasp, something of which we are ignorant.

1:59 Not everyone is willing to consider what may lie beyond their immediate assumptions and beliefs about the nature of their own existence. Those open to such investigation, however, frequently come to the conclusion that they don't know—that they don't experience their own existential nature, or how it is they came to exist, what life really is, or who and what they actually are. It's not impossible to grasp that we are ignorant of our own true nature. With some reflection, we can notice that we're not directly conscious of the true nature of *anything*—that we are not enlightened, or perhaps not enlightened enough.

1:60 Beyond this existential ignorance, a corresponding challenge we have is that we're also unconscious of the foundational underpinnings of our own perceptive-experience. We don't understand the real workings of our own minds and selves. If change is our goal, then it is essential to learn how one's mind works and what drives us to behave and react in the ways that we do. We need to experience what keeps us stuck in the "forms" to which we are attached. Why do we have these particular emotions? Why do we insist on certain opinions and moods, personality traits and behavioral patterns? Real transformation requires that we experientially grasp the nature and workings of the self-mind so that we can free ourselves from it.

1:61 We should be clear that we probably have two goals. One is to know the truth, to become conscious of our own true nature and the nature and the workings of our mind. The other is to become a better person, what we consider transformed. We need to understand that being a better person is a relative affair, having nothing to do with being conscious of our true nature or the absolute truth. We don't know whether such direct-consciousness would change our experience in any way, although rumor suggests that it will. Whether it will or not is really unimportant when it comes to the truth. It's only important if what we want is transformation, and think that knowing the truth will give that to us. In any case, "better" is a subjective notion. It comes from whatever we're socialized to believe is good, and what we have learned or imagine are the characteristics of a "good" person, which is an ideal. As we will discover, trying to achieve an ideal is a fool's errand. When it comes to enlightenment, the absolute is not relative, so it can't be an imagined ideal.

1:62 Enlightenment does not guarantee transformation, nor vice versa. Yet together these two goals are charged with bringing us freedom and happiness. Unfortunately, our motive to pursue freedom and happiness comes from an experience that is neither free nor happy. As we've seen, this motive is based on some form of suffering which is, by definition, an experience that is not free or happy. Our pursuit of both these goals is founded on a fundamental ignorance about what they actually are. Our imaginings regarding what pursuing either goal might lead to are likely inadequate and misleading.

1:63   As if all these hurdles aren't enough, the mechanisms that drive the self-mind are formed for a purpose that is contrary to the pursuit of both enlightenment and transformation. From this design and purpose come strategies in perception, interpretation, and interaction that serve only one objective, and that is the persistence of the self. This means that the strategies behind our self-agenda cannot lead us to freedom or happiness; and no matter how much effort is made or what is accomplished in this domain, it will not create the resolution we seek. Understanding this condition may be difficult, but it's necessary if we're going to break out of the resultant closed loops of fruitless activity.

1:64   Try to refrain from being discouraged, however, for you have already begun the work. Being alerted to these challenges allows you to tackle them straight on and with intelligence. In this way, although you may have your hands full, you can make real and significant progress toward both freedom and happiness.

1:65   Because this work is about you and your experience, clearly it all hinges on you. What you personally do or don't understand is critical to your pursuit of either consciousness or personal growth. If you truly want to know what you are or take on the possibility of changing yourself, the next chapter will set you on the right path. We'll be starting this endeavor with an approach to transformation, which appears to be a more accessible topic than enlightenment. But whatever your goals, since you are both the agent of change and the subject to be changed, it's useful to understand the nature and origins of being a self.

*It's best not to begin,
but once you've begun it's best to finish.*
—Chöygam Trungpa Rinpoche

CHAPTER TWO

Self-Transformation

What Is a Self?

2:1 If we want to transform the self, it would be useful to know what we're talking about. When I say "self," I mean you. Not *you* as an absolute—not what's ultimately your true nature and existence—but *you* as the experience that you're having of yourself right now. It seems I've just made a distinction between two versions of you, but the assertion here isn't that there is a "real-you" in your experience and a "self-you" in your experience. I'm simply saying that whatever is ultimately true about you is unknown, and what we're addressing now is what you *experience* as you.

2:2 The next thing to grasp is that "self" refers to all of you. The word "self" is often taken to mean some "part within," some particular aspect of your experience. Perhaps one reason for this is our habit of confusing the notion of self with ego. Since common terms like *self-centered* and *self-absorbed* are often related to egocentricity, it's easy to assume that I'm referring to some mere aspect of your experience. But self and its operating principle, survival, (which also determines and shapes all that you perceive as *not* you) is everything you experience as you, inside and out. This experience, this entire existence that you know of as yourself, is what I'm referring to as the self.

2:3 We're tackling this matter with the idea of becoming conscious of what's ultimately true about self, and also the possibility of changing it, so it's wise to have a basic understanding of the principle and context that creates the self in the first place. This is challenging, so I'm going offer a model or story as a way of grasping the idea with some clarity. Recall the dangers and limitations of using models and analogies, and take care not to confuse the images drawn with the truth they're meant to point out.

2:4 In order to get to the root of this business, I want to begin in a rather "existential" manner. This is a bit like returning to the beginning of the creation of life and self. As a starting place, imagine a world in which there are only inanimate objects. There is no self here, and no survival or persistence. Everything simply exists, and disintegrates without resistance.

2:5 Now imagine that some new phenomenon occurs, something we call *life*. In ancient times there was a reference to the "spark" of life, indicating something other than inanimate objects arose and created a new domain of existence. This spark is the distinction we make when we perceive something as alive, *ergo* we sense that an entity is present and not merely an object. Arising along with this spark of life seems to be a will to persist, a drive to maintain itself despite changes in circumstance and to survive beyond the normal and natural disintegration of objects. Unlike our previous inanimate-object world, dissolution is actively resisted.

2:6 Within this domain of purposeful persistence, a necessary distinction is made by the entity between what's *it* and what's not, so it can know what to protect and promote and what is irrelevant to that purpose. For example, if a worm can't somehow tell the difference between its own worm parameters and a blade of grass, how would it know what to attend to and what to ignore, what to use and what to avoid? If we couldn't distinguish between our arm and a tree branch, or an emotion we're having and the wind we feel on our face, we couldn't relate effectively to our own needs or well-being. From this distinction, we can see that we'll then identify with being one thing and not another thing—and a self is born.

2:7 Imagine that the self principle is like a formless force that can be applied to anything. The moment something is adopted by self, or inhabited by self, or perhaps identified as self, it becomes an aspect of self. In that instant, whatever this something may be—object, emotion, idea, activity, image, belief, characteristic, or whatever—it is suddenly included in the self's need to be protected and to persist, and so self-survival becomes active.

2:8 A self can be very simple and without any "knowledge" of its own beingness, or it can be complex and self-reflective. We are the latter. The human self then is whatever we identify with and consider to be self. If we experience the body as us, then this will be a part of ourselves. If we associate with an emotion, a belief, a sense of presence, an awareness, the activities of our internal state or mind, a self-image, a sense of worth, point of view, history, and so on, then all of these will be included in what we experience as our selves. Thus the human self becomes highly conceptualized.

2:9 You may be able to see that everything you experience as yourself—everything you can list as you or as characteristic of you, including the core sense of simply existing—is that way because you identify with those attributes or experiences. If this is so, then there is a possibility that you could let go of any particular aspect and perhaps change what it is you consider to be your self. Doing so, you would experience yourself differently. Given the dynamics involved, however, such transformation doesn't sit well with self-survival.

You are not your cluster of memorized ideas about yourself.
—Vernon Howard

Confusing Self-Improvement with Transformation

2:10   Concurrent with your desire to manage life and take care of yourself, you've developed ideas and made plans aimed at accomplishing this task—this is what I call the *self-agenda*. The manifestation of this agenda forms your character and personality, determines your hopes and fears, and dominates your mental processes and emotions. All of this is the self principle in action, trying to manage life in relation to whatever you identify with, arising in your experience as the content of the self's job of persistence. This is the very experience you're having right now. You might sometimes think of changing yourself in some way in order to create a better self-experience. But attempting to improve yourself by adopting a system of beliefs and shuffling the content of your agenda is a rather superficial undertaking.

2:11   The main thrust of many self-improvement methods involves enrolling in a certain image of the "world," and so of oneself within it, and then reinforcing this image through a belief in a set of conceptual add-ons. These notions don't demand real change in you but ask only that you learn to present yourself, and perhaps try to think about yourself, as someone more like what you wish or are invited to be. This doesn't change you. It adds concepts to you the way you already are. There's nothing wrong with adopting a new concept that works for you. But that's the point. It works *for* you, it doesn't *change* you.

2:12 Changing the very person that we are is usually not even considered because we stand on the assumption that "who we are" as a person is a *fait accompli,* making our selves the source of change rather than the subject of change. We assume that it's *this one* who needs to accomplish something called transformation—improving ourselves, experiencing a better life, or becoming more successful. This leaves ourselves fundamentally as-is and the focus becomes altering the presentation or behavior rather than changing the very person. This is not transformation. It's what we already attempt to do, whether we're successful at it or not.

2:13 What I'm referring to here may be difficult to grasp since our shared assumption is that we *are* our selves, and thus the self is sacrosanct. This assumption precludes the kind of perspective that would allow us to consider any significant change. We don't look at our fundamental "person" as changeable or even in need of change. We assume that it is this very "person" that we want to have attain a better experience. What we don't understand is that this person will continue to experience himself or herself in much the same way regardless of any adopted practice or belief system, and so will also experience life fundamentally the same way. In order to change this experience we need to change the person that we are *being.*

2:14 This change shouldn't be confused with simply attempting to eliminate negative qualities, the side effects or consequences of which you find undesirable. Your personal negative characteristics are really just the manifestation of your self-agenda manipulations and behaviors that are socially, and perhaps personally, unacceptable or ineffective. For example, if one of your characteristics is to be quick to anger, you may want to be calmer and more in control. If this is your desire, it's at least partly because the community disapproves of the behavior. As part of the community, you may also disapprove of it, and may also want to eliminate this reaction because you've noticed that it just feels bad. Some people are quite attached to and even proud of their temper so wouldn't think of it as something they want to change. Those that would do so because they understand the causal relationship between their behavior and suffering negative consequences.

2:15 Changing the fundamental person that we experience being is not simply trying to do away with a few negative aspects. We're already called to modify or compensate for any attributes that are seen as potentially detrimental to our success. Our self-agenda ranges anywhere from dealing with insignificant discomforts and minor needs to pursuing deeply important resolutions and achievements. One goal of this agenda is to fit in socially—be approved of, respected, considered worthwhile, etc. This includes, but is not limited to, managing undesirable self-aspects, even if our response is only to ignore, cover up, or desire to "fix" them. Changing ourselves fundamentally can't be done through any manipulations of our self-agenda, because the agenda's purpose is to *maintain* the very person it serves.

Manipulating Ourselves versus Changing Ourselves

2:16 The desire to make such a change is one thing, action is another. We have to admit that we still have unwanted characteristics even though we talk about getting rid of them. This is because we really don't *want* to get rid of them. We may wish we didn't have a particular characteristic, but it serves us. It does something for us that we think important. It is actually a self-agenda manipulation trying to fulfill some need. In order to entertain dropping it, we need to acknowledge that our "needs" trump our "wishes."

2:17 When we imagine that these characteristics are something inflicted upon us by an external cause, or something that we just can't help, then of course we find it difficult or impossible to change them. On the other hand, if these characteristics are something we are "doing," even if we don't understand how or why, then we must concede that we either don't want to give them up, or we just don't know how.

2:18 Negative internal states are pretty much the definition of suffering. Who doesn't want to get rid of suffering? If these internal states are manipulations generated by our own minds, then what we want to change is what we ourselves are *doing*. When we grasp the truth of the matter, we realize that underneath our protestations to the contrary we really don't want to stop doing what we're doing. What we're doing is "being our selves," and this is not something we want to give up.

2:19 If transformation means changing ourselves completely, then the self we are now would have to become a new self. It is not actually transformation if our approach to such a change is focused simply on bettering the self by changing something about our behavior or internal state so that we appear closer to our ideals of how we should be. That's nothing more than attempting to achieve the ideal goals already held by the self.

2:20 The reason we don't attain, or have a hard time attaining, even this existing goal (or some newly adopted spiritual goal) is because the self we think we *are* is identified with *how* this self behaves, reacts, and emotes. In other words, we are attached to the activities that are experienced and identified as the self. Yet we also hold ourselves to be the source of these expressions or manifestations. So, persisting as this self—both source and manifestation—produces the same stuff, and thus the same basic experience. Altering the stuff doesn't change the self. Chasing ideals by embracing a belief system is just adding more stuff, and probably includes adopting a pretense—behavior inconsistent with what's experienced internally as the self-identity.

2:21 As we'll see more clearly further on, in order to continue pursuing a real transformation beyond your ideals, you'll find that your motives and objectives will of necessity have to change over time. As you discover and become more conscious of what's true about the nature of your mind and self, you will start to see things differently. What drove you before may well become a non-issue or be seen as inappropriate to your newly created objective, one you couldn't have fathomed from your previous perspective.

2:22 You can't correctly understand where you need to go or how to get there if you've never been there before. The only starting point is an idea of some condition called "being transformed." From this concept, you will create images and build a process that you imagine will accomplish getting you there. This provides a direction in which to move but neither image nor process will be accurate, and as you proceed you will need to make corrections and alter your course. It's a bit like imagining that you must go north to reach the ocean, but as you climb up on a hill you see that the ocean is actually to the west and so change your direction.

2:23 Holding transformation as changing the very person that you are is likely to be a new idea for you, and so would necessitate creating a new objective from any you've previously held. Independent of any improvements that might accompany such a change, there are very good reasons for holding it in this extreme way.

How Transformation Relates to Consciousness and Enlightenment

2:24 Achieving enlightenment may be challenging, but it is straightforward. Few people, however, have this as a serious goal. Transformation, on the other hand, is even more difficult than having a first enlightenment. But it appears doable and accessible because it is found within the world of process, as is the self. I suspect far more people are interested in the idea of transformation than enlightenment—and often mistake enlightenment for transformation and vice versa.

2:25 To be honest, until recently I had little interest in the domain of transformation. For decades, my focus has been discovering the truth about what everything really is. I also had an interest in discovering and creating more effectiveness in life activities, and some people characterized this work as "transformative." But self-transformation is about changing the form of what we're *being*. Since I see the form as ultimately meaningless to begin with, I saw no reason to promote changing it—with the exception of becoming more effective or skillful. These latter goals call for change, but they don't require completely transforming the fundamental person.

2:26 Seeking greater effectiveness demands significantly altering the way the mind works. We must learn to make new distinctions in what we experience or perceive, while recognizing and getting free of the ineffective assumptions and programs that prevent us from achieving our goals. This in turn teaches us more about ourselves and the workings of the mind in general, and increases our consciousness about these activities. Although pursuing enlightenment or effectiveness are very different goals, in both cases the real heart of the matter is consciousness.

2:27 To be clear, effectiveness doesn't lead to discovering the Truth. Being effective is only meaningful within the context of human enterprise, but that's where we live. Since this is where we seem to be stuck, we're obliged to study this human condition and learn to base our actions on the most valid principles and workable methods we can find, as we also try to understand what *this*—self, life, reality—is all about.

---

*Act only according to that maxim by which you can
at the same time will that it should become a universal law.*
—Immanuel Kant

2:28 In my own studies, regardless of the subject, my central focus has always been to understand what "is." Toward that end, an essential pursuit has been enlightenment—becoming conscious of what I am, what life is, what reality is; in other words, the Truth. It wasn't until working with consciousness apprentices that I recognized the value of using transformation to assist in uncovering the Truth.

2:29 As mentioned, I've long observed that people learn best when what they learn is grounded in attainable goals that demand action, which in turn provides feedback about their real understanding and progress. Otherwise they tend to remain abstract and conclude that merely thinking they're making progress makes it true, and this goes unchallenged. So I always ask my apprentices to accomplish something specific. In this case, I asked them to transform themselves. It was amazingly difficult. As we worked through obstacles and misunderstandings, it became clear that the first valuable function of transformation work was to help clarify just how strong the anchors are that bind consciousness to one's self-identity.

2:30 Investigating our inability to change some central aspect of our emotional reactions, thinking, or characteristic behavior helps reveal the very source of these aspects of self. In order to get free of these anchors, we need to discover what keeps us stuck—not just noticing it intellectually, but uncovering it on an experiential level. Just trying to get free makes it increasingly clear what the impediment is, and how strongly it dominates our experience. Aside from any progress toward transforming, this feedback and clarity alone is worth the effort. The demands of this path lead right through the necessity of becoming conscious of deeply buried assumptions about one's own self-mind.

2:31 Beyond becoming more conscious of the foundations of your self-mind, an even greater reason for transforming actually relates to enlightenment. If transformation is changing yourself so completely that you are now a new self, what does this say about your real nature? It may not be obvious at first, but there are profound implications to accomplishing transformation, and these align with the consciousness gained from enlightenment. If you transform from the person that you now identify with into a new person, then you must realize that you can't actually *be* either.

2:32   Did you get that? You'd have to realize that the "old you" can't actually *be* you since you're still conscious and exist but are no longer that person. In fact, you could never have *been* that person or you wouldn't exist presently in any form at all. You must also realize that you can't be the person that you've transformed into, since you weren't that person before and still somehow you existed. Get it? This must lead to at least an implicit understanding that you ultimately don't exist as any self or self-identity.

2:33   It only takes once. If you can transform once, you could do it again and again to infinity. But you don't need to, because in doing it once, you must grasp that you can't be any of what you thought you were—that your nature is somehow not formed at all, even if you don't have an enlightenment experience.

2:34   In this case, it doesn't matter what person you transform into as long as it's different from who you are now. The realization that you can't *be* any form at all must occur no matter what you become. Yet also adopting a secondary goal of increasing consciousness through becoming more effective and combining the two (transformation and mastery) gives you particular and testable objectives, while providing the opportunity to pursue a consciousness consistent with enlightenment.

2:35   In the past I discouraged students from fantasizing about self-improvement, since it had nothing to do with the Truth and I didn't want them to think it did. I would invite people to pursue mastery, however, in whatever field they wanted to master. I knew it would lead them to become more conscious, to learn so much about themselves, and even change their self-identity to some degree. But mastery doesn't transform the fundamental self-principle at its root, and so I was always quick to clarify that becoming more effective is a different domain than becoming conscious of the Truth. This is still true, but now we can combine these pursuits while remaining aware of the difference. Instead of confusing the two, we use change to serve as a tool for Consciousness.

Bliss Is Not the Truth

2:36 Attempting to directly experience what's absolutely True, or even the truth about the human condition, is generally considered daunting. When it is attempted, it's often quickly abandoned, so obviously serious motivation is required. If everything in your experience were positive, would you care about the Truth or want to pursue any change? In theory, one might want to know what reality really is simply because it's what *is*. This would need to stand on a realization or at least an idea that you are currently ignorant of this Truth, and the intention to pursue what's true without any other impulse except to know what it is.

2:37 You might like to think that you would do this because you are serious about knowing what's true. But the fact is, such a disposition is so rare that maybe Prince Gautama was the only already "contented" guy who ever started down that path. The few who pursue the Absolute truth almost certainly do so because they think it will provide them a better experience and perhaps freedom from suffering. Without these motivators, would you really go for the truth solely for its own sake?

2:38   In my own contemplations, I reached a point in 1977 where I spent a good deal of time basking in a deep state of "oneness" with the absolute. I was very happy to just sit and disappear into a state I called "being with God." From time to time, I'd leave my loft behind the school only long enough to drop down and teach, then I was always excited to go back up and sit once more. Over time I began to notice that I wasn't really contemplating; I was simply shifting my state into one of bliss and Nothingness. I was very happy and felt quite fulfilled.

2:39   I did not, however, know what the human condition was really all about. I was not directly conscious of what self was or why a self arose, why suffering existed, and so on. Once I realized that I had forsaken the complete truth for my own happiness, I stopped this routine and threw myself back into investigating the world of self and suffering so that I could continue to learn and deepen my consciousness of the Truth. Once it became clear what I was actually doing with my sitting, there really wasn't any other option than to give up what was, in the end, simply a deeply pleasurable experience and continue to pursue the complete Truth.

2:40   I relate this story because at some point it may ring true for you. It's possible to think that you're committed to enlightenment or discovering what's true when you're really seeking a greater sense of pleasure in the form of bliss or some other ideal state. This is not the Truth and should not be the goal. It's important to watch out for the siren of idyllic experience and not be distracted by this temptation.

Grounding Our Pursuit

2:41 Rather than focusing only on what you're trying to accomplish or attain, you should also investigate why you feel a need to pursue anything at all. To do this, start with what's right in front of you. If you're motivated to change yourself, you need to acknowledge that how you're currently experiencing self and life is in some way lacking. Improving yourself is seen as offering a better experience. Exactly what that might look like depends on the system of beliefs it's held within. Yet regardless of what you imagine as the outcome, you first need to look at and dig into your current experience. What drives you toward wanting transformation? What are the underlying dynamics that are keeping you stuck in your present undesirable—or at least less desirable—experience of yourself?

2:42 Contemplating our current experience rather than striving for our imagined ideals not only changes our focus, it creates an immediate and significant alteration in our experience. Life becomes an open question. Instead of just being something to enjoy, put up with, or suffer, everything we experience becomes an object of investigation. With this shift in perspective nothing is overlooked or resisted. Rather than being something to deny, ignore, or struggle against, our challenges represent opportunities to discover more about what's true. If we hold the possibility that these difficulties are unnecessary and occur simply because of a lack of consciousness, our relationship to them changes radically even prior to eliminating them.

2:43 Admittedly, this takes *discipline* (from a Latin root meaning "to learn"), since discipline is steadily pursuing something that doesn't just befall you. In order to get to the bottom of what drives you—what pushes you to feel, react, and behave as you do, which is seemingly caused by circumstance—you have to investigate it rather than succumb to it. This means overriding the impulses and whims that are characteristic of your self-mind, but at the same time not denying or suppressing them. Instead, you examine them for the purpose of understanding them.

2:44 In this way, rather than gazing off toward some ideal or trying to mimic some adopted belief, you're invited to stay present and question beyond the face value of whatever arises. The good news is that this discipline offers endless possibilities for greater freedom and understanding, which, once you grasp this, will provide all the motivation you need to pursue it.

2:45 Although I want to ground the idea of transformation in practical and visible action, investigation, and contemplation, first we need to lay some groundwork that will not appear accessible at all. I want to talk to you a bit about enlightenment. If it seems incomprehensible to you, it only needs to be held as a goal or possibility until such time as you grasp it for yourself. In addition, some of the communications will be for those who've had enlightenment experiences, assisting them in clearing up misconceptions and encouraging them to acknowledge and take on remaining ignorance. So remember, I'm speaking to two audiences, those who've yet to directly grasp their true natures, and those who have at least begun this adventure.

CHAPTER THREE

What Is and Isn't Enlightenment

Clarifying Enlightenment—sort of

3:1 It's a ridiculous idea that I, or anyone, could possibly convey what enlightenment really is. The most accurate relationship to the matter would demand that I just shut up. Although that leaves you with nothing, that's actually the best thing to be left with. Of course, the problem is you aren't really left with nothing—you're left with everything you assume, have heard, or think you know. Because this is unfortunately so much *less* than nothing, I'll try to provide a doorway to a better understanding of the matter. Even so, this "door" can only be discovered personally, by connecting the dots through multiple layers of disparate communications. Forgive me in advance for the presumptuousness of the attempt, and try to look beyond the words to grasp what's really meant.

3:2 Many misconceptions and myths have been built up over time and we need to shake these off of the word "enlightenment." In Chapter One we touched on some of the ideas and beliefs surrounding the word. You know that we're not talking about a seventeenth-century movement, a modern outlook, or being informed of something. Our focus is more akin to a Zen usage, referring to what's thought of as a "spiritual" awakening of some sort. But even here, people are often misled to believe that becoming enlightened means transforming from an ordinary "caterpillar" of a human into the "butterfly" of a transcendent soul, or some such.

3:3 Whatever methods may purport to achieve such an end—whether it's to be highly disciplined and monk-like, sit endlessly in contemplation, or learn to surrender to a higher power—at some point we're supposed to be rewarded with a dramatic change in state, experiencing something blissfully "transcendent." The good news about this view is that it encourages personal participation, as opposed to merely asking one to believe in religious, spiritual, or even scientific assertions. The bad news is that it's fundamentally a false view. A change in state is irrelevant to the truth. Freeing the term "enlightenment" from the baggage of rumor and myth is useful if our goal is to know what's true about it. When considering what enlightenment really is, it's important to get beyond the word and hearsay, and to realize that this Consciousness is prior to any idea, image, term, or belief.

3:4 Consider that at some point in human history, even after someone had already become deeply and directly conscious, there was no "enlightenment." In other words, no one was seeking enlightenment; they were seeking the Truth. If the legend of Gautama Buddha is to be trusted, even he wasn't searching for something called "enlightenment." He was trying to become free, to completely understand and transcend life and death. This is a different focus.

3:5 Turns out, of course, that you can't transcend anything without becoming fully conscious of what it is. Ultimately, enlightenment—knowing what is absolutely true about self and reality, life and death—must occur in order to achieve such freedom. But having one or two enlightenment experiences isn't enough or

What Is and Isn't Enlightenment

Gautama would have stopped his search early on. He undoubtedly had a number of enlightenment experiences but knew that he still wasn't completely free of life and death, and that an even deeper consciousness was necessary. He couldn't have known whether it was possible, much less what it would be, only that it had to be whatever is really true about existence.

3:6 In the work of trying to personally understand what self, life, and reality are all about, "enlightenment" is a term used to indicate a direct-consciousness of the Absolute truth, whatever is absolutely true regarding what "is." In the case of you, which is the primary subject for enlightenment, it is your true nature, what you really are, the absolute reality of your existence.

3:7 Even disregarding how it's used in other domains, the term "enlightenment" can be confusing. Although enlightenment is always about what's True, there are various degrees of consciousness to be had, and the term refers to *all* direct-consciousness, whether shallow or deep, about self or reality. While it always refers to being directly conscious of the true nature of something, it's not always referring to the same subject matter or the same level or depth of consciousness.

3:8 Although defining or explaining enlightenment isn't possible with any kind of accuracy, that doesn't mean that it is ambiguous or that it is something open for debate, about which each individual should draw their own conclusions—like what kind of diet is best for them, or whether or not to believe in god. Such intellectual pursuits are a completely different matter from direct-consciousness. By definition, a direct encounter can't be found in anything heard or imagined. It also can't be found within opinion or conclusion, thought or feeling. These are all activities that relate indirectly to things. Being conscious of what's absolutely true is not something to decide about within one's world of opinions. Even though all this may be challenging to sort out, enlightenment is exactly and only what it is.

Truth is not a matter of personal viewpoint.
—Vernon Howard

The Challenge of the "Object"-ive Mind

3:9 Why is it so difficult to understand the domain of enlightenment? Because comprehension comes from the mind, and the mind best grasps only what can be categorized and objectified. In other words, the way our minds work is to take meaningless indirect input and carve it up into distinct and separate aspects, and then give meaning to these distinctions as they relate to us and to every other distinction.

3:10 Stated simply, our minds like to think in terms of objects. This "objective" domain isn't restricted to physical objects, however, but includes process and all relational distinctions such as speed, distance, condition, location, time, images, and so on. This domain presents us with our primary form of thought. We perceive objects as separate from one another and so can relate all objects to each other. When we relate them to ourselves, we immediately apply to them qualities of function, association, and meaning. Our minds are constructed to represent and relate to every aspect of reality in order to form an experience that is consistent with this "object" framework.

3:11　The word "object" originally referred to an item "presented to the senses." What we perceive both physically and mentally is the "object" of perception. When we think about something that is not an actual object, we still use objectification as a mental reference, either as image, metaphor, or representation. It's the way we create and relate to whatever is imagined, perceived, or thought. When you "imagine" something, for example, you create an image or mental "object" in your mind. Since image is a function of sight, you must mentally form an object to view. In similar ways, this object-relating is involved in how we create thought, memory, emotion, and so on.

3:12　Our whole mind is framed upon object relations. For example, we speak of an emotion as if it's a particular and separate "thing" located inside the body, and even somehow imposed upon us, although it is neither. We know what's meant when someone says "it was like sticking a knife in my heart," or when we hear that someone is "a political lightweight," or that a conversation was "a *heavy* discussion." Time itself is not an object, but notice how we think of the past as a "place" where "things" happened, and the future as the next "objective reality" we will enter. The depth and reality of this mental framework go far beyond my simplistic examples and in ways that are difficult to describe or notice. Even with further explanation, it's likely that much will be overlooked, but the reality of this matter will arise again and again. I'm suggesting that this "objectified" framework for thinking is the foundation for our entire perceived world, which makes it well worth considering on your own.

3:13　In any case, because of this natural limitation of mind, we are challenged when tackling thought outside this framework, and further, are incapable of grasping what can't be grasped by the mind. Direct-consciousness or enlightenment is of that kind. It cannot be understood short of having it, because it does not fit into any framework whatsoever.

3:14　This is why so many of the communications around enlightenment seem enigmatic, confusing, vague, or mysterious. Sometimes this might be because the speaker really doesn't know what he's talking about and wants to obscure this fact, or make enlightenment sound more interesting. But even without any monkey business, the matter is still impossible to express in any meaningful way to anyone who hasn't had at least one enlightenment experience. Even then it can be challenging, but the person has some foundation—if only as a previously inconceivable openness—from which to consider the dialogue.

3:15　Because the Absolute can't be grasped by the mind, it's impossible to imagine what enlightenment is. Trying to conceive of something inconceivable is doomed to failure. Since the mind functions by making distinctions—basically "knowing" everything as if separate objects—and relating these distinctions to each other, this creates what we call "experience" and so what we perceive as reality. That being the case, the mind is ill-equipped for the job of being conscious of absolutes. An absolute lacks objective or even subjective distinctions. The Absolute truth isn't separate from anything. It *is* everything, but not *any* thing, nor is it several things or even all things. The absolute nature of *Being* is the source of reality *and* reality itself.

3:16　See? That just doesn't communicate anything useful, does it? There is no use in talking too much about direct-consciousness since it will of necessity sound like gobbledygook. Just consider that it is not anything you think or imagine. Enlightenment is not a change of state, an experience, a conclusion, or a philosophy. It's not even an insight or realization. It is not a function of the mind or perception, which is all we have access to. It is only *you*. It is the thing itself. That is why we call it "direct." But as I've said, even "direct" is too far.

3:17   Using the word "direct" implies "immediate and without buffer," but even that implies a separation, as though some action needs to be taken to *be* direct. This is not the case with enlightenment because you are already there, so to speak. There is no action, there is no perception, there is no separation—no matter how infinitely small or close. There is NO separation, NO process. It IS *you*. It IS *reality*. It IS the nature of existence. It is NOT a perception of these. It is NOT an experience of any kind, subjective or objective.

3:18   You can see then that if your mind struggles to identify and so "know" the *object* (physical or ethereal) that is your true nature, it can never happen. We must consciously "be" in the very same place and reality that *is* the "thing-itself." So if we use a term like "direct experience," it is only for lack of any more accurate means of conveying what's meant. That's to be expected, however, since no term or idea *can* be accurate. Enlightenment is not something "experienced," and although "direct" is the modifier—indicating something different about this use of the word "experience"—it will inevitably be misunderstood.

3:19   Nothing in our culture or language can adequately represent this Consciousness. One reason is that almost no one ever has such deep direct-consciousness and so there is very little that is widely shared—which is necessary for something to be culturally acceptable and "known" by people in general. Yet even if it were represented and we had ways to speak about it that were more closely aligned with what's true, these would still only be representations and not the real deal. More than any other aspect of human existence, enlightenment can only be grasped directly. Short of that, it cannot be understood.

Being Trapped within Experience

3:20 Let's try to clear up what I mean by "experience" since it's crucial to this discussion. Your experience, in this moment and every moment, is all that you know and perceive. It is everything you are aware of in any way—your internal state, mental activities, what you perceive as your environment, everything you feel or sense, intuit, imagine, remember, think, believe, and even the influence of the content of your unconscious mind. It is the whole world for you; it is what you experience as you and reality, others, and everything else.

3:21 Think of it this way: There is nothing in your awareness that is *outside* of your experience. If you think there is, then you aren't grasping what I'm calling experience. People with a "spiritual" bent or imagination often seem to hold that they can experience something outside of what I'm referring to as experience. If you're doing that, stop it.

3:22 Experience is created by mind; and the predominant, although not exclusive, contributor to this "knowing of our reality" is perception. Perception is not a direct encounter of what is—it is always indirect, different than, and separate from whatever is perceived. Enlightenment requires a direct-consciousness of the truth, not an indirect perception or experience. Our "consciousness" is stuck within this indirect perceptive-experience. It's as if we are "looking out from" rather than "being conscious of" the very place we exist.

3:23 The perceived reality in which we live is very difficult to get free of because its nature isn't recognized. Our perceived-experience is a bit like being in a dream. Within the dream, no matter where you look or what you do, there is nothing outside the dream world that constitutes your entire experience. Grasping that it's a dream will suddenly end the search because it becomes clear there is nothing within the dream that you could possibly use to free you of it. This is because the perceived dream reality itself is not real. Once you wake up from the dream, that entire perceived reality falls away. The problem with this analogy, however, is that when you wake up, you are immediately in a very similar reality. It's basically the same kind of perceptive-experience, with the added distinction of being the "real" one, allowing you to make a distinction between the dream world and the real world, grasping that the dream world isn't real. But you're still stuck in perception and experience, and the context of object-reality.

3:24 It is this "object" context that creates the most significant difference between these two worlds. Because of this context, we see that in the dream world there are no lasting consequences, while in the real world there are. This difference makes it almost impossible to deny the reality of our real world. The thing is, nothing needs to be denied. It's the true nature or absolute reality that we're considering. Whatever is true about the world is already true. Our problem in grasping that, however, is a lot like searching within a domain that can never provide the answer. In that way, this analogy of the dream world—where there is no way out of that experience without grasping the true nature of it—is apt.

3:25 Enlightenment is not an aspect of experience or mind on any level or in any way. This is not to say that one's mind goes unaffected when having an enlightenment experience. It is affected, and always in a positive way. There is increased freedom from previously binding aspects of mind—not every aspect, and usually not most, but some. This may be why, in some circles, it has come to be called an enlightenment "experience." But any changes in one's experience or mind are *not* the enlightenment itself. This often goes unnoticed, even by people having some direct-consciousness.

3:26 Accompanying an enlightenment is often a temporary euphoria, the length of which depends on the depth of the consciousness. This doesn't mean that having an insight or realization and being euphoric about it constitutes an enlightenment. The only essential aspect of enlightenment is an increase in consciousness, and specifically becoming directly conscious of the true nature of some aspect of existence. From this consciousness, the mind will create some form of "knowing" what's true in the matter. It will be as accurate as the mind can be, but it will not be the consciousness itself. You may have a genuine insight or realization but, without this clear consciousness that is the same as the "thing itself," you have not had an enlightenment.

3:27 When you have a genuine enlightenment, you become conscious that your nature is nothing. You have no quality, no aspect, and you exist in no location, so there is no objective aspect for the mind to grasp. The true nature is absolute, and so paradox is an aspect of this consciousness, making it incomprehensible to the mind.

3:28 Although much of this can't be understood prior to having an enlightenment or two—which I highly recommend for everyone—the idea at least provides a possibility to which you can relate in some way. Yet I can't overemphasize that this is not something to believe. If you *believe* what I said about being nothing, etc., then you are believing in the wrong thing. No matter what you think or believe about this, it is not the truth.

3:29 Having an experience about which you might say "there is nothing" or you experienced "emptiness" or some such, is NOT an enlightenment. It is a *perceptive-experience,* and *any* experience is a function of mind. People who work hard to contemplate these matters can and do come up with many altered states, realizations, conclusions, and experiences, many of which might be described in similar terms. But these are not direct-consciousness. Enlightenment is a consciousness of the true nature of *you,* not an experience of any kind. These statements about enlightenment are made only to provide a springboard from which to leap, and to shake up the fixed mind-set about something that is literally inconceivable. Please hear them in that context.

3:30 The Consciousness that is enlightenment is grasping the Absolute truth about the nature of existence (fill in the blank as to the existence of what). It turns out that there is absolutely nothing here, but this isn't an absence of anything, nor separate from "what is," because it *is* existence—it's not an aspect or quality or perception. There is no objective reference for understanding this. What I just said will be confusing because, of necessity, you will search experience, mind, perception, thought, and feeling in order to translate what's said, and no matter what you come up with, it won't be what I meant. The Absolute truth does not and will never lend itself to something that can be thought, felt, sensed, intuited, or perceived in any way—not even in an unusual or special way.

Why Becoming Conscious Doesn't Always Create Change

3:31   Creating the possibility of dropping some aspect of the person you are opens the space to do so, but it doesn't do it *for* you. Recognizing, for example, that you're not your anger, or even one who needs to use anger as a tool to manage his needs, does not eliminate anger from your automatic impulses. It does, however, create the opportunity for you to see anger for what it is and stop using it, or begin to use it in a very different and conscious way. This is true for any aspect of yourself, such as the idea that you are superior or worthless, wanting to control others, your fear of rejection, your habit of interrupting, your urge to smoke, the need to be right, being pretentious, or any other characteristic within your self-experience. But you'll instinctively hang on to anything that is seen *as you*, so how is it possible to let go of it?

3:32   In order to let go of or eliminate any characteristic feeling-impulse or behavior, it must be recognized as *not-you* and not needed. The operative word here is "recognized." Whether it is in fact not-you does little unless you experience it as such. Once something is experienced clearly as not-you, the mental-emotional impulse that creates the characteristic in question can then be released from the lexicon of aspects identified as "you" or as a tool of yours. Depending on the depth of your experiential consciousness, this may be as easy as simply dropping it, or you may find yourself undergoing a process of long-term hard work. No matter how it goes, the first requisite to free yourself of anything is that you recognize it is not you. Very powerful and embedded human assumptions make this difficult.

3:33 Enlightenment allows one to grasp that the self is unreal and that your true nature is inconceivable and not formed at all. This provides a "platform" upon which to truly transform. At this first level of direct-consciousness it is likely not to be all that deep or clear, but this distinction will eventually evolve as you become even more conscious. With this consciousness you create the possibility of more readily letting go of any aspect of your self-experience, since, with some attentiveness and work, you can see it as *not-you*. In that case, it seems less like destroying something called "you" and is instead freeing yourself from limitations that you are not. If you hold that something *is* you, "you" can't let go of it because it's "you." If it's experienced as not-you, then obviously *you* can let go of it. See how this works?

3:34 Don't confuse disliking something about yourself for seeing it as not-you. Rejection of some self-aspect isn't the same as grasping that it isn't you. The very fact that you feel compelled to reject it already acknowledges that you experience it as yourself and want that to be otherwise.

3:35 Wanting, liking, disliking, denying, ignoring, believing, and so on are not the same as the distinction of you and not-you. You can apply all these reactions to anything perceived. What makes something "you" is that you identify it as you. Multiple aspects exist in what you call yourself, both positive and negative. With enlightenment, you become conscious of what is really true about your nature and existence—what you actually are—and realize that you are not what you previously *experienced* as yourself.

3:36 But make no mistake, enlightenment is not a panacea. Simply having an enlightenment experience, or several, doesn't change

WHAT ARE WE DEALING WITH?

you without your participation. As I've said, enlightenment isn't the end, as people often think. It's the beginning.

3:37   Whatever occurs within the mind is never a consciousness of one's true nature. Mind is about brain and mental activity, concept and perspective, perception and experience. Your true nature is about the actual or fundamental existence of the being that you are. You *are* your true nature; you *generate* and *perceive* the content of mind. Consciousness isn't mind, but mind is a form of consciousness.

3:38   Becoming conscious of your true nature doesn't necessarily change the mind. Consciousness, mind, and brain aren't all references to the same thing. For clarification, we could hold the brain as a tool, and mind as using the tool. Sort of like a piano is the tool and music is what arises from playing it. Music isn't the piano, and the piano isn't music, but they are related. Consciousness, in this analogy, is like the player-listener, which is neither music nor piano, but the creator of both.

3:39   I'm just trying to make some distinctions here so that you have a better way to understand what I'm saying. In this depiction, enlightenment is becoming conscious that you are the player-listener (sort of), and not the tool being played, or the resultant content of the playing. Don't take all this too seriously; it is just a way to provide you with an inaccurate understanding of what I mean by saying enlightenment doesn't necessarily change the mind. Grasping that your nature is neither an object (the brain) nor the activity of experiencing and understanding (the mind) doesn't change the object or activity. Only changing those changes those.

3:40   Of course, realizing that you are the player-listener when you formerly experienced yourself as music or piano would be quite an awakening. This would likely change the way the music comes out, or what is played, but much would remain the same. After all, the keys and notes are still the same ones, and most of the music has already been written. Furthermore, since so much of the brain-mind has been ingrained as automatic and repeated patterns of reaction and activity that have been deemed necessary for self-survival, this forceful activity is likely to continue. It is *the* activity of life, and this proceeds as if of its own accord.

3:41   We need to take care not to divide up these distinctions too sharply for fear of falling into the trap of oversimplifying the matter by "object"-ifying everything. Unfortunately, such objectification is supported by the very use of an analogy. In fact, the analogy only works because it does just that. It divides the references into distinct and known "objects" that are more easily understood. This is its purpose and strength, but also its weakness. It demonstrates the assertion I made about how mind works to grasp things. This is unavoidable.

3:42   But, as can be seen within this piano analogy, there is an even greater danger of misunderstanding. Please don't hear "player-listener" as the "observer" or "witness" or awareness. These are already the accepted forms of self-as-consciousness and they are NOT what I'm talking about. To make this mistake would be a significant setback. Remember, although Consciousness is not mind, mind is a form of Consciousness, so in our piano analogy, you would actually be all of it and none of it at the same time. But you will be ignorant of this fact if you are identified as any of the elements experienced, rather than the Absolute Consciousness that is *you*. This is why we need to take care to reach beyond the presentation of any analogy or model to seek out the truth.

3:43   Changing anything about oneself takes a personal commitment. Yet there's a cultural reason why people confuse enlightenment with transformation. Because contemplation is the accepted road to enlightenment, it appears that it's a task of searching for something. This something might be held as grand, life-altering, and the greatest thing since sliced bread—otherwise why would anyone work so hard to pursue it? I suspect people imagine that anything with such a reputation would transform them merely upon its encounter. This is false. As I've said, consciousness of the truth doesn't change anything—the truth is already that way.

3:44   Becoming conscious of who and what you really are is invaluable for transformation, but this awakening alone doesn't accomplish it for you. For the most part, any personal changes that occur must be done consciously and deliberately, or else little about the self is changed. Without intervention, the automatic programmed self-mind will still tend to dominate your experience, and so, shy of profoundly deep or "complete enlightenment," some ignorance or lack of consciousness will remain. Because of this, enlightenment degrades into a form of "knowing" but not *being*. This knowing is correct as a reference, but inaccurate if it's considered to be the thing-itself, or the true nature of "being."

Enlightenment and the Human Condition

3:45   Enlightenment only occurs suddenly, since it is outside of time or process. When someone has what is called an enlightenment experience, it is a sudden glimpse of the true nature of something, usually oneself. Although such consciousness is absolute and true, it is rarely universal. It isn't becoming conscious of "everything," so to speak. This is obvious to anyone who's had a first enlightenment and is confused by the fact that there still remains much unknown and the self remains pretty much intact. Remember, after realizing his true nature, one of my students said, "It's now obvious that I am not this mind or this self, so why do I continue to be trapped within both mind and self?" This is a good question, and requires some attention.

3:46 As I've said, becoming conscious of what's true isn't about changing anything. Most of the attachments and identifications that comprise the self-experience usually remain intact. The consciousness of your true nature doesn't necessarily provide any depth of consciousness about the workings of the self-mind. With such direct-consciousness, however, experience, self, and mind will be viewed from a different perspective—sort of like seeing them from the outside for the first time, and with the understanding of not *being* any of them, thus providing the possibility of not identifying with them. This creates a new relationship to all that, but it doesn't *change* all that.

3:47 As one's consciousness increasingly deepens, the confusion, or remaining ignorance, regarding consciousness and mind begins to clarify over time. Still, this is only likely to occur if the self and mind are studied and observed through the lens of this consciousness. Such clarity is usually a gradual process, since it occurs within the normal activities of being human and within human understanding. Although enlightenment is sudden and "outside of" mind, understanding is usually slow, as the mind is steadily recreated to include a new function capable of paradoxical thought. We might call that developing "wisdom."

3:48   Even with this depth of consciousness and understanding, there usually remains in the mind a separation of self and being, of consciousness and perceived reality. Eventually, there should be no such separation. The entire matter of absolute existence can have nothing left out or left unconscious. Existence and non-existence can't be seen as separate or different. Enlightenment *is* absolute existence and must include the direct-consciousness of the self, the mind, reality, and all that is, or it isn't complete.

3:49   Eventually, when Absolute Consciousness is grasped to be the same as "existence," a natural transformation must occur since, at that point, being human wouldn't be separate from the Absolute. This would change the whole foundation of experience—it would both exist and not exist, and these would be the same. This may be an ultimate goal for some, but not for many, and is exceptionally rare. The truth is almost no one is going to achieve it. Upon his own complete enlightenment, Gautama Buddha himself didn't think people could possibly grasp it, and he was only convinced to teach because of the slim possibility that someone *might*. Yet this shouldn't stop anyone from pursing it, accomplishing whatever depth of consciousness can be had and freedom attained.

3:50   Most people who pursue enlightenment don't actually want the complete and Absolute truth. Perhaps they want to directly experience their own true nature and "have" that as an accomplishment. This is fine, and a good outcome for most. From here, transformation can be undertaken in earnest and with a much better foundation. Some sort of transformation was probably their real goal in the first place. Of course, just as in the case of enlightenment, they will find that their fantasies were wrong about transformation too; but that is how it always begins.

What Is and Isn't Enlightenment

> *If we knew what it was we were doing,*
> *it wouldn't be called research, would it?*
> —Albert Einstein

The Absolute Is Beyond Distinctions

3:51 Although it can't be stated any more clearly, people just don't believe that enlightenment is not something perceived in any way. Since perception is how we "know" or experience reality, we don't imagine any other real possibility, and certainly not something weird called "direct-consciousness." How can you relate to a statement such as: *Absolute Consciousness does not exist in the domain of experience, and yet is not elsewhere*? The response to such an assertion is to imagine that it is a very special form of experience, or a unique domain of perception. No. This is simply what *can* be thought when trying to conceptualize the matter. Of course, it is mistaken.

3:52 It may be impossible to communicate, but it really can't be said much better than this:

> *Form is no different from emptiness.*
> *Emptiness is no different from form.*
> *Form is precisely emptiness,*
> *emptiness is precisely form.*
> —The Heart Sutra

3:53 Try not to see this in relative terms or as a metaphor or poetry. Another option would be to say that objective reality is Nothing or does not exist; and Nothing *is* objective reality. Here, form is everything that *is* or exists. Nothing is an absolute and is the true nature of form. Since it's a translation as well as a reference, we can reword this description a bit without changing the meaning but perhaps clarifying the message:

> *The nature of form is Absolute Nothing.*
> *Nothing isn't the absence of anything.*
> *Everything is the same as Nothing,*
> *Nothing is the same as something.*

3:54 That didn't help much, did it? I'm sorry that it's not easier to get. The above communication represents a very deep level of consciousness. This depth of realization goes beyond self and into the heart of the real nature of reality. Even those who've had their first few enlightenments don't really grasp the truth of what's being said. Although it sounds neat, doesn't it?

3:55 Enlightenment is not an experience or something experienced. It is not a perception or something perceived. It is not an object or even a subject. It isn't what you may define or figure out. It is not an idea or conclusion. It isn't a state of mind of any kind, nor a really big and wonderful world of magical phenomena. All of these things may happen, but none of them are enlightenment, no matter how hard you may assert that they are.

3:56 Enlightenment simply "reveals" to your consciousness that there is absolutely nothing here, and it *is you*, and it is reality, and it is everything. Since the mind can't hold such an absolute consciousness, this will degrade into a form of "knowing" that can be related to; and even those who've had such consciousness often take this "knowing" for the consciousness itself. They are mistaken.

3:57 If you've had a *kensho* ("first glimpse") or two, all this may make some sense to you, although you've likely found such acknowledgments absent from the "enlightenment discourse." Hearing my assertions, however, you can probably relate to them in some way. Some of what I'm saying (and will continue to say throughout this book) is directed to those who've had at least one enlightenment experience. Regarding such experiences, there is precious little communication available, and most of it is kept on a very cryptic level. I understand why this is so—trying to explain these matters, one has to be willing to come off as a pontificating fool. Although my attempted communications will run into more serious challenges than that and may be misunderstood, know that I'm trying to speak to you as seriously and candidly as possible.

3:58 If you haven't had your first enlightenment experiences yet, much of what's said here won't make any sense, but you should hear the story and possibility anyway—it plants a seed—and it's useful to hear that it doesn't automatically transform you, since transformation exists in the domain of process. Therefore you can begin transformation without enlightenment.

3:59 Of course, enlightenment can help a great deal but much can be done without any enlightenment whatsoever. If transformation is your goal, you would be ill-advised to wait for complete enlightenment. There is much in the next chapter to assist you in beginning to tackle transformation—with or without enlightenment.

PART TWO

Getting Down to Work

CHAPTER FOUR

Setting the Stage for Transformation

Letting Go Rather Than Attaining

4:1 When we're interested in self-improvement, we'll naturally try to come up with a set of characteristics that we think would be inherent in the person we want to become. This occasions crafting our ideals—often combined with the ideals of a chosen belief system—into an image of what we'll be like when we succeed. In this way, however, our attention goes to our imagination rather than to ourselves.

4:2 Transformation begins at home. Unless you comprehend the internal "mechanisms" of your own mind, there is little chance that you can make any significant or lasting changes. You need to understand that you've already been pursuing "self-improvement" in some form via your already ingrained ideals. These exist as images of how you *should* be—whether your goal is to be a better person, to have a better life, to attain what you believe is needed to resolve your suffering, or to accomplish some imagined destiny that will finally set things right in your heart. If you've already been living with these goals in mind, however, whatever you've attained or failed to attain is unlikely to change using this same perspective.

GETTING DOWN TO WORK

4:3 Transformation is changing the very person that you experience being—the "you" that's looking out from your eyes right now. This means that what you identify with as a self—your various characteristics and beliefs, your reactions and emotional justifications, how you view yourself and reality—all must end, be destroyed, dissolved.

4:4 That doesn't sound so good now, does it? This is rarely what people hold as the goal of transformation. The annihilating aspect of transformation isn't the whole story, but it is one that needs to be taken seriously and confronted.

4:5 I want to be clear: I'm not talking about change because there's anything wrong with you. We're not tackling transformation because you are wrong or bad or broken. If something is broken, fix it. If you merely *believe* you are broken, stop believing that. Those are different matters. If being wrong or broken is your reason to transform, it's not the best motive. What that's about is healing or improving, and that's important to do but is a different effort than transforming. Healing, if needed—and it's often needed—is only a first step.

4:6 The domain of transformation that I'm talking about demands a confrontation with letting go of yourself, the "death" of what you've come to know and experience and identify with *as yourself*. This shouldn't be confused with trying to eliminate the bad in you, or to correct what's wrong. Still, such an idea as letting go of yourself is probably a rather new one. Outside of morbid nihilism or other such dark or suicidal ideas—which is absolutely not what I'm suggesting—the thought of becoming free of the person you experience yourself to be doesn't appear desirable. It exists in the same domain as dying, and death isn't something people embrace.

4:7 I suspect that you'd be surprised at how incapable people are of confronting death. Everyone has some ideas about death—they fear it or think they've come to grips with it, but mostly they ignore it. This relationship to death, however, is strictly conceptual. People are actually incapable of really comprehending death or even thinking about it as a reality. Try it. I'll bet that if you try to simply imagine your own death—not a fantasy of you surviving in some fashion or being reborn, but actually dying—you'll not only find it difficult to do, but in a matter of minutes your mind will slip off the subject as a reality. Death is anti-self. No more self. At all. How can a self imagine this? How can a self confront it? It is no-self, and that is antithetical to the very heart and soul of *being* a self.

4:8 Death isn't a process or even your destruction. It is *no you*. That is a different matter than "dying." Since a self can't fathom or "think" of no-self, death is not something we can successfully confront. Managing to transcend the primal fear of no "you" is also central to transformation because, no matter what you become or don't become, it would have to be something other than you-as-you-are, and so in some way it would be not-you or no you. Can you even imagine an experience of no-you? Notice that every experience you have or can have is inherently based on you. You are the primary feature in all experience.

4:9 This may be why all sorts of "survival-in-some-form" scenarios have been created throughout human history. The mere idea that all your efforts to survive, to attain, to resolve, to grow, to build and so on are actually meaningless and will fail in the end is unthinkable. It invalidates your very existence as a self, so some other notion is needed to fill that space. No matter what it is, it

GETTING DOWN TO WORK

has to be better than fruitlessly striving in a meaningless life ending in non-existence, doesn't it?

4:10   Even indulging the drama that what I'm saying is in any way negative is not grasping the matter. Neither the fact of death nor the freeing aspect of transformation is negative. Instead, it is a principle, one we can put to good use. If this unconscious aversion, however, is an automatic human relationship to death, you can see that such an ignoring-force might well apply itself when attempting to let go of any self-aspect.

4:11   We need to pay attention to the fact that the self constantly pushes to remain unchanged and to have its needs met. That is its purpose and function. When thwarted in some way—when you force yourself to act uncharacteristically or stop responding to arising impulses—the self will cry out with increasing vigor until you're back living from a familiar disposition. Any attempt to eliminate or change what you identify with will be met with resistance that will need to be overcome.

4:12   Don't suppose that I'm inviting you to war with what you consider to be your "self." It would be unwise to adopt a negative perspective regarding your present experience. This would just create more self-judgments and difficulties, alienating you from your own process. Although the principle of elimination must be active, this shouldn't be accompanied by disassociation. Instead, you should embrace what you experience.

4:13   For example, say you find yourself with a character trait of being outwardly fearful or shy. You may find these attributes unpleasant and desire to be free of them. What you aren't noticing is that you *want* these reactions to take place, otherwise they wouldn't. They are a form you've chosen as a method to protect or persist as yourself in some way. To fight with them or consider them negative isn't doing much, since you already consider them negative and have likely struggled with them throughout your life. Investigating your fear demands that you fully experience it for the purpose of getting why it exists and what you're accomplishing by creating it.

4:14 Turning your attention toward grasping what you're purposely doing changes your perspective in the matter. Learning to create the activity of investigating what you're accomplishing—both existentially as well as psychologically—by doing what you're doing moves your consciousness to the source of the doing. Being able to create this disposition at will, independent of the stimulus of circumstance, goes a long way toward freeing you of these entrenched activities. If you become conscious that you are the source, you can change what you're doing.

4:15 The principle of change means that whatever currently exists becomes different than it is right now. In the case of transformation, this means that not only is there some difference in how you act, but that you yourself are different. If you're unwilling to give up the experience you have of yourself, including what you consider to be permanent, correct, or cherished, transformation cannot proceed. Do you think you can remain the same and change?

4:16 The very person who is reading these words is the you I'm talking about, not something else. This experience of "you" includes everything you're attached to, such as your moods, your perspectives, how you think, what you believe, and so on. It also includes that aspect you consider the very core of you. Without changing that core, how is it really possible to change you? Make no mistake, this one that you think you are, this one that you know and love, cannot survive any real transformation. Does that sound like something you want to pursue?

4:17 Letting go of your very person would mean that your character and opinions, your dispositions and attitudes, your quirks and familiar internal states won't exist any longer—or at least won't exist as *you*. If eliminating aspects of yourself evokes self's knee-jerk reaction to death, this may prevent any real pursuit of change. It's not hard to imagine that the fundamental disposition humans have toward death will interfere with letting go of anything to which you are attached, anything that is seen as one's self.

4:18 The truth may be that what you really are, like an absolute, can't die since there is already nothing there. As it turns out, you are not a self or a process, and so there is no life or death. But since you probably don't experience that, the death of your self will still be experienced as the very real death of yourself. This is one reason it is useful to grasp who and what you really are before you die.

In the case of everyone there is observed supreme love for one's self,
and as happiness alone is the cause for love,
in order to gain happiness one should truly "know" one's self.
—Ramana Maharshi

4:19 We tend to focus on what we might get out of transformation, not what we'll lose. But most of our focus needs to be on what we can let go of or get rid of, which is often looked on as a negative. Certainly, the imagined positive aspects of transformation are the reason we would attempt it. We wouldn't consider such a path if we didn't think it would turn out better than what we already experience. Basing such a pursuit on our ideals, however, is a closed loop.

Why Ideals Become Objectives for Transformation

4:20   Ideals are as complex as we are. They exist in every domain that our self-minds and self-identities operate—from the subtle and mundane to the ambitious and grandiose. This complex content dominates our experience more than we think. The underlying dynamics of ideals, however, can be difficult to ferret out.

4:21   We really don't have much of a choice when it comes to choosing an objective for transformation. Since the end product of transformation is unknown, we can't form an accurate idea or image of it. And yet we probably already have such images. Where do these come from? They come from our ideals, what we imagine is a better life, a better self. Within this taken-for-granted conceptual domain exists the person we think we should be, as well as images of attaining total happiness and being fulfilled. How could this not influence our idea of transformation?

4:22   Ideals constitute the part of our experience that suggests what is missing or lacking in ourselves, and what would, in theory, make us complete if attained. Ideals represent—both consciously and unconsciously—all of what we believe are the attainments that would resolve our personal struggles, and thus end them. As pointed out in *The Book of Not Knowing*, this will never happen but lives as if it should. We believe that if achieving our ideals doesn't resolve everything, we'll have failed our ultimate life mission. We often succumb to a lesser experience of self than we think we should, but even this is in contrast to our ideals since that's what makes it "lesser."

---

*Hope is a bad thing.
It means that you are not what you want to be.
It means that you entertain illusions.*
—Henry Miller

4:23   Our experience of ourselves is made up of, among other things, what we think we are or have settled on as our self content. The contrast of our ideals to our accepted self content attaches an ongoing sense of incompleteness to whatever we currently experience as ourselves. This is something that is overlooked and taken for granted. We generally accept it as simply our experience of "life," and perhaps it's absorbed into that category we refer to as "I'm only human." The thing to notice here, however, is that whenever we have a positive, we must have a negative; when we have a better we must have a worse or lesser. From this, we can see the diminishing impact that our ideals have on our experience of self and life.

4:24   We certainly wouldn't *knowingly* create a lesser experience of ourselves, so why would we do it at all? We overlook the fact that needing to be better than we are now creates in our current experience a context of being lesser or incomplete, since negative and positive are inseparable. Beyond overlooking this relationship, we are also driven to pursue "ideals" based on mechanisms of mind and experience of which we are not aware.

Penetrating Your Core Experience

4:25 Personal ideals are founded on an underlying framework where we believe our nature has specific traits that shape the individual we are. We think that as a person, we inherently have particular attributes at our core, forming taken-for-granted truisms of our very being. These unrecognized assumptions and core beliefs are what I call the framework or matrix of uncognized mind.

4:26 What virtually no one grasps is that this domain of self-experience isn't a *reaction* to circumstance, it's what generates reactions to circumstance. It isn't a feeling or emotional disposition, it creates feelings and emotional dispositions. Your reactions and behavior, your self-agenda and performance, all relate to and are based upon these usually simple but unrecognized core beliefs. These unnoticed convictions dominate your character and personality.

4:27 Common among foundational self-aspects are such "certainties" as being incapable, vulnerable, broken, unreal, inauthentic, worthless, insignificant, and so on. The reason they are most often negative is that only the negative "facts" about your nature need to be resolved. This is what dominates your character by dictating your self-agenda as well as forming your ideals—images of something better *must* be based on and relate to a less-than-perfect experience.

4:28 What you consider positive aspects of yourself are actually rather irrelevant for the task of life because they don't need to be resolved or managed. Ideals can't be based on them since there's nothing lacking. All you really need as a positive is simply *being* itself. Any other attributes assigned only limit and degrade, even if they appear positive. Often, however, what are considered positive attributes are covering up or compensating for a core sense of something negative.

4:29　We might think having a sense of worthiness or significance would be a positive thing. But why would these exist except through either past programming or as a need to compensate for feeling unworthy or insignificant? Any *feeling* of being worthwhile or significant is unlikely to be an aspect of our unrecognized nature, but rather a willful affirmative conclusion about ourselves compensating for the opposite. When it comes to what we believe is true of our core, we can see that positive attributes aren't really needed, even such positives as being real or capable. What is more real than *is-ness* itself? What is more capable than *life* itself? The mere fact of being and being alive already inherently provides these. There's no need for a belief or attribute to assert them. When there is such a need, it's only because these are lacking or in doubt. *Being is.* That's the end of that story. So when we unconsciously believe we have inherent attributes, these will tend to appear negative. But for the most part they don't appear at all, remaining as the unrecognized foundation for what *is* experienced.

4:30　Ideal beliefs only exist in relationship to beliefs of personal deficiency. Yet these bottom-line beliefs aren't present in your experience as beliefs, they're there as facts. They're present as "you." These core experiences exist as if they *are* you, as if they are part of your very nature. They are not just assessments of your self-performance, as one might think. They live as if they *are* your true nature, but their existence is rarely acknowledged or recognized.

4:31　The reason they're overlooked is that your perceptive-experience is committed to resolving them rather than grasping them. An eye doesn't look at itself; it looks at what it's seeing—that is an eye's function. Looking at itself would serve no purpose so isn't part of the design. Just so, bottom-line core beliefs aren't experienced by you for what they are. Instead, they generate and dominate the experience you have of yourself and of everything else. They are so foundational—and below the surface of your normally cognized experience—that they aren't questioned or challenged, but assumed.

4:32 You need to understand this aspect of your experience in order to understand the relationship your ideals have to these unresolved and overlooked bottom-line assumptions about your nature or very person. We'll confront this issue more as we progress. For now, it's useful to be aware of the relationship between what you assume is a positive (your ideals) and the negative foundation that these ideals are hoping to resolve.

4:33 We are still left with having to create a direction in which to proceed, however, and so need to formulate an objective to start the wheels rolling. Even if we adopt some established belief system's conception of a "transformed" person—or whatever name is given by that system—this image will still be related to and re-formed within the experience of our own ideals. Nevertheless, to make progress we must proceed, and this requires an objective.

Creating a Transformation Objective

4:34 It is difficult to have an accurate idea about where we need to go when our view affords us no clue about our destination. If we knew the "answer" to our "problem," so to speak, we'd have solved it already. We frequently believe that we know what ails us and know how to fix it, or at least we've adopted someone else's belief system on that. Yet, if we are correct in our view, then why have we failed to transform or even to resolve our personal struggles? We must confront the possibility that we are probably wrong about what transformation is all about.

4:35 When I used to do private instruction in interactive skill, it was common for someone to walk in and relate to me what their problem was and what they needed to fix it, and then ask me to do that. I would always start with "if you knew what the problem was, you wouldn't need me; you would have corrected it already." Of course it turned out that I was right and, after investigating what they were actually doing—how they thought, moved, conceived of success, and so forth—the means of correcting their inability to accomplish desired goals was always found in areas they hadn't looked nor conceived before. How could they? If they weren't ignorant of the cause, they wouldn't have the problem.

> *No problem can be solved from the same level*
> *of consciousness that created it.*
> —Albert Einstein

4:36 A new and deeper consciousness needs to occur. With this in mind, how do we address creating goals for transformation? Steadily increasing consciousness and making breakthroughs are essential contributions to this work. But beyond any sudden insights, transformation is a process. Proceeding from one form to another requires change—changing from this experience to a different experience, from your way of thinking to a new way of thinking, from habitual behavior to unfamiliar behavior, from one set of impulses to a new set of impulses or no impulses at all. This means that we must somehow go from where we are now to a place unknown. If it's unknown, we need to *create* some objective, some image or direction that works to get us going, yet one that we can and must change as we progress.

4:37 When we speak of transformation we're not considering what ultimately "is." We're considering changing the processes we're identified with into some other form or process. Therefore, in order to proceed toward transformation we must try to imagine or define the result of this process, which is what it is we're trying to achieve. Otherwise, how would we begin?

4:38 We need to come up with some image of a "transformed person," or a list of attributes we'd recognize as a transformed experience. But this must only serve as our objective temporarily. It won't be where we'll ultimately end up, since by definition this is beyond our ability to imagine from our "pre-transformed" perspective. But the real function of creating an objective is to have it operate as a catalyst—something applied to make a change that itself doesn't remain after the change. Introducing something temporarily that allows a process to move forward is the point of the story of the wandering Abdul.

4:39 Abdul is traveling with his camel in the desert. He comes across a heated inheritance dispute among three brothers. Their father recently died and has left them seventeen camels, decreeing that half should go to his eldest son, a third to the middle son, and one-ninth to the youngest. But seventeen camels don't divide up in that way. To solve this dilemma, Abdul donates his camel to the dead man's estate. Then, with eighteen camels, they can be divided with half (nine) going to the oldest son, one-third (six) to the middle son, and one-ninth (two) to the youngest, thus

GETTING DOWN TO WORK

totaling seventeen. Abdul then takes back his camel and goes on his way.

4:40 Our main concern is to use the image of "who we would be if transformed" as a temporary goal—an inserted camel, so to speak—and yet not fixate on it as a final goal, but rather a stepping stone. Forming an idea of an objective so we can determine "who we want to become" is in some way inherent in the idea of transformation. So where do people usually look for such a concept?

4:41 One source for images of a transformed self is found in examples of or tales about people who've asserted they are enlightened. We notice that when such people are engaged in the role of representing enlightenment, they generally take on certain qualities. They may not take on these qualities when engaged in another role, or the qualities may appear differently. Yet when they are charged to represent enlightenment, they tend to be honest, clear, present, uninterested in self, often compassionate, sometimes brutal but only to facilitate others, fearless, apparently freed of many of the normal social constraints regarding self-image and self-agenda, etc. These are generalizations that vary from person to person, but they're also backed up by stories about the unusual nature of such people, and further supported by our desire for them to fit our ideas of what an "enlightened one" should look like. From this kind of input, we can form an image of what a transformed person might be like, and then set about trying to be like that.

4:42 If we adopt of all those characteristics, would we be transformed? Or would we just be pretending? Remember, these "enlightened" people didn't *adopt* those characteristics (unless they aren't enlightened and are just pretending). Such characteristics came about as a side effect of increased consciousness as well as the impulse to represent the truth as accurately as possible so as to remain aligned with this consciousness. The shift in consciousness comes first; the characteristics may or may not follow. But this tendency toward certain characteristics does indicate a direction that suggests there are perhaps hidden principles involved.

4:43 Would it be harmful to adopt those characteristics? That depends. As an affectation, it would hurt very much. Such pretentious activity only draws our attention elsewhere and pulls us away from what is so for us, and is therefore inconsistent with grasping what's *true*. We are also drawn to fall into the trap of thinking we've accomplished some degree of transformation just because we can adopt certain behaviors, or even attitudes and internal states. This may not be true at all, especially if the reason for doing so is to attain an ideal self-image—in our own mind or in the minds of others. That's not much more of a feat than putting on a set of new clothes. If the behavior doesn't naturally come from our sense of *being*, and as a reflection of it, then it is only a pretense. Rather than pretending to be some way, adopting and using these characteristics as a contrast and challenge to our current experience can help ground us in a more realistic and honest relationship to the matter.

4:44 Staying as close as possible to being authentic seems like the best way to proceed. It turns out that when it comes to the make-up of an individual—the arena in which transformation manifests— the real truth is that it's not *you,* so one's makeup doesn't matter. The true nature of existence doesn't care what is "existing," so to speak. If we find that none of it is real and we're caught in a meaningless and unresolvable battle within the form of self, what difference does it make whether we change any of it? If this assertion is true, it makes no difference, but we'd have to actually see it that

GETTING DOWN TO WORK

way for such a detached freedom to contribute to our perspective, and for the most part, we don't. Some people may *believe* it's all an illusion, but that certainly doesn't mean they experience that to be true.

4:45 Even though the Absolute truth may be unknown, we can't base our objective on hearsay. Regarding any list of characteristics we might come up with, whatever seems most true—as well as it can be discerned beyond personal preference—will provide one component or principle to help lead us toward determining what should constitute our objective. Along with another principle we've introduced, that of letting go or getting free, honesty helps us get past the overlooked barrier of being vague or unrealistic. Together these directives can ground us in specific action.

Clarifying Your Objective by Being Specific

4:46 Since you exist within the "maze" of mind and perceptive-experience you find little possibility, much less the impulse, to let go of your self-experience. Why is this so? Because self identifies with this mind, and so you've become confused with your own "experience"—thought, emotion, beliefs, impulses, drives, and characteristic behavioral patterns. You must grasp in some real and experiential way that you are NOT any of the things that you experience and identify with.

4:47 In order to free yourself from any characteristic self-experience it's best to be unambiguous about what it is you're identified with; otherwise you won't be clear enough to let go of this aspect of your experience. Also, if your transformational objective isn't specific, it will be hard to contrast and clarify what exactly in your experience is *not* that, and *how* it isn't that. Although this imagined objective may only be as temporary as Abdul's camel, it has to be real and specific in order to do its job.

4:48 What you choose as your objective may be up for grabs, but you need to make it something specific and clear or it will be difficult to direct your efforts and ground your work in real and verifiable results. You can better clarify your personal traits and characteristics by contrasting your self-experience with a clearly imagined alternative experience. Conversely, developing an alternative experience is largely done by becoming increasingly clear about your current experience—starting with specifying what you experience that you don't want and why. Because these reactive patterns are unique to you, they will have to be personally determined. You also need specificity so that you can receive clear feedback within your interactions regarding the consequences of your reactions. Avoid fooling yourself by using vagueness, thus allowing your mind to bias the results, or pretend that something is true when it is not. Strange as it may sound, being specific empowers freedom.

4:49 For example, if you experience being frequently irritated by the behavior of others, you may simply blame them for causing this disposition in you and not see this as a personal characteristic. But when tackling the notion of an all-encompassing-change, this vague recurring sense of being disgruntled starts to be seen more clearly as some feeling you characteristically generate. Why do you react in that way? What really irritates you? Forcing yourself to acknowledge the presence of this tendency allows you to investigate it more thoroughly.

4:50 Once you clarify the repeated presence of this reaction and get to know the real feeling you're having, you can begin to unearth why you do it. Unexpectedly perhaps, you find that your irritation is founded on a feeling of sadness that in turn reveals a sense of personal grief at being misunderstood and feeling like an outsider, not accepted by others. So whenever you interpret that you aren't being heard or heeded, you react with a sense of despair that quickly turns into irritation. Clarifying what your experience is really about and why it exists, you become far more capable of freeing yourself from it by recognizing the concepts and beliefs, history and programming that make it seem necessary. You can then change or eliminate those conceptions.

4:51 When I was young, I was boxing with a student once and he cowered under a fast barrage of punches. I stopped and asked him why he just gave up. He said that he became confused because the punches were coming "all at once." Since I knew I threw them one at a time, albeit quickly, I saw that confusion here was created by "fusing" one moment of experience with others. In his experience, he related to many punches as if occurring simultaneously. How would he dodge "punches all at once"? Yet as I pointed out, he could dodge them one at a time. By forcing his mind to be specific and clear, without muddling or confusing experience into a vague mishmash, he could then deal with each one specifically and effectively (albeit quickly).

4:52 This same principle applies when you find yourself living within a general or vague background sense of self that seems to arise into particular but uninspected experiences that make it difficult to free yourself from anything. As you clarify your experiences, and what you're identified with and attached to, you increase your ability to see them for what they are, get to the source of them, and take action to get free.

Four Principles to Help Design an Objective

4:53   Even though any vision of who we want to become will at first be largely based on our ideals and beliefs, it not only has to be specific, it needs to align with certain principles. Any objective we imagine must be based on the following: on *honesty*—in order to align with the truth; on *freedom*—to activate the principle requiring the dissolution of what binds; on *grounding*—so that we remain healthy and balanced within the physical and psychological; and it needs to be *far-reaching*—to make it a challenge for us, demanding that we extend beyond what's familiar.

4:54   When crafting an objective it's useful to develop a grounded idea of a new experience that is different from your current experience. You want something that's attainable and yet still difficult to become, something that you cannot reach without surrendering some of the patterns and familiar internal states and behaviors that you currently identify with.

4:55   Such a far-reaching objective creates a contrast and a friction with your current identity, which helps reveal the limitations and binding force of your specific self-attachments. By having these self-aspects exposed and amplified through the attempt to change or eliminate them, you can more experientially and consciously contemplate the root of these characteristics and get to the bottom of them.

4:56   Work on transformation must also involve the elimination of or letting go of aspects of yourself. This is consistent with the pursuit of freedom and is not anything that should be held as a negative. How could you transform or get free without such a principle at work? Do you see how embracing this principle also changes the focus and the design of any goal you might choose to adopt?

4:57 Once the far-reaching and freeing principles are active, thus creating a contrasting direction in which to grow, you can focus specifically on what *not* to be. Proceed to identify and drop individual aspects of your experience one by one—such as some idea you assume about yourself, or an emotional reactive pattern, or a belief, or a minor characteristic. You can replace each of these with a healthier way of being, or with openness, or with nothing. In the end you'll have fewer aspects, patterns, and characteristics to identify with. This direction will be simpler, healthier, and *less*—which, strange as it sounds, has the effect of expanding consciousness.

Decreasing self increases consciousness.

4:58 As we've seen, one of the most important of these four principles is over-the-top honesty. You have to learn to be ruthlessly honest with yourself, especially about the real motives for everything you do. Genuine transformation demands such extremes in order to balance your automatic and overwhelming "self"-defenses. It is only when you force your mind to confront what's really true about yourself that you begin to know your inner workings and assumptions well enough to change them. You can't change something of which you're unaware.

4:59 Working with what you only think or hope or even fear is true of you is a little like trying to lift a box by reaching to your left when the box sits on your right. You will be unsuccessful and not know why—'cause you're ignorant! To address the "illusions" generated

Setting the Stage for Transformation

by the bias of your self-mind, you need to strongly activate the principle of honesty. This will allow you to go beyond anything you believe and instead seek out what's true.

4:60   The primary requisite for being honest is an ability to recognize and acknowledge when something is true. It's not whether you like it, or whether it does you any good or harm. It's not whether it fits into what you believe or want to believe. It doesn't matter how you feel about it. The only thing that matters with honesty is whether or not something is true.

4:61   This honesty principle should be applied even to the taken-for-granted and the mundane experiences that occur for you, such as observing what you say to yourself, or what you're thinking or feeling at any given moment. Is what you're saying to yourself actually the truth? Don't stop with asking whether you think it's true, or whether you really feel that way. Is it *actually* true? People assume that any thought or feeling they have is true simply because it's thought or felt. Don't assume this.

4:62   Question your self and all your experiences: are you being honest with yourself? For example, is what you think of others true? Are you being honest about your assessments or are they biased and self-serving? Of course they're biased and self-serving—that's what a self does! So work to get beyond these automatic judgments and interpretations and try to experience what's *true* without any self-serving judgment or distortion. This takes effort, and a deepening honesty is necessary to grasp what is really true about anything. Apply this principle to every aspect of your experience. It will be difficult but in the long run it will pay off the most in helping increase your consciousness.

GETTING DOWN TO WORK

> *Anyone who doesn't take truth seriously in small matters cannot be trusted in large ones either.*
> —Albert Einstein

4:63   By including these four principles as qualities when you create your imagined objective, you should be able to come up with a functioning idea of who it is you want to become—and so design an imagined person different from yourself, one that you feel would be worth being. This can serve as your transformation objective. It is a good beginning. As you undergo the changes required to free yourself of those aspects and experiences that don't match your objective, you will mature and begin to shift away from your former ideals and beliefs into a more conscious and open process.

Divide and Conquer

4:64   When working toward your objective, it's OK to focus on freeing yourself of negative and unwanted characteristics. These are what you'll be drawn to focus on anyway since, in your idealized self-image, they are not how you want to see or experience yourself. You'll also have to address what you consider positive aspects and be willing to drop those as well but, since you want to cling to them, it's hard to find the motivation to do so. That's all right. If you start with the negative, you will eventually get to the positive.

4:65   One way this will play out is found in the fact that negative and positive depend on each other, and your self depends on them. As a matter of fact, self creates them. You can't manage self-interests without determining what's negative and what's positive as it relates to you. So, if you eliminate some negative characteristic, the remaining characteristics—even those held as positive prior to this change—will divide themselves up into positive and negative. You will find negative aspects to formerly positive experiences. Eliminate these negatives and once again the remaining positives will divide up into something negative as well as positive.

4:66 So you see the trend. Just by eliminating the negative you will whittle down your experience more and more, so that very little is left, or it shifts into a domain that defies being called "yours." This is a more "painless" way to go about letting go of something personal, and it joins with your already occurring desire to eliminate the negative. As long as you remain honest, you will continue to find some new negative aspect, even if it's now in a very different domain or level of your experience than you had previously considered. The increased consciousness necessary for actually eliminating or freeing yourself from some aspect of your identity will in turn assist you in discovering and recognizing aspects about your self and your experience that you wouldn't have noticed before.

4:67 Your mind and emotions, and everything you're attached to, are only aspects of experience that you've crafted together and learned to think of and identify as your self. If you hadn't done that, you couldn't have discerned anything to call yourself within the field of perceptive-experience. It is inevitable for each person to create and form an identity in order to experience being a self, but that doesn't make it true, and it doesn't make it *you*. This is an important principle to get, without which you will be endlessly confused with, and so trapped within, mind and experience.

4:68 Your self-experience and self-identity are not *you*. As you become directly conscious of who you actually are, you will realize this. A deepening consciousness of who and what you really are must be pursued or your attempt at transformation will not go far. Such a pursuit needs an experiential distinction between *you* and your self-mind. Enlightenment is the only way to provide that distinction.

4:69 Not only is our conception of what it takes to transform inadequate, shared existential assumptions about self and reality make it difficult to address real change. So in the next chapter, we'll revisit the subject of enlightenment and its relationship to transformation. Refreshing and deepening our look at self and consciousness provides a stronger platform from which to proceed in our work.

CHAPTER FIVE

Freeing Self from Object-Identity

The Usefulness of Feedback in Pursuing Consciousness

5:1 Even if consciousness of the Absolute truth is your only goal, when you have some successes with this objective, you're likely to exaggerate the depth of your consciousness. Mind tends to lie a lot. Remember, the job of the self-mind is to protect and promote the self, not to know what's true. This being the case, it's very useful for you to have some sort of grounded feedback to help prevent you from "misreading" the depth of your consciousness, as well as to assist you in discovering aspects of self and reality that may have eluded your attention. Undertaking a real transformation provides this feedback and revelation. Transformation is as useful to those who pursue or have had an enlightenment experience as it is for anyone.

5:2 Attempting transformation but finding some self-aspect that you're unable to change reveals a specific remaining unconsciousness—an assumption or attachment you're still overlooking, unwilling to confront, or unwilling to part with. Without such feedback you are likely to remain stuck and unconscious of this aspect of yourself. With such feedback, however, you can clearly focus on the "location" of this unconsciousness or resistance and set out to experience what's holding you back. Recognizing this buried aspect of your self-identity and its role in creating certain aspects of your experience will enable you to let go of it.

5:3 A powerful and viable practice for anyone interested in either enlightenment or transformation would be to purposefully work on letting go of everything to which you are attached—all beliefs, emotional reactivity, opinions, self-image, limited ways of thinking and learning, characteristic behaviors, assumptions, everything taken for granted, habits, needs, addictions, judgments, and everything else with which you identify. Just trying to clarify exactly what all that is will be a big step forward. What matters most, however, is what you let go of, and that you let go of it, even if only temporarily. This will help to reveal the true state of your consciousness.

5:4 Can you imagine what such a practice might be like and what it would lead to? Not only an increased sense of freedom, but increased consciousness on many levels, including clarifying and changing your particular self make-up, and more thoroughly grasping the nature of mind, possibly even your true nature. Though transformation occurs within the limits of experience, this investigation tends to lead you back to consciousness. But trying to change this self is no easy task, and even to imagine it is difficult.

Becoming a Cloud—A Mental Exercise

5:5 For a moment, think of the endeavor of transformation like trying to change from being the Golden Gate Bridge to being a cloud. In order to accomplish such a transformation, much would have to

Freeing Self from Object-Identity

change, and as a bridge you can't even imagine how to become a cloud. Still, you know that you're going to have to start letting go of your bridge identity—such as being identified with steel and cement, being long, fixed, and having a purpose of supporting cars—and to somehow begin to identify with water vapor. Perhaps you could do that all at once. More likely it will take undergoing considerable process, discovery, and breakthroughs to make it happen.

5:6 The starting point, however, is to acknowledge that it's impossible. Yes, you read that correctly. There is no way that as a steel bridge you can imagine how to turn into a cloud, so you need to acknowledge that right off. It is within this "impossibility," however, that the *possibility* exists.

5:7 Facing the reality that your mind doesn't know how to accomplish this change and views the task as impossible will help ground you in the very experience that needs to be transformed. It's only here, in your experience, that the possibility can be created as anything more than wishful thinking. Beyond confronting the impossibility of the matter, you need to recognize that there is also no desire on the part of the bridge to become a cloud. Such obstacles not withstanding, can you imagine the huge difference in perspective and experience that you would have if you *were* a cloud rather than being a bridge?

5:8 Your function and purpose would be different, you'd see life totally differently, your relationship to—and so experience of and reaction to—everything encountered would be different. Your job wouldn't be to support cars moving from one place to another, nor would you be fixed in one place. You would no longer be made of strong steel and beloved by all in the San Francisco Bay Area.

An earthquake would be meaningless and your location would be directed by the wind. Try to imagine the multidimensional difference that would occur with such a change. You can see that you would no longer be the same "person" nor have the same experiences. Although this is a simplistic metaphor, the point should be clear.

5:9 Now try imagining this for yourself. Pick some experience that is as far-reaching and absolutely different for you as becoming a cloud would be if you were a bridge. Once you've imagined this alternate human experience, then really try to experience or imagine what that would be like. What could not be and so would not be the same? What kind of perspectives would you have? How might even the little things or mundane moments appear if viewed from this new perspective? Actually try to ground it and make it as close to a real experience as you can. Delve into it, stay with it for some time, and discover assumptions you've overlooked or aspects you forgot to include in your consideration.

5:10 I'm inviting you to realize that we're not talking about changing from an apple to an orange, which is too easy and still in the domain of familiar things, as is simply imagining a "better self." The demand here is more like transforming from being an apple to being the color blue, or infinite space. You can see that the mind shift necessary to even think in this way demands a greater degree of openness, since it addresses the essence or nature of your self-experience. This draws you to try to imagine a way of being that is far-reaching and skirts the edges of the unimaginable and impossible, which is a necessary exercise for moving toward an unknown goal that still needs to be consistent with your purpose.

5:11 Such an exercise helps ground you in the matter of transformation a bit more, even though you are only using your imagination. At least in this way you are drawn to imagine concrete and specific experiences and behaviors that provide you with a temporary alternative to your current experience. It also creates and grounds the possibility that you can be some way other than the way you are now. This contrast helps you better recognize what you're up to as a self, and to confront the conglomerate of experiences to which you are attached. In so doing, you begin to open the can of worms that is the subject matter for transformation. But don't just imagine this change. Once imagined, move beyond mere imagination and work hard to "go there" as a real experience of yourself, even if just as an exercise. And do it now, not later. Don't confuse extrapolation with the journey, imagination with the truth, or concept for direct experience.

Using Transformation to Pursue Consciousness

5:12 Contrary to prevailing beliefs, you don't have to change your mood, your emotions, or your thinking in order to have an enlightenment experience. Inevitably people assume that such a change is necessary but, in pursuing a direct-consciousness, you can be in the middle of a negative or mundane experience and need not change a thing. This is because grasping your true nature isn't an *experience*. It's not a feeling or a thought or even a perception, so no change in any of these is required. Certainly, you need to be open to being conscious beyond thinking, emotion, and perception, but that isn't something you can do *within* thinking and emotion or through perception, so these don't need to change. You must simply become conscious of what is already true.

> *Zen monks are instructed to refrain from sex, thinking this is necessary to bring about enlightenment. One monk left after decades in the monastery, discouraged at having failed to achieve enlightenment. He proceeded straight to a brothel, where upon having sex he also had his first enlightenment experience.*

5:13   Although enlightenment requires no change, transformation is founded on it. Self-transformation can't really happen unless the "self" changes. Yet you probably find no desire to give up your self and, perhaps more importantly, find no capacity to do so. No matter what you take on, pretend, or practice, self will still be at the heart of it. Any experience that arises is not a direct-consciousness of your true nature but something crafted by this self. Even if you worked hard to act selflessly, and deny yourself any self-serving activity—although this would certainly be a significant change and quite a practice—it still wouldn't eliminate "you." It just alters what you are doing in a very disciplined way. It's antithetical to self to give up self. You can't use the same impetus, which is a complete commitment to self-survival, to accomplish its opposite. So how can you let go of the self? The truth is you can't. But you can realize that you are already not that.

5:14   Consider that the self is a manifestation of the core event of *life*, the commitment and struggle to exist and stay alive. This is a strong force, isn't it? Perhaps the strongest you have. If you can consciously and experientially connect this powerful force to the survival of your self, you begin to understand the inexorable drive of self-survival. As you know now, one problem is that whatever you identify with *as* "self" takes on this same force, and there is much that you identify with that is not only unnecessary but false, and none that *is*, or even represents, your true nature. As long as

Freeing Self from Object-Identity

you remain in any way confused with process or life, some self-mind will remain.

Like vanishing dew, a passing apparition
or the sudden flash of lightning
— already gone —
thus should one regard one's self.
—Ikkyu,
Kyoto, Japan, 1393

5:15   So our practice becomes a "chicken and egg" approach: working toward Absolute Consciousness while pursuing transformation in order to provide groundedness and feedback; or working toward transformation with a requisite need to pursue Absolute Consciousness in order to fully transform. Toward that end, challenging some of the existential assumptions that comprise our experience can help open the mind to deeper contemplations. It is essential to pry open these overlooked assumptions to get a handle on how and why the self-experience is constructed. Core assumptions about yourself, about being a person, and about the nature of reality may be the most significant barriers to deeper and deeper enlightenment. So discovering these will open doors previously locked shut. This is worth far more than getting "better." One example of an existential assumption can be found in the fact that all one's experience and pursuits are based upon self-existence, but there may be no such thing as a self to begin with.

You Already Don't Exist

5:16   You naturally assume that reality is objectively occurring and that your perceptions are a reflection of this reality. It is literally inconceivable that this is not the case because it is the case for you, and is the *only* case, the only world in which you exist. You don't have anything else to identify with except what you *can* identify, and you can only identify with something experienced or recognized. What remains unknown or unrecognized can't be identified as you since it isn't perceived or conceived.

5:17   The act of identifying with something is a bit like looking around at all the objects in a room and identifying that the table and chair are yours but those golf clubs and bicycle are someone else's. When you perceive everything you can possibly perceive or experience, every object, thought, feeling, sense, etc., some of it you will identify as you and some of it you will identify as not you. Who you actually are, however, can only be considered if you postulate that it is unknown, and that you may not be whatever you currently identify as yourself.

5:18   When people adopt the idea that they don't know who or what they really are, they may set out to "find" this one, since what's known to be the self is now open to question. That attempt is usually called contemplation. What they mistakenly do then is search for an "experience" of their true nature. It's a natural and irresistible activity, but it's not going to help because *you* are not anything experienced or an experience itself. Remember, I'm not talking about a special or transcendent sort of experience that you can eventually find. I'm certainly not talking about a concept or an abstraction that you somehow simply "know" or conclude in the mind. I'm really just talking about *you*. But within your self-experience, you can't recognize *you* since the only thing you can recognize is perceived experience. See how this works?

5:19   There is a common and major assumption that prevents understanding much of what I'm saying about self and you, and that is confusing Consciousness with awareness. The act of being aware, and thus aware of everything you experience, is not the same as Consciousness. We usually think of consciousness and awareness as different words for essentially the same thing—you are *conscious* of the apple on the table, you are *aware* of the apple on the table, not much difference. Even in the dictionary they are defined in similar terms and refer to "knowing" a perception or object. But I am using the word Consciousness very differently, and that's why I capitalize it when I want to emphasize this difference, or speak about it as an absolute. I invite you to consider the possibility that you can be conscious beyond, or independent of, or prior to, any awareness or perception. I also want to invite you to consider that your very nature is of that kind.

Concepts which have proved useful for ordering things easily assume so great an authority over us, that we forget their terrestrial origin and accept them as unalterable facts.
—Albert Einstein

5:20   Even though you know that this Consciousness is impossible to imagine—because imagination requires an object of perception—it does give you at least an idea of a different way to hold Consciousness, and therefore a distinction between "that" and everything experienced and perceived. Without making this distinction, "you" can only be found and identified within experience and perception, which is what everyone assumes is the nature of their existence.

5:21　Some form of experience is necessary for cognition to take place, for a perception of some kind to arise. As we've seen, some kind of "object" or "form," be it physical or not, needs to exist in order for your mind to grasp or "perceive" and identify something. Because of this relationship between perception and form, you carry a lifelong assumption that you are some kind object, seen or unseen, existing somewhere. Perhaps you are a body, or a mind, or a soul, or some "little man within," or a spirit, or perhaps something ethereal and diffuse, or whatever. But even if you don't consider the matter, you assume—live as-if—you are *something*, existing somewhere in some form, known or unknown.

5:22　If I say that this isn't the case except in your world of assumption and perception, on its face my statement seems obviously untrue. You have solid and accessible experiences to back up the assumption that you are some kind of "object," even if you don't consider yourself just a body. If you look very carefully, however, you'll discover that you can't actually find the real source-object that *is* you. But you may still assume that you simply exist "behind the scenes" and so just can't get a good view of this you-object. Since there is no way for you to validate my assertion without a direct-consciousness, the matter will degrade immediately into belief or disbelief, neither of which will help. Despite such drawbacks, you can't fundamentally change the self-experience without recognizing it as not *you*, grasping what you really are reveals that you are not any self-identity.

Freeing Self from Object-Identity

5:23 You don't have to do anything to not exist. You already don't exist. Really. With deep enlightenment, you become conscious that *you* are not a self. It is likely, however, that you're ignorant of this as a reality. But even if you have grasped this truth to some degree, you probably still hold that you, as unformed consciousness, are separate from self, objects, and life. This assumption that you exist elsewhere makes you an "object" once again. This is a natural and quite common mistake. It suggests that you don't really know, at the very root and heart, what a self is, what mind is, and what reality is. Nothing needs to change, however, to truly grasp these things, because you are already involved in manifesting as them. The ultimate truth is that your nature is inconceivable and not anything you experience or *can* experience, think or *can* think, and so it is literally impossible to separate out or pin down. Pursuing a deeper consciousness will resolve this confusion. Until then, life goes on. After that, life goes on as well.

5:24 Recognizing that you aren't your mind creates the possibility of changing it, but doesn't free you from the "necessity" of mind as long as you still identify with being a self. There are aspects of being a "person"—perception, experience, interpretation, thinking, feeling, identity, and interaction—that come with the package and are required in order to participate in being human. It's like playing Monopoly. In order to participate you have to choose one of the pieces to represent you, but you don't really confuse yourself with the piece (not too much anyway) and you have no issue with tossing it back in the box when the game is over. A certain freedom arises with the recognition that no form is you, and all form is unnecessary, just as after the game the pieces become meaningless. When this is known to be the case, the form of you can change, and what exists now can be let go. (And it's OK—you didn't really want to spend your life being the thimble anyway.)

GETTING DOWN TO WORK

5:25   Just so, the whole self-world is very much like playing a game. The game doesn't exist outside the mind that creates it, makes it up, and gives it "life." Although when you're "in" the game it appears as real and really occurring, when you stop playing it is gone. Even when you are playing, it still doesn't actually exist except as a figment of mind. While you're playing, you may be aware of this, or not. Either way, in order to play the game this self-world must occur and be specifically what it is. It doesn't actually exist whether played or not played.

5:26   And to further work the analogy, just like a game, self, life, and even the Universe don't need to exist. Nothing would be lost if any of these were to disappear, since they already don't exist, or to say it another way, their true nature is Absolute "Nothing." Sounds pretty stupid, doesn't it? Don't blame me, I didn't make it that way. This isn't a matter for speculation or belief, it is a matter of being conscious or ignorant about the real nature of existence. Freedom, *ergo* transformation, is ultimately dependent on this principle.

5:27   Yet as long as life occurs, then *process* and "being something in particular" are going to take place. It's the degree of one's consciousness of the Real that makes the difference between being stuck as a "piece on the board" and being free—with or without life. This freedom creates a very different perspective of self and life, but it doesn't eliminate either. Remember, even Gautama himself, post- "complete enlightenment," continued to walk and talk and eat and sleep and live out his life to the end. If we're conscious enough to realize total freedom from self, life, and living, then transformation is both very possible *and* not really an issue.

5:28   This is all heady stuff and, although all these assertions are likely to remain merely hearsay for the time being, there's a reason for my broaching these subjects. Laying down this rather "existential" framework provides a much more effective perspective from which to view the work of self-transformation. Without it, you're much more likely to be stuck spinning your wheels within the same experiential limitations and assumptions that found your current experience.

5:29   To further help us get free of these dynamics, there are principles that must be addressed and there is a need to better understand how mind and perceptions are created. As we break some of this down and make more distinctions in what appears to us as just the experience of life—which is really a mush of many unexamined elements working together—we can better craft a practice in which to pursue consciousness and transformation.

CHAPTER SIX

Mechanisms of Experience

Approaching Change

6:1 When a person comes to me with some seemingly insurmountable challenge regarding their behavior or emotions—say, an insatiable desire to eat chocolate, the fear of going on stage, feeling depressed, or being angry at life—they're often shocked when I respond, "Well, *stop* that!" They think I'm merely joking, but I'm not.

6:2 When you set out to address something undesirable about your personality or character, one option is to simply let it go on the spot. In other words, the first thing to try is "magic"—simply free yourself from the unwanted attachment or behavior, or shoot for letting go of the whole self-identity all at once. There is no reason to enter into a long and grueling process if a short and easy one will work. You may find that you can simply stop feeling this, or thinking that, or even being a certain way just by adopting a real intention to do so.

6:3 No kidding. If you can create a thought, you can stop creating a thought. If you believe in something, you can toss that belief. If you feel a certain way, you can change your mind and instantly stop feeling that way, or feel another way. This is a real possibility, yet few use it.

> *Rather than continuing to seek the truth, simply let go of your views.*
> —Buddha

6:4 Since most people find it difficult to change in a heartbeat, this "magic" isn't readily accessible to them. Even if this is the case for you, take it seriously and try it repeatedly. It is the best way to discover your connection to the source of your own internal state. Whenever you experience being in the driver's seat, then steer your experience immediately. If not, then contemplate to find the source.

6:5 If the first approach doesn't work, you can then take on the more long-term process of discovery. When you find some self-aspect stubbornly persisting, contemplate it to become conscious of its source and let it go. In this way, over time, transformation can occur in a real and steady way. The first approach may be more accessible after an initial enlightenment experience or two, but neither approach is dependent on it.

6:6 As I've explained, enlightenment takes place independent of mind and therefore outside of perception. What we're addressing in this chapter is transformation, which may assist you in moving toward enlightenment only insofar as it helps you clarify and de-identify with your self-experience. The "direct" of direct-consciousness means that it occurs *prior* to thoughts, emotions, experience, and self, so change is irrelevant. Transformation, on the other hand, occurs by changing the foundation mechanisms of your self-experience. Unfolding the composition of mind and perception can facilitate such changes. The most grounded avenue for making change is through learning how self, mind, and experience are constructed.

Unseen Layers of Our Emotions

6:7   How will you know if you're transforming? You'll probably examine your internal state for clues and, if you seem to be as emotionally reactive as ever and in the same ways, you'll assume that no change has occurred. You will be correct. It might seem like the thing to do then is to change your emotions, but there is a big difference between changing the source of emotion and attempting to cover up or alter the emotion—which is like ignoring the cause of a disease in favor of modifying the symptoms. Trying to "force" yourself into an acceptable internal state is not unlike taking a large dose of cold medicine in order to feel better for a while, even though it does nothing to cure your cold.

6:8   Suppressing your emotions doesn't mean you've transformed anything. To focus on changing your emotional "appearance"—believing that this indicates you are transforming—is backwards and a waste of effort. Transformation leads to a change in your experience, and that will change your emotions, but trying to suppress your emotions and alter your behavior to fit some ideal image doesn't lead to transformation.

6:9   That said, there is still an important role for challenging your habitual mental-emotional patterns and attempting to adopt a different state. Such practices help reveal what is at the heart of your reactions and clarify specifically where your challenges lie. So, rather than suppressing your reaction or pretending some idealized new experience, a more effective approach is to attempt to genuinely free yourself of this reaction. What is there to lose? If you fail, it will draw your attention to feel and isolate your resistance; if you succeed, you get free.

> *Although nature commences with reason and ends in experience,
> it is necessary for us to do the opposite, that is to commence with
> experience and from this to proceed to investigate the reason.*
> —Leonardo da Vinci

6:10　Have you ever wondered why emotions exist? What purpose they serve? Why your internal state unfolds as it does? Most people quickly become mired in confusion if they even attempt to look into it, which is why simply learning to question the overlooked obvious is addressed at such length in *The Book of Not Knowing*. Since understanding the nature, purpose, and origins of your experience is essential to transformation, from time to time I may briefly review points made in that book and perhaps expand on them.

6:11　Our feelings often seem to arise like some mysterious force from deep within. Even when we experience a mild and appropriate response to what's occurring, our emotions seem to be sourced from some hidden place over which we have little or no control. When we consider the suffering that our emotional states can produce, it's not surprising how difficult it is to grasp that each of us is an active participant in these "spontaneous" reactions, but why on earth would we want to produce our own suffering?

6:12　It doesn't take a huge leap to see that your internal state—the domain of your emotions, moods, thinking, and internal dialogue—governs your behavior. What's harder to grasp is that the content of this domain has an even more obscure function and character.

GETTING DOWN TO WORK

6:13   We generally think of manipulation as an activity that shows up only in our behavior and communications with other people. Since we assume that emotions are largely caused by circumstance, it doesn't occur to us that our feelings arise for the sole purpose of creating some effect in us in order to manipulate our own state of mind, or motivate certain behavior to manipulate others or the environment. Emotions are manipulations, not perceptions.

6:14   Emotions occur when we interpret circumstances—both within the environment and within our minds—and then relate this interpretation to our own self-identity. This produces a disposition or reaction that serves us in some way that is consistent with our self-agenda. Because we remain oblivious to the source of the feeling, we're also oblivious to our participation in creating it, even when it causes us great pain. Perhaps we should take a look at how emotions evolved and for what purpose.

The Evolution of Emotion

6:15   We make a distinction between simple and complex organisms and consider ourselves to be the most complex life form on Earth. In our grounded theories and observations about evolution, we see life evolving from the most rudimentary forms, like single-cell organisms, all the way up to the complex multi-celled and multi-faceted organisms like our wonderful selves.

6:16   Considering this movement, we can postulate that even though there may be an expansion from the simple into the complex, the complex is still founded on the same basic components and principles as the simple. In other words, what allows life to exist and to function in a bacterium or worm is basically the same for a dog, a horse, or a human. The difference is what's added. In the higher organisms, we rarely see an absence of the ingredients found in the lower; instead we see more ingredients.

6:17 This may seem like a point without a difference, but stay with me here. There's a reason for going down this road, and it relates directly to your emotions and your self-identity. When we observe simpler animals, we often anthropomorphize, interpreting their behavior as if it's motivated by emotions like ours. This is a mistake that doesn't allow us to consider what may be there instead, assuming that the animal's experience is just like ours. If, however, we consider the possibility that what's there is a *predecessor* to what we experience as emotion, we can more clearly investigate our own experience.

6:18 When we assume that a dog's behavior is motivated by the same kind of fear or anger or joy that we experience, we miss the fact that it's actually not reacting from any of these, but from something far more basic that precedes human emotion. It's easier to consider in bacteria, since few of us have them as pets. They have no eyes, ears, or brain, only a very primitive perceptive sense, even compared to that of a snail. But the perceptive organs of the snail developed from the same principles and purpose that produced the bacterium's, and Rover's, and yours. The difference in more complex animals is the addition of collective groups of specialized cells, all interacting to produce new ways of perceiving through a brain and sense organs. They still function to create perception, just in a more sophisticated way.

6:19 Applying this analogy to emotions reveals the same pattern. Consider: perception is a function of survival, allowing us to interact successfully with both the physical environment and the "environment" of our internal state. Our emotions and thoughts are more sophisticated out of necessity, but they provide for the same need that a single-cell organism has to manipulate its environment.

6:20 We are motivated to act via specific mechanisms that show up mostly as emotional activity—moods, urges, impulses, attractions, repulsions, and many other feelings too subtle to name. This whole emotional field determines and directs all of our dispositions and behavior. It influences what we perceive and everything we do.

6:21 In a moment we're going to examine the formation of these internal manipulations to show how they exist to serve the self. First, let's consider the fairly obvious fact that everything a worm does is in the interest of its own survival. Each action—perceiving its surroundings, wiggling, reproducing, making distinctions between what's edible and what's detrimental, and whatever else worms may do—is done to keep it (and so its species) alive. We don't suppose a worm has anything like emotions, but something motivates it to relate to particular circumstances in specific ways.

6:22 Now apply the same logic to a dog. Each behavior is motivated by a purpose: to relate to danger, get a treat, show subservience or dominance, and so forth. These too are purposeful survival activities and may appear to us as fear, anger, happiness, etc., even if they're not prompted by anything as sophisticated or conceptually complex as human emotions. As most of us relate more readily to a dog than a worm, it becomes clearer that our emotions may serve the same purpose. What sets humans apart is that this purpose includes the survival of complex self-identities. We identify with a complex conceptualized self and conceptually

Mechanisms of Experience

created social relations, and these are what generate the activity we know as emotions. Human emotions spring from the very same impulses that motivate a worm to move this way or that, but they are applied to a more sophisticated conceptual domain, demanding a more complex set of conceptual distinctions. This activity arises as the conceptually based feeling-state we experience as an emotion.

6:23   In modern culture, people generally acknowledge that emotions are, on some level, generated by our "selves" and so by implication are consistent with what each person is up to. Unfortunately, most people also believe that these same emotions are caused by circumstances and are merely reactions to them. Let's look more closely at how this activity might actually occur. I am going to present another set of important but challenging distinctions in what we generally call our "experience."

6:24   As with much that is presented in *The Book of Not Knowing*, I'm sure most readers will not understand how I came up with such distinctions. It could be seen as simply my opinion, or as beliefs I've developed, or perhaps a theory that I'm asking you to consider. We live in a world in which those are pretty much all that are available to us, short of scientific research providing hard data that we regard as fact, but even then we might question the interpretation of this data.

6:25   There is another possibility that remains virtually unknown in human culture, and that is to directly encounter these "observations" or "experiences" as they take place. This occurs outside of belief and conjecture. Certainly, even after such direct experience, the mind can, and often will, take what's "known" in this way and degrade it into fabricated conclusions in order to make it more

GETTING DOWN TO WORK

compatible with personal beliefs. But barring erroneous twists and turns, staying true to what's "seen" provides information that is *not* simply a matter of opinion nor is it negotiable. It's not a belief. It is something directly experienced as *so*.

6:26 The need for quotation marks when writing about these matters indicates that our language doesn't have words to accurately convey what I'm saying, and yet communication is obviously needed. This "direct method" of "knowing" is the primary source of all the communications in this book as well as in *The Book of Not Knowing*. I'm not claiming that I am free of error, but that the source is direct experience rather than something merely believed, and that I do my best to keep my mind from misinterpreting what is grasped. I maintain with confidence that if you too grasp what's true in these matters, you will clearly recognize what is asserted. The only proof you need is your own conscious experience, so by all means, investigate. Don't just believe me, even if you do believe me.

The Sequence of Encounter

6:27 Our experience occurs for us as a process, one that seemingly unfolds automatically and at light speed. Let's break this down a bit:

>Direct Experience -> Perception -> Interpretation -> Meaning -> Effect -> Reaction

6:28 If we start with what is at this point only the notion of *direct experience*, we have the possibility of being directly conscious of *what is*. This is like "being one" with what's there, so there is no process or separation involved. Don't equate that with enlightenment for the moment and just work to grasp this as a new distinction in what we call experience. We may not have any consciousness of this starting point, but it gives us a place to begin. From here, consciousness separates from "direct" and moves into process and the sequence unfolds.

6:29   *Perception* is the first distinction that people can acknowledge, so we normally overlook the fact that the very nature of perception implies a separation from the thing being perceived, making it necessary to bridge this gap. Since we need some form of feedback to provide information about what's encountered, this separation means that perception *must* be indirect.

6:30   The information we receive is *not* the thing encountered. Perception is more like discerning a ripple in the water and using it to deduce some manner of contact or encounter, or like a radar screen providing a particular blip but no other information. One can only know whatever the perceptive method—sight, sensation, sound, smell, taste, conceptualizing—can provide. For example, color isn't available in sound or sensation, and temperature isn't provided by sight or sound, and so on. This reveals that the method of perception is inherently limited and cannot provide the "whole story." Yet even if it could, it would still be indirect in that it will never be the "thing itself."

6:31   Grasping the distinction I'm referring to as perception is quite difficult since we only know perception as the end product of this whole process and we don't make these distinctions individually. In this model, perception is a meaningless phenomenon. Consider that perception is not anything we are aware of, and what I'm talking about is not anything we've considered or encountered because it is not a distinction that we're aware of. We don't recognize perception itself because we only grasp what makes sense and has meaning. Perception is meaningless because it occurs prior to meaning. Making sense and giving meaning is a function of the rest of this process, which next unfolds as *interpretation*.

6:32   Once again, you need to allow that what I mean by "interpretation" is not what is normally meant when we use that word. None of these distinctions are "normal" usage, since in conversation we often use these words interchangeably. I'm speaking of each of these as distinct from the others. Interpretation is the part of this process where the meaningless feedback determined by perception is related to our selves and so becomes something specific and therefore useful. It's not related to our self-agenda yet, but merely to the fact that we exist, because a self needs to make sense of what something "is" in a basic and immediate way. We still don't know what it means to us or how we should relate to it, only that we've encountered something specific in relation to everything else—it is a chair, a person, a color, a smell, fast, an idea, a feeling. Once this basic interpretation has been formed, we give it meaning.

6:33   *Meaning* relates the interpretation to our particular self-identity and self-agenda. In this part of the process, our automatic mind functions rapidly to relate what's perceived and interpreted to ourselves and our needs. This is where we establish what it means to us—how we can use it, whether it's a threat, how it fits into our overall and immediate survival needs. This meaning immediately shows up as a charged feeling, isolating it as positive or negative, as well as providing the information about how we should relate to it. If you like the color yellow, the "like" demonstrates the positive meaning you apply to that color. It is this charged meaning that affects us.

Mechanisms of Experience

6:34 Whatever is "cognized" as an experience—cognition being the aggregate of Interpretation, Meaning, and Effect—is what occurs for us as an internal "experience." This is the *effect,* and it's this end product that we recognize. The result of this sequence forms into a feeling-impulse that tells us what we need to know in order to react consistently with our self-interest. This effect is always in the form of a positive or negative, and it is the creation of the feeling disposition that motivates us to respond in some way. Liking yellow might indicate the meaning to you, but feeling good and having an uplifted mood when seeing yellow is the effect.

6:35 This *effect* arrives as an internal impulse, the purpose of which is to push us to take action—called *reaction* in this model—to somehow manage whatever is encountered in a way considered to be most self-beneficial. With reaction, we either manipulate our own internal state by altering (or attempting to alter) our thoughts and emotions, or we go further and take physical action in order to manipulate via our behavior or communications. What we normally call our "experience" is usually limited to these end results. For example, the interpretation of seeing a snarling dog is simply that it's a creature in action; the meaning, however, is that it's dangerous to us; the effect is fear, and the reaction is to run. For us what dominates our consciousness is the fear and running to protect ourselves. This is all that's needed to manage the job of survival, and so it's all that the self is aware of.

It's All about You

6:36 Although it's hard to believe and difficult to experience, this means that all effects and reactions are about you. They are created by the particular self that you are and the ways that you've developed to interpret everything in relation to you.

6:37 When an effect arises, its positive or negative charge determines your general relationship to what's perceived. You will be moved to avoid it, resist it, embrace it, nurture it, ignore it, hide it, fix it, or whatever your interpretation and meaning indicate is best. Your course of action will be a manipulation that attempts to accomplish some goal to manage the effect. Remember, for the most part this happens lightning-fast and automatically, without your recognition. From a self's point of view, what leads up to being motivated to act isn't important; what to do about it is.

6:38 Managing effects is a full-time job and occurs from minute to minute in your experience. Your reactions can be physical, as in behavior or speaking, or they can be mental, such as talking to yourself, generating a feeling, or adopting an attitude. Your immediate goal with a negative reaction will be to make the effect go away. Physical discomfort might move you to adjust yourself in your chair. A feeling of fear may compel you to cross the street to avoid a dangerous-looking person. In an attempt to alleviate the emotional pain that generates anger, you might yell at your spouse; or when you encounter feedback about yourself that is inconsistent with your own self-image, you may well attempt to deny its validity in order to maintain your positive sense of self.

6:39 A positive reaction will induce you to maintain the effect. When caught up in feelings of romantic intimacy with someone, you may continue to speak in soft and loving tones. The taste of delicious food will move you to keep this pleasure around by continuing to put it in your mouth. Hearing music you like moves you to turn up the radio. Yet each self will react differently to the same stimulus. For instance, someone afraid of intimacy might push away an embrace, while another craves it. One person may see the ocean waves as an exciting opportunity, but someone else may view them as dangerous, and a third as simply a pleasant encounter with nature. I might feel partial about blue and hate orange, while the effect on you is quite the reverse.

6:40 No matter how subtle or dramatic an effect is, this whole dynamic is based upon an unnoticed mechanism, the foundation of which exists in a matrix of uncognized mind. Since we don't make comprehensive distinctions like this in our conscious experience, changing the processes that create experience eludes us.

6:41 Making these distinctions can be especially difficult because they're not made within our culture or in our language, and so we don't experience them in our feelings or thinking. It is the nature of perception that if we don't make a distinction within our perceptive-experience, it does not *occur* in our perceptive-experience. If it does, then we're already making that distinction.

6:42 People assume that experience occurs whether or not we make any "distinctions" at all. It seems to us that experience comes first and making distinctions within the experience comes next. This is a misunderstanding of what I'm talking about. The distinction *is* the experience—that's what makes it *that* experience. I know this is hard to understand, so I refer you back to *The Book of Not Knowing*, Chapter 24 (even this may not be enough, but it could help).

6:43 It is possible to make the distinctions I'm talking about in the sequence of encounter. They are already present but overlooked aspects of our experience. It simply takes a lot of attention and the willingness to notice normally indistinct aspects in more subtle domains of consciousness than what we imagine are available to us. One of the first challenges is the fact that this process occurs more rapidly than we can discern through normal perceptive methods. It's much faster than we can think and, prior to effect, it doesn't show up as a feeling or reaction. For the most part, recognizing concepts and feelings is all that we're aware of within our internal perceptive field.

6:44   Most people won't be able to discern these distinctions first-hand but can still grasp that there is more going on within their perceptive-experience than what is commonly recognized on the surface. The fact that our experience is *constructed*—and depends on association, interpretation, and relating what's interpreted to ourselves—gives us room to consider that what we perceive may not be a simple matter of what's there but instead something particular to and generated by us.

6:45   Grasping this allows us to look into just how the self-identity constructs our experience. In this way we might be able to learn something that can create the possibility of transforming our emotions rather than just putting up with them, acting them out, or suppressing them. Since emotions seem to be the primary impulse dictating our behavior, it's important to understand more about how they are created.

6:46   If our emotions are not of our own making but "caused" by circumstance, then we have no choice about whether or not they arise. If, on the other hand, they are something we ourselves are generating, then we do have a choice, and also the possibility of transforming them by changing what we're doing. This totally depends on one's level of consciousness.

6:47 We can't change a self-mechanism that we aren't aware of or don't recognize as occurring. By contemplating our unseen motives for reacting in the ways that we do, we can discern not only that we're up to something, but even what it is. Investigating the very mechanism that puts together our experience, we can learn to recognize, without passion or bias, how and for what purpose both passion and bias are created. We are no longer sentenced to a life limited to merely suffering reactions. Recognizing how we generate our experience creates a different way of relating to it, and once this is the case, change becomes possible.

6:48 We transform what we are *doing* by transforming what we are "being." In the above sequence of encounter, both interpretation and meaning are created by relating perception to an "uncognized matrix of mind"—the content of which I call "bottom-lines." This unrecognized aspect of self-mind constitutes our most fundamental core identity and is the source of our reactions. It is here that transformation must occur if we are actually going to transform. If we change this domain, our experience will change. Let me explain how this is so.

The importance and unimportance of the self cannot be exaggerated.
—R. H. Blyth

How the Self-Identity Creates "Perception"

6:49 A self-identity always has a particular character—a consistency of action, reaction, and self-presentation. It may seem obvious that we're all different, but did you ever wonder why all humans don't have the same personality? A character can only be formed

GETTING DOWN TO WORK

by repeatedly engaging in patterns of behavior and reaction that then become identified as "characteristic" of you. But why would one person's behavior be different from another's who has the same basic series of life circumstances? We just assume we act this way because this is how we *are*. In other words, we think our behavior is a result of something inherent that forces us to act in consistent ways. It is far more complex than that, and quite circular and self-referential.

6:50 As reflected in your behavior, your character demonstrates your internal state as it manifests in relation to your environment—your "mind" being physically expressed, so to speak. Your particular ways of relating to and managing life circumstances are perceived as "acting like yourself." But how you relate to anything is determined by the way you perceive it—or more accurately by the way you *interpret* it and the *meaning* you assign. And what determines how you perceive something? Strangely, as convoluted as it sounds, you do.

6:51 The dynamic of recognition and interpretation is part of a loop created by comparing your experience of self to whatever is perceived, and then "inventing" how to see what is there. Your interpretation differs from someone else's because the information you need is different from what someone else might need. Neither of you needs to know merely what's there. The information you need depends on the unique needs of your self, so your judgment, bias, and perspective will be tailored to inform and fulfill the specific needs of your identity. This automatic self-referencing function is an important aspect of what's called in *The Book of Not Knowing* "perceiving things *for-me*."

6:52　The only way you can know how something relates to you—whether it is useful or harmful, good or bad, and the specific ways and degrees to which it is so—is by having some experience called your self. You can't compare you to "it" unless you have a "you." Your generic human experience allows you to quickly assess something's parameters and characteristics—its physical features like location, size, shape, etc., or its conceptual parameters if it's an idea or communication, or what have you—as well as to attribute to it function, and so on. These are generally the same for most people in any given culture. But this is not enough information to determine your *particular* relationship. You also need to compare the specific "parameters" and characteristics of your individual self to this perception in order to know how to relate to and manage it appropriately for your particular needs.

6:53　Are you beginning to see the loop here? Your personal characteristics are generated through your repeated behavior toward life circumstances, and your behavior is generated by relating your personal characteristics to life circumstances. This can seem pretty baffling, like an Escher drawing, so it's normal if you're confused. I'll continue trying to clarify.

6:54　As mentioned earlier, all that comprises your self-experience—the details of your self-identity, the ways you think of yourself, every belief, assumption, viewpoint, impulse, idea, and program, every facet of your self-esteem, and everything else that makes up your experience of you as a unique and particular person—combines to form the "shape" of you.

6:55　Everything you encounter is viewed in relation to this shape to determine how it fits. It's like you're a puzzle piece and everything you encounter is another piece. You see it all in terms of yes or no,

GETTING DOWN TO WORK

a fit or not? Your shape is far more intricate and unique than any puzzle piece, but the principle is the same and it influences your every perception. Once you grasp this, it starts to become clear how your particular identity determines the way you perceive and experience everything, including what you call yourself.

6:56   In an attempt to further simplify: try to imagine what you would perceive if you identified yourself as a butterfly. You'd perceive a flower completely differently than if you were a human or a dog. As a butterfly, you would see the flower as a source of food. To a human, it is likely to be a pretty decoration, and to a dog it probably wouldn't register and so won't be seen at all. Among humans each "self shape" is unique and so each will relate to what's perceived as it relates specifically to that self. Your perception of the world is only that particular way because of what you assume yourself to be. It is much more complex and subtle than these simplistic examples, but there are no examples that can do justice to what I'm talking about. Another way to put it: take a look around you—every single perception you're having right now is an example.

6:57   What makes recognizing this all the more challenging is that the foundation of your unique self-shape is an uncognized matrix of mind. So, much of what you experience as your identity includes unconscious assumptions that you have about yourself. If you want to change the self-shape and its influence over your perceptions, it's necessary to recognize and eliminate the buried assumptions and convictions you have about the nature of your fundamental person.

6:58   This complicated dynamic is hard to follow and even harder to experience. Most people need to get several "hits" on it to even

begin wrapping their heads around it all. Here is a simple overview in bite-sized pieces that might help.
- Everything is experienced in relation to what it means to your self.
- This self—and so its perception—is experienced *from* and *as* the attachments you have and the identity you've formed.
- What is perceived influences your internal state, which then motivates your behavior.
- All this combines to create your character through repeated behavior patterns.
- This forms a closed loop of activity, with the "shape" or form of your self creating your interpretations by passing whatever is perceived through a process that relates what's there to your own identity.
- This process builds and reinforces your self-identity, and also influences and validates your perception of reality.

6:59 Your perceptions, and so your reactions to them, are a direct function of what you identify with. This isn't easy to see because you take for granted a very different and simple reality, one in which you merely observe a world around you that "causes" you to react as you do. Such an outlook, although almost universal, is not true, and so could be called an illusion. You don't necessarily need to understand all of this to begin to study it, but you do need to get a feel for the dynamics involved and work toward a deeper consciousness in the matter as you proceed.

6:60 Contemplating the core beliefs and assumptions that source and ground our basic reactive tendencies is essential. Beyond contemplating these matters, however, we should remember that our goal is to free ourselves of them. Our goal is not to act them out, nor is it to endlessly contemplate them. Unfortunately, most of the time we find that we continue to either act out or suppress our reactivity, and even our contemplations don't seem to produce any real freedom or serious change. So, what keeps us stuck in this way?

6:61 One thing that holds us back from discovering the source of our intransigence is our tendency to justify the emotional reactions and behaviors that arise for us. They are always justified in our own mind because the stimulus or conditions encountered seems to "cause" our reactivity. This will always be the case. Why else would a reaction arise if the self-mind didn't see it as necessary and justified? We can tell ourselves that it isn't, and this might create some space to investigate it. Yet how long can we hold onto such a thought? Emotions and gut motivations always tend to override any rationally adopted thought or belief.

6:62 Until we can perceive these source motivations and circular dynamics for what they really are, and recognize them as created for a self-imagined and meaningless purpose—and so see them as unjustified, ineffective, and damaging—we will not let them go. No amount of suppression or pretending or overriding will be effective. As with weeds, no matter what we manage to cut down on the surface, the root will sprout again, in the same place or in another. Therefore, understanding the foundations of our emotions, impulses, drives, and reactivity is at the heart of changing the person that we are.

The dissatisfied nature of the mind itself is suffering.
No matter how much of something you get, it never satisfies
your desire for better or more. This unceasing desire is suffering;
its nature is emotional frustration.
—Lama Tubten Yeshe

CHAPTER SEVEN

Transforming Your Emotions

Emotional Dominance Revisited

7:1 It should be obvious by now that more than any other single factor, feeling-states dominate your experience and behavior. You're certainly attached to your thoughts, beliefs, and values, but what makes any of these influential, gives them meaning and determines their significance? It's the way you *feel* about your mental processes that gives them substance. So clearly the domain of emotions needs close attention as you attempt to transform.

7:2 Recall some major life event and the feelings you had at the time, whether the incident was positive or negative. Notice that you could have made an intellectual assessment about the significance of it, but your experience of the incident would have been radically different without your emotional reactions because the magnitude of any event comes to you as a feeling and not as a thought. Absent any emotional charge, you would not be invested with the motivation to adopt a "self-appropriate" disposition, much less the drive to act upon it.

7:3 Right now, notice your current experience. Take a moment, breathe, and just observe how you're feeling. Notice that you are always maintaining some sort of feeling. Even if there is no obvious emotional reaction taking place, there is still a feeling-sense telling you generally how you're doing, whether you're OK or not, satisfied, happy, irritated, sleepy, etc. Your current mood is determined by feeling, as is your disposition, temperament, and so on. These provide the outlook and attitude with which you'll approach the next circumstance, while also influencing how you'll perceive it.

7:4 Emotional orientation determines the quality and meaning of your world—what and how you suffer, your judgment of anything as good or bad, your level of happiness, your mood, and the general tone of your entire experience. Without emotion—and all those feelings too subtle or too far in the background to be named but that nevertheless saturate your experience—how could you possibly assess any of this? What would you use to decide whether you're doing well or poorly? The quality of your experience, your relationships, and your life are determined by how you *feel* at any given time.

7:5 We're all driven by emotions, but each of us is driven by particular emotions, and in reaction to particular circumstances. We've already seen how the self-identity demands an adherence to specific patterns of emotion so that in most encounters they arise to serve and promote that self and that self's agenda. Since these reactions seem unique to us and are regularly occurring, we come to view them as expressing our one-of-a-kind personality. Given that this "self-shape" creates both the interpretation and the reaction to everything encountered, our perception of reality will remain intact as long as we do.

7:6 Obviously if we're going to successfully change our behavior, we must change our impulses and internal states, but we can only accomplish this by changing our self-agenda, and that will only happen if we change our self-identity. In the pursuit of genuine transformation, we continually find ourselves grasping some matter and then "slipping back" into the habitual patterns that keep our self-identity intact. This is to be expected, since thwarting the drives of the self is on a par with a kind of self-annihilation. Therefore, it is essential that we discover what's at the bottom of our self-identity and the impulses that keep it that way.

> *When angry, count to Zen.*
> —Leonard Scheff

Learning to Relate to Emotions Differently

7:7 Before we look further into getting to the source of our emotions, let's consider what we can do prior to achieving such consciousness. We can either work to change an emotion or, failing that, learn to live with it differently. The practice of changing or eliminating emotions as they turn up is useful in a way that's similar to stretching a muscle. In the process of developing an experiential ability to change emotional habits, we loosen our attachment to them. With such a practice, we're empowered to shift from our old context of patterned *reactions* to a new context of consciously created *responses*.

7:8 Although ridding ourselves of negative emotions is already something we want, it might be harder to notice the challenges caused by what we consider to be more "positive" emotions. But the characterization of "positive" or "negative" is not what indicates which emotional habits will be difficult to change. What matters most is how deeply we're attached to them. When they are so ingrained as to seem a part of our character, we miss the fact that we actually *want* to keep these feeling-reactions around, even if we find them distressful. We see them as protecting us or helping us get our way, and unconsciously view them as vital to the pursuit of our self-agenda. Because of this, they dominate much of our internal state, indirectly attempting to manipulate our relationship to life. Although we may balk at the pain caused by some of these reactions, we continue allowing them to dominate much of our internal state, covertly manipulating our relationship to life.

7:9   We use many such feeling manipulations to pursue our self-agenda—being angry, fearful, hurt, arrogant, withdrawn, stubborn, scornful, seductive, intimidating, flattering, frantic, pitiful, and many more. Consistent with our goal of transforming, however, it's useful to consider that it's possible to create more direct avenues for getting what we want instead of emotionally manipulating others and ourselves. When we investigate these emotional-manipulations more thoroughly, we realize that they aren't actually needed or even useful. Eliminating the root would eliminate the impulse, but prior to achieving that, we can still learn to live with these impulses differently.

7:10   Even if immediate change isn't forthcoming, you can stop taking your emotions so seriously, and refuse to let them dominate your behavior. Their whole *raison d'être* is to provoke you into certain behaviors or dispositions, but they don't *make* you behave in that way. You still have a choice, and each time you opt out of reacting to the presence of an emotion, and the impulse to manipulate because of it, it will lose power. If you regularly acknowledge your emotions and yet don't assume them to be something useful to act upon, you will eventually short-circuit their purpose. As this new disposition becomes familiar and reliable, the impulse itself is likely to arise less and less frequently because it serves no purpose. Of course, since there are self-agenda reasons that cause you to react as you do, this may be easier said than done.

7:11 Remember, you must make a clear distinction between what I'm suggesting here and suppressing your emotions. I'm recommending that you fully feel the emotional activity, but avoid attaching any particular meaning to it, which is what would cause you to react. It's sort of like laughing it off, no matter what it is. You can see that if you felt angry or sad or afraid and yet uncharacteristically *laughed* at these feeling-impulses, your entire attitude toward them would change—even without trying to make them disappear.

7:12 Options for dealing with emotions increase commensurate with an increased consciousness of their nature, but emotions will continue to arise. Their insistence on playing a role in our experience is similar to that of our internal dialogue, which seems in our control until we attempt to completely shut it off. That's when we discover that this internal chatter (instead of being just some negligible background noise) is actually a powerful, nearly unstoppable impulse. Once we grasp the raw, primal force behind any of these activities, investigating them becomes both more realistic and more personal (also more interesting). Our preferred option, of course, is to get to the source of their generation and change them there.

The search for truth is but the honest searching out of everything that interferes with truth.
—A Course in Miracles

GETTING DOWN TO WORK

Experiencing the Source of Your Emotions

7:13   To ground our investigation of emotions, in Chapter Six we outlined the foundation mechanisms in which perception and experience are created. Some of what will be said in this chapter is similar, but any review here should be seen as an opportunity to go deeper as we focus our attention on getting to the source of our emotions and reactivity. Understanding the nature of these underpinnings can be daunting because they are not to be found in any of our current perspectives, experiences, or beliefs. Just to locate the domain of this endeavor takes a willingness to consider matters outside the conventional, and the courage to go beyond accepted assumptions about human experience. But we'll start off slowly and work our way into it.

7:14   Although the dominance, the patterns, and even the purpose of your emotions are probably becoming clearer, one aspect that remains inscrutable is the "place" from which your emotions arise. You might be able to see your unique "self-shape" manifesting in your personal preferences and characteristic behaviors as you interact with the world, but there is a framework beneath this experience that has nothing to do with the world and everything to do with the deep core assumptions that you have about yourself. These hidden but powerful convictions were introduced earlier as "bottom-lines," and I want to extend this consideration into a deeper aspect I call "source assumptions."

7:15   A bottom-line is the origin of your motive to react in some way, the starting place for creating a strategy that will dictate your reaction. This is the foundation of the attempt to manage or resolve something thought to be true about you. Although the distinction

Transforming Your Emotions

between bottom-line and source assumption might seem like splitting hairs, it does help us better understand our self-nature and emotional patterns.

7:16 A source assumption is what you assume is true of yourself without even noticing. It is taken for granted and simply experienced as "you." This uncognized source is what drives your emotional and behavioral patterns. It is the root, the foundation aspect of mind that makes emotional reactions seem necessary. We've already looked into the way your perceptions and reactions are "all about you" in relation to others and reality. Source assumptions consist of what you deeply identify with and hold as true about yourself. They're what you think—prior to logic or reason—is true of you, your fundamental nature. A source assumption is not the reactivity you experience, it is the source of the reaction.

*You will not be punished for your anger,
you will be punished by your anger.*
—Buddha

7:17 It's quite difficult for people to grasp, let alone experience, the deep and primal way in which bottom-line convictions and source assumptions operate. These convictions and assumptions are reflected in your experience in such a way that makes them seem to be merely a perception of others or life. For instance, you might think that your emotions are based on correct observations about the people or circumstances that seem to cause your reactions. From this perspective your emotions seem clearly justified, but that perspective is not actually true. The accuracy of your assessment of others and circumstances is completely irrelevant to your reactivity. The reaction is based upon and relating to a domain of unnoticed source assumptions that you have about your nature, and your bottom-line core beliefs about how to manage these assumptions.

7:18   For example, say you have an unconscious core conviction: "people are dangerous." This may be true in some sense, but when you consider the assumption in light of your deep internal experience, you realize that your bottom-line is actually: "people are dangerous *to me*." Such a "perceived reality" would of course call for some way to manage this danger, and so strategic emotional reactions and interactive behaviors will arise for you as a result.

7:19   Beyond any impulse to manipulate, notice the conviction that "people are dangerous" to you can only arise relative to something you believe is true of yourself, not of others. Your experience of yourself must have some aspect that makes you vulnerable to others—some assumption that your very *being* is incapable, or weak, or less-than, or broken. Whatever it is, this assumption acts as a foundation reality so that you live inside of a sense that others are dangerous. If you experienced yourself as invulnerable, or capable of handling any possible action created by others, they would not be seen as a threat. See how this works?

7:20   In addition to your sense of capability or incapability, the domain of core assumptions about the "is-ness" of your fundamental nature consists of convictions regarding personal worth or lack of worth, perhaps a sense of being unreal or inauthentic, insignificant, fragile, or what have you. These core assumptions regarding what is true about you determine your essential needs and fears. You may be unaware of them, but they are the foundation of your self-identity, generating your drives and emotions as well as piloting your strategies for accomplishing particular goals, all of which show up in your feelings and behavior. These assumptions generate how you feel in relation to others and life because your experience is created by relating others and life to your core assumptions regarding yourself.

7:21 I hope it's becoming apparent by now that this aspect of mind exists *prior* to emotion and charge. In other words, none of these core personal "truisms" will be in the form of an emotion because they are used to *create* emotions. But even if you think you have a handle on what's being said here, be aware that intellect alone won't get you there. And if much of this is unclear, the best way to explore these matters is available within your emotions themselves.

7:22 The best avenue for grasping a bottom-line or source assumption goes right through the heart of your emotional drives. Now that you have clarified your emotional patterns and gotten in touch with the force of the impulse to feel and behave in those ways, you are better equipped to contemplate your emotions. Becoming conscious of why they arise is necessary in order to free yourself from them. This work is covered more thoroughly in *The Book of Not Knowing* (Chapter 22, "Awakening the Uncognized Mind") but below is a quick review. By following this contemplative process, you can get to the bottom of what drives you.

7:23 ***Bottom-line Contemplation***
When contemplating for the purpose of becoming conscious of the source of your emotional reactivity, you need to fully feel the emotion and the impulse to act in the ways that you do, yet dwell on this feeling without bias or presumption.

Rivet your attention on this experience with the intent of discovering what's behind it, why it is that way . . . existentially. I say "existentially" because you aren't trying to discern what it means or how it drives you; you're already assuming and so experiencing these.

What you want now is to know directly the root cause of the emotional activity, the source that exists independent of what you "do" about it—what you do about it is have an emotion and adopt a particular disposition. Instead, keep trying to discover what is *prior to* that reaction.

Stay with the feeling and don't limit your contemplation to speculation or veer off the subject. Continue to open up to discovering what is true but unrecognized in your experience. It is not elsewhere, it is right in the same place that is your cognized experience, you're just not conscious of it yet.

What do you hold to be true about the reality of you that founds such an emotion and reaction? Keep going. When you get to the bottom, you'll discover the fundamental building-block assumption upon which probably more than that one reaction is generated.

7:24 Once you are conscious of the source "beliefs," assumptions, and attachments that construct your self-view—and are the root of your ways of thinking and emoting—you can dissolve these core beliefs. Being conscious of this domain of mind allows you to begin the process of letting go of previously unknown convictions and assumptions that you hold as your very nature, thus freeing yourself from the resulting emotional reactions. Because your emotions and behavior reflect your "self" expressed via your character and personality, freeing yourself from your core emotional patterns is a tremendous step toward changing. I recommend entering into a deliberate and committed contemplation practice to transcend all attachment to familiar driving impulses and reactions.

The Negative Building Blocks of Self-Identity

7:25 The reality of such a practice is likely to draw you into areas that you didn't expect or intend, including areas that you hadn't wanted to go but must in order to continue to deepen the process. This effort will lead you to deeper and more primal building blocks of your self make-up. If you look at or, more accurately, feel your background sense of "you," you may be able to discern something unsettled or not quite right—some form of dissatisfaction. It will be familiar and perhaps vague enough to escape notice, falling into that overall sense of living "life." But with careful and open probing, you can recognize some core sense that inherently has a less than perfect quality to it.

7:26 While taking on some kind of self-improvement carries a built-in implication that you're currently not OK the way you are, glossing over this fact with talk of fulfilling your potential or becoming a better human being helps obscure any uneasiness you might feel about your own personal worth and completeness. Because you view others via their actions and communications, you might suppose that all around you are relatively competent and functional people. It's easy to miss a deeper truth about them, which is that virtually *every* human being suffers from a sense that they are in some way "broken" or not whole.

7:27 Whether or not we acknowledge it or recognize the universality of this condition, most of us experience a sense of incompleteness, feeling worthless, ignorant, or wrong—somehow *less than* we should be. This domain of mind generally remains obscure for us. At times, however, and through certain triggers—perhaps recalling some past emotions or behaviors of which we're ashamed—our self-concept is likely to be significantly influenced by buried feelings that emanate from this domain. The creation of these feelings and reactions might remain a mystery, but it's clear that they arise from us. The fact that we aren't conscious of how and why we create these impulses forces us to view them as part of our core self, assuming that the objectionable thoughts and emotions which surface now and then are somehow a reflection of our very "person." This assumption is based on ignorance not consciousness, and it causes a great deal of unnecessary pain.

---

*You secretly feel broken,
not realizing that this defective person is something you're DOING,
rather than someone you ARE.*

7:28   The deeper framework of mind that assumes such existential traits leads to many impulses to think or behave in ways that you consider objectionable. To get around this unacceptable condition, you'll use suppression, denial, justification, counterbalancing, and feeling shame or guilt, all as ways of dealing with what comes out of "you" as selfish or hurtful acts, or other personally distasteful reactions and behavior. You might work very hard to make changes, but coming to grips with this aspect of your character is all the more daunting because, even if you struggle past the suppression or justifications, you remain ignorant of the cause.

7:29   If you become conscious of the foundation that makes such activity seem necessary, you will realize that it's all based on previously unrecognized core assumptions regarding your self. Core assumptions such as thinking you're incapable or worthless or in some way broken as a human being do not support your social or physical survival, so the self-mind immediately catalogues them

Transforming Your Emotions

as aspects to be suppressed, denied, and hidden away. Even while they are being overlooked, however, they are still experienced as fundamental to your self—they too are self-aspects that must survive and, as such, they persist as part of your experience of the very person who must "make it in life." So, you enter a relationship of trying to manage the presence of these seemingly existential core self-aspects while denying their reality.

7:30 Why does it seem like such assumptions are always negative? We touched on this earlier, but let's take a deeper look. Outside of the buried love you have for everyone, and perhaps other such positive dispositions, there are reasons why the only things that show up as the source of reaction and struggle appear negative.

7:31 First off, when you look for a bottom-line, you consider the matter in relation to your behavior and your emotional reactions. What behavior and reactions will you choose to investigate for the purpose of getting free? Negative ones, of course—experiences that in some way seem undesirable or a limitation. So right there the stage is set to look for whatever exists in you that supports this negative experience. Whether investigating negative or seemingly positive emotional patterns, however, you'll find that these reactions are attempts at resolving or managing something considered off-kilter about yourself, therefore the source assumption is going to be of that nature.

7:32 Other than believing that some aspect of you is a flaw or broken, what could be assumed? When followed to the bottom, any positive aspect is simply that you "are." No quality appears as positive or negative there—in this case, positive just "is." The mere is-ness of something is just its existence, its appearance; there is really no negative or positive there. Even if you add descriptive qualities as an assessment of what "is," it's akin to saying it's a tree or a ball or light—no further judgment is necessary or relevant. Indeed, if this is then held to be an aspect of self, it will need to persist, requiring only to "be" or function as that thing or activity in order to survive, thus fading into the automatic flow of unfettered activity called living.

7:33 For example, you might say that breathing is a positive activity, but really it is just a necessary activity for survival. You don't think about it or notice it, for the most part—you just do it. If you pay attention and appreciate the "fact" of breathing, you may enjoy this and consider it positive, but your breathing will fade back into an unrecognized life function soon enough. Only if you have a problem with breathing do you put attention on it and act to manage or resolve the difficulty. If it is a constant problem, then you'll create ongoing strategies to manage it. It doesn't really come to the fore except as a malady that needs to be resolved, and then it shows up as a negative.

7:34 When it comes to the plethora of personal and social, psychological and physical aspects that construct your self, what requires resolution or managing and what doesn't? For example, if you *exist* as "real" or "capable" or "significant," what is there to do about that? It's simply a given and a place from which you view things. There is no need to enter reactive and convoluted struggles of emotion and manipulation relative to such assessed qualities. Because they don't show up in your self-agenda as something that needs resolution or managing, they won't appear in your reactivity and drives. What does show up as self-agenda activity will arise from taking for granted that some core aspect of yourself is unacceptable and needs to be corrected in some way, such as being inauthentic, incapable, or insignificant, and these will of course be held as negative.

7:35 To "correct" something you identify with that's seen as existentially negative, your impulse would be to obtain the positive. In matters that drive your reactions and manipulations, negative and positive are part of the same world. A drive to create the positive is frequently relating to a negative, trying to resolve it. If you *are* unreal, you may work hard to seem real. If you *are* insignificant, you could try to become significant. If you *are* stupid, you might work to become very knowledgeable and prove to yourself and others that you're smart. But none of these apparently positive assertions or efforts alter the source. They can't, because they are reactions to it.

7:36 You might have all sorts of reactions and dispositions in relation to some believed "fact" of you, and many could easily appear opposite to this core sense. You could feel fundamentally incapable of life and living it, and yet your experience is one of being a very capable person and you demonstrate this by being successful at what you do. This could well be based on a core belief of incapacity, and your agenda is proving to yourself and others that you really are capable. But no matter how hard you try or how much success you have, you'll find it won't be enough. If the "fact" of your deeper experience is that you're actually incapable, then no demonstration of capacity is going to change that. This would be true for any dysfunctional core sense you have. You may well spend your whole life countering it, trying to mend it. A gentle priest might think he is really evil, or a rich man worthless, maybe an affectionate woman feels incomplete, or a professor of knowledge thinks she's inherently wrong.

7:37 This source will be something you consider a "fact" of your very nature, some self-aspect that is held as unacceptable and in need of struggle and manipulation to set right. These source assumptions, which constitute a primary part of your self-framework, exist for you as an "is"—not a feeling or reaction, but just a "so." If you experience this core self-sense it seems like experiencing just what's true for you, your nature. But this doesn't necessarily show up anywhere in your recognized experience so it isn't in the same domain as the experience and behavior that come about because of it, whether emerging as some negative reaction or as a lifelong commitment to some "positive" counterbalance.

7:38 Since most of what's being said here will be heard as psychology, and related to what you experience as good and bad in your cognized internal state and behaviors, I want to reiterate that this is not what I'm referring to. I'm not even stopping with those buried feelings and doubts you have about yourself, which you may acknowledge in secret or on occasion when you reflect upon them in private moments. What I'm speaking about here is not a part of the conscious experience you recognize. Instead, it is the source self-framework that *determines* your experience. The domain where there is a fundamental core-belief of being "broken" in some way is not an experience or a manipulation. It's more like a taken-for-granted and unrecognized *fact*, something that "is" you, and is "lived" by you. It is assumed to be a fundamental aspect of you, but remains unseen in a similar way that the eyeball remains hidden even as you view everything from its perspective.

7:39 When some seemingly existential self-aspect is assumed to be a flaw—if you are somehow worthless in a world that demands worth, or incapable when survival is the prime principle—then all you can do is try to compensate for this flaw. Your interpretation of everything encountered will be generated in relation to this "fact" of you, and so all sorts of reactions and manipulations will be undertaken in an attempt to manage this state of affairs.

7:40　Are you getting all this? Can you see the non-random dynamics involved such that the bottom-lines and source assumptions you unearth will tend to appear negative? The source assumption will be something you consider a "fact" of your very nature that is held as flawed and in need of correction. You might have many reactions intended to counter this core, and some may simply be expressive of it. But there is a big difference in domains from the efforts and reactions—which are all agenda-related manipulations—and the core assumptions that are lived simply as facts of your nature. This unacceptable source will be held as a negative when encountered by a self-mind, but the whole thing is really just a mistake born of ignorance. Therefore, it can change.

7:41　If you were fundamentally whole and complete, real and capable, without qualification—not living as someone that is somehow in error or incapable or undeserving, or whatever—you'd require far less struggle or machinations to survive, especially socially. The matter of persistence becomes quite straightforward when you're dealing with nothing but uncorrupted essential human components. Perhaps something like the experience of a healthy deer or the mind of a mentally unfettered bird. To be clear, this is not enlightenment. It is simply freedom from all of the stuff that constitutes being "broken" in some way. Even with this freedom, you will still suffer the basic existential stuff that everyone suffers—a sense of separation, the need to survive, the assumption that you are an object, and so on. But you won't need to engage in meaningless unresolvable struggles attempting to fix what's wrong or broken. The immense realm of manipulation that is undertaken to try to resolve these flaws would not exist, and so would not be a dominant feature of your self-agenda and life.

Relating to the Negative Building Blocks

7:42 All of the above is difficult to get because people's thinking and experiencing is assumed to be all that's available to them—a limited surface-level consciousness. As an analogy, if your experience and consciousness is all about boats, then the surface of the water is all you'll be aware of or concerned about. If you consider what supports or makes possible the water's surface, you become conscious of the depth and volume of water as if from a fish's perspective, not just a boat's. If you ask further what supports or "holds" the water, you may discover the seabed and thus the earth, and so on. This sea-bottom depth of "consciousness," however, is a far cry from sailing, and seems useless to you as a sailor because all you need to know for sailing is on the water's surface. Since the survival of what you assume is yourself and your world is all that your mind is concerned with, the depth of consciousness needed for this work appears equally unimportant and goes unvisited, which is why it's difficult to grasp and even harder to transcend.

7:43 A certain amount of struggle while confronting these aspects of your self-experience is appropriate and necessary. Prior to completely freeing yourself from your bottom-lines, at some point you will have to genuinely experience the presence of these so-called flaws. Make a commitment to come to grips with the reality of your deep personal defects or "brokenness" and acknowledge these as a part of your self-structure. You'll need this in order to experience the truth that these "facts" of your person are only beliefs and programs—in other words, just concepts. They are not real. Their nature is conceptual and so an activity you're *doing* rather than what you *are*.

7:44   Transforming this structure also requires forgiving yourself for the really stupid and selfish things you've done in the process of maintaining those beliefs about yourself. Such forgiveness becomes genuine when you realize that there was no other way "you" could have been, and that your "brokenness" is in fact not in any way an aspect of your true nature. Your goal now must be to transcend what binds you to the past and these core self-beliefs.

7:45   Your self-experience is only what you designed in formulating a self in order to "be." You are not wrong or broken—or any of the deeply held core or foundation assumptions that pretty much everyone has. You are exactly the way you are, and no one could have done "you" better. You did a perfect job. If you can become deeply conscious of the real nature of this self that you've created, you can also realize that there really was no way around being exactly the way you are.

> *Today you are you, that is truer than true.*
> *There is no one alive who is youer than you.*
> —Dr. Seuss

7:46   This isn't to say that somehow your self has only manifested as it was destined to become. None of that is true, and not what I mean. What I mean is, *you* created your self, and in order to create a self, you had to create some form. A form was needed to fulfill all the functions demanded of a self to survive and "become." You did that, and really couldn't have avoided it, so there is nothing wrong with what you created. You are perfectly yourself. Your challenge now is to become conscious of the bottom-lines and source assumptions that you think you "are," grasp their conceptual nature, and free yourself from them.

7:47   When it comes to what's really true about your very existence, your true nature, there's nothing there. What comes to exist as some "thing" is an exercise in creating a self. In truth, Consciousness is *doing* you; *you* are doing you. To change you, *you* have to stop doing "you" the way you've been, and do something else. But don't do it because you aren't OK the way you are, because you are OK. Do it to know the truth and to be free.

Freedom from Emotions

7:48   As we work to increase our personal consciousness of the depths and framework of our emotions, it's good to remember that our goal here is not just to become conscious of what we're doing, but to become free of what we're doing. In other words, to be free of emotional dominance altogether. This goal will likely lead some people to confuse emotional freedom with becoming emotionless. When we try to imagine being free of emotion, we might conjure up an idea of some bland non-descript state, or an overly dry intellectual person overriding the emotional domain with the rational, or adopting a forced disinterest. Except for people who are predisposed to shutting down their emotions, this doesn't sound particularly attractive. It's also not what being free of emotional domination means.

7:49   Transcending emotional dominance is not a feeling-less state. Instead, consider that the shift to such freedom creates a similar condition to what happens post-enlightenment. A common "state" after an enlightenment experience seems to consist of something close to "bliss," or love, or compassion. This experiential shift arises as a natural human response to enlightenment. Being at least temporarily freed of the self-identity and the commitment

Transforming Your Emotions

to survival, the constant fear and struggle that generally accompany those are dissipated. Therefore, you are free to be open in relationship to others and life without being overwhelmed by the constant fear of consequence that contracts consciousness into the self and its concerns. This results in a kind of love or compassion not usually felt. Sounds nice, but take caution and note that the goal must be freedom, not one of trying to attain an imagined form of ecstasy, since such a goal would be totally counterproductive to the freedom necessary to attain this so-called "euphoric" state.

7:50 Consider: does your experience normally consist of anything that you could honestly call blissful, or unconditional love, or selfless compassion? Probably not. The idea of such a state, however, does provide a contrast to everything else that one might struggle with in the emotional domain, and this helps clarify the nature of the human experience within which you live, because all self-experience is dominated by charged interpretation dedicated to self-persistence. The ceaseless drive to persist by implication affirms the ever-present possibility of self-annihilation. To a self this is never a blissful experience, although it is the universal underpinning to all self-experience.

7:51 In order to become free of emotional dominance, at some point you'll need to confront trying to free yourself from two key ingredients of emotion, which are pain and desire. Pain is an ingredient in every negative emotion, and the main ingredient, in one form or another, of all forms of suffering. Understanding and being able to transcend the domination of pain and suffering are pivotal for engaging transformation. Toward that end, you should realize that desire is also a form of suffering. If you could manage to transcend both pain and desire, a transformation will have already occurred.

GETTING DOWN TO WORK

A new way of being would spontaneously be created because you would no longer have what we consider a normal human experience. It's not necessarily an *abnormal* experience, but one that is rather more genuinely human, with your perceptive-experience appearing in an altogether new light.

7:52　This "new light" stands on the freedom we've been speaking about. It isn't emotionless, it is simply free. It's not bound to a world in which experience is compelled to arise for the purpose of pursuing survival, and it turns out that this is a rather "blissful" experience. Just as with enlightenment, this sense of blissful compassion will be impossible to imagine this side of a personal encounter. Such bliss and love are not emotions, which doesn't make sense to us since we only know their emotional counterparts. It's worth noting that even this bliss is simply the human mind's response to a freer and more enlightened consciousness.

You are, but the mind is utterly empty.
That's the moment of enlightenment.
That is the moment that you become for the first time
an unconditioned, sane, really free human being.
—Osho

7:53　I've purposely avoiding using the word "happiness" because it's so easily confused with our emotional reaction to success in some self-agenda goal. There is no way the bliss of which I speak can arise if it is in any way desired, and it will disappear the moment it is clung to. The word "bliss" is such a weird word, however; so if we substitute the word "happiness" we need to know it is not the emotion we normally associate with that word. When experiencing this state, whatever it's called, there is no desire for it

Transforming Your Emotions

to remain or even for it to exist. It is not a focus of attention, nor does it require any thought or manipulation to exist. Instead, it arises as a side effect of an enlightened consciousness acting on the mind. So keep in mind that, although the idea of such a state provides a more attractive possibility than suffering, it is not something to actively pursue. It is simply an outcome of freeing yourself from emotional dominance.

Transcending Your "Real Self"

7:54 Beyond investigating the source of your patterns of emotion and behavior, you can and should look right into your present and *existential* experience of yourself—putting attention on your very "soul," the very heart of what you *live* as you. In addition to a self-identity composed of unique and discernible self "experiences," you have an unshakable and unalterable existential sense of being. This core sense is assumed to be the place where the "real" you resides. It seems to be the only ingredient that you absolutely cannot be without since it is held as your essence, your existence, *you*. You may think of this as the conscious entity that you are, upon which all other self traits and activities depend. Yet when you look more closely into this sense of your "soul," you find that it isn't open, free, or generic. It too has a "character," which suggests that, although it might seem indivisible, it is in fact composed of specific qualities.

7:55 In order to see this more clearly, imagine having an experience of being deeply and completely free and whole and happy, without one speck of disturbance or attachment or fear, free of limitation and desire, without any disposition at all, nothing in any way positive or negative. Does this sound descriptive of you? If not, you can see that some "formation" is held as your fundamental nature, and you'll also notice that there is an "intrinsic" suffering to this sense of self-existence.

7:56 I suppose this talk of inherent suffering in one's experience could be confusing. Some will insist that they rarely suffer and generally have a happy life. I'm glad that's true for them, but it's not related to what I'm suggesting. I guess one way to explain what I mean is to relate a new awareness that took place after I had my first direct-consciousness. One thing I was instantly aware of was being happy. I got that I had never been happy throughout my entire life, but hadn't known it since there was no comparison with which I could have grasped such a thing. In life there are good and bad experiences, and it seems only the bad is suffering. But the constriction of consciousness into a self that is always automatically concerned with survival is itself a form of suffering that is hard to notice until you're suddenly freed from it. Trying to discern your fundamental self-nature could help reveal this condition.

7:57 As you reach into your "soul," you will discover core emotional dispositions that act as a frame for what you consider to be simply your experience of "you." It's important to investigate your self at this level. Delve into this most basic sense of you and see what you can find. Your mere existence as an entity isn't the only thing that's there. You are attached to a unique sense of *being* that has a character or form to it, even though it usually goes unnoticed and lives in the background as the core "place" of you. You will find there seems to be something substantial there that you cling to as your *real* self. It may be possible for you to survive the loss of this or that character trait or ability, or some emotional pattern, even your memory, or a perceptive faculty. But you're certain that losing this "soul" part of you means your death. It's difficult to even think that this might not be so, that even this most core sense of you is not *you*, and that it too can be transcended.

7:58   Again, I invite you to consider that if you can identify with character traits, qualities, thinking, or experiences other than what you identify with now, then you must not actually be any of these elements. If this is so, who are you? What are you? If you try to pin down who you really are, you will search your mind and attempt to grab onto an idea, or feeling, or sense. Yet that very idea, feeling, or sense itself can be let go, and so it can't be you either. See how this works?

7:59   If you follow this letting-go principle to its end, it must lead you to your true nature, since nothing else will be left! Of course, this has to be done for oneself and not merely accepted as an extrapolated fact. An openness to this possibility is useful to consider, but only direct-consciousness will confirm it. The truth of you must *be you*, rather than some idea or experience *about* you. Needless to say, since enlightenment isn't had through any method, it won't occur as a process. But the attempt may be quite fruitful, nevertheless—and you can't tell, it may work. Enlightenment is not the result of a process, but that doesn't mean it can't occur while engaging in some method or process. In any case, entertaining the mere possibility that *you* aren't anything that you experience could open a door in your contemplations.

7:60   As we proceed to scrutinize the nature and components of self, and to free our consciousness from attachments, we'll run into pitfalls and confront barriers that impede our progress. In the next chapter, we'll work on becoming aware of these complicated and often overlooked traps so that we can recognize them more quickly and move beyond them.

CHAPTER EIGHT

Predictable Pitfalls

Some Immediate Obstacles

8:1   A sobering reality that we need to confront again and again is that we're unlikely to have the will or even desire to actually change the very *person* that seems to be the source and core of our experience. The ideas we have about transformation are too often limited to merely tweaking our behavior or struggling to eliminate personal characteristics that we've wanted to change for a long time. Our entire existence and everything we think we *are* is devoted to the particular person that we experience being. Give *that* up? Ridiculous.

8:2   Even so, it is possible. Such work usually starts off slowly and builds as your consciousness in the matter increases and the benefits become more clear. Toward that end, I suggest you discipline yourself to keep attention on contemplating what's going on with you, seeking to understand in detail why your experience is the way it is. Since you're likely to slip from this contemplative disposition, you need to create some means of continually bringing your attention back, and find ways to override your resistance. Over time, regular practice will become more familiar and engaging, adding momentum that makes it easier to maintain your practice through more painful or tedious times.

8:3   Despite your best efforts, from the outset this pursuit will lead to many hidden traps. One common entanglement is identifying with the practice such that the self becomes attached to the "character" who's pursuing transformation. When you make progress, take care not to slip into identifying with being superior simply because you've managed to adopt a "better person" persona for a while. Such a course is only helpful if the appeal inspires you to take on a transformative practice. After that, you must drop this persona, or risk sabotaging your own goals by indulging in "spiritual snobbery." Repeatedly freeing yourself from this trap is the perennial "next step" to be taken whenever such an attachment forms. In fact, much of the work of transformation is continually extricating yourself from the inevitable traps and pitfalls that such work entails. These are not just wrong turns or blundering detours, per se, but are often obstacles right in the middle of the road.

8:4   Probably one of the most important attitudes to have is one of being undaunted by failure. I can't tell you how many times I gave it my all and still fell flat on my face—far more often than I succeeded, and by a huge margin. In my younger days, each time I failed to accomplish what I had set out to accomplish, I would rally myself with a vow that went something like: "I renew my commitment to do it now." Failure is to be expected. If you like, you can use my "mantra" or create your own, but learn to relate successfully to the times you fail.

I have not failed. I've just found 10,000 ways that won't work.
—Thomas Edison

8:5   When it comes to making a breakthrough in consciousness or having an enlightenment experience, one can contemplate and attempt to grasp what's being considered and fail to get it again and again. How many moments of intent does one put into a contemplation and yet make no significant breakthrough? It is completely up in the air. A breakthrough can occur in the first instant of contemplation. It can also take millions of attempts before a single enlightenment occurs. That's a million to one. So we must learn to cope with failure—refusing to let it diminish our intent and commitment—or we could easily become discouraged and quit.

8:6 When trying to become a better person by adopting new attitudes, working to change your emotional reactivity, or taking on new behaviors, you often have success only for as long as your focus remains on your commitment to that shift. As we all know, a self's habitual programs are tenacious. The moment you stray from your commitment, your characteristic defenses will automatically arise in relation to particular stimuli. When you've thrown yourself into making some change, and especially after making some progress, what often follows is a relapse into old ways. If this is typical of your efforts, chances are you're trying to solve a deep problem with shallow solutions.

8:7 Redesigning the foundations of mind that are responsible for emotional reaction is not a superficial task. The self-agenda is pervasive and primal, and "designed" to withstand any assault by mere intellect. Since our entire experience is founded on a complex and virtually inaccessible self-mind, the primary and ongoing task of transformation demands that we become conscious of deeper aspects of mind. Addressing the foundations that keep us stuck in our current experience is a bit like pulling up a weed by the root rather than just chopping off whatever's visible.

8:8 One activity we can use to deepen our understanding of ourselves is communication. Interacting with others and observing our reactivity in real time provides a great deal of feedback that's missing when we try to work everything out alone. There are some important distinctions and breakthroughs to be made about communication that not only express change but also *empower* it. Of course, the motives behind our communications are what determine the strategies that design an interaction. Here too, pitfalls and misunderstandings need attention.

> Deception and "con games" are a way of life
> in all species and throughout nature.
> Organisms that do not improve their ability to deceive—
> and to detect deception—
> are less apt to survive.
> —Harriet Lerner

Manipulation versus Communication

8:9 Suppose you could hit a pause button in the middle of emotionally reacting. If in that moment you were to experience that the reaction was itself a manipulation, and also experience what you were trying to achieve with that manipulation, this alone would radically change your disposition. You might still react, but you couldn't take it as seriously as you would if you were unaware of the real motivations behind your impulses. Your reactions would not reflexively appear to be somehow true and right in and of themselves.

GETTING DOWN TO WORK

8:10   To go further, however, is the real change. In this section we'll look more deeply into several aspects and hidden layers of manipulation that are so commonly confused with communication. This will require making new distinctions within your experience to shed light on previously unnoticed motivations. For example, once you ascertain the real goal of any particular manipulation, you will find that its purpose is actually to resolve some internal drive or to fulfill some need—maybe to get love, or to feel safe, be respected, feel capable, satisfy a desire, escape from a dilemma, be seen in a certain light, be nurtured, acknowledged, receive assistance, feel connected, or what have you. Consciously interacting from this core-objective is a very different experience from manipulating your own behavior in an unconscious attempt to bring it about.

8:11   If we make a distinction between honest communication and acting out internal drives, we can see that one is sharing our internal state while the other is manipulating because of it. Honest or actual communication is getting an unaltered experience across to another person for the purpose of being understood. Trying to elicit some response or produce an effect in the other is not an attempt to communicate, it's an attempt to *manipulate*.

8:12   Manipulation is what most people do most of the time. We speak or interact non-verbally for the purpose of producing some effect or reaction in the other person. We're attempting to generate an impression or to alter another's experience in some way that serves a purpose of our own. Recall some of your past interactions in this light and notice how much was actually not communication at all but simply verbal manipulation. No matter how innocently it's done or how well-intentioned it seems, it is still a manipulation.

8:13　Communication, on the other hand, is simply and honestly sharing an experience, period. The only motivation behind it is to get it across. The communication may provide information, or create understanding, or some such, but that is a result of the shared experience itself. It is not an attempt to indirectly handle your needs by creating some effect in the receiver. Can you see the distinction here?

8:14　Honesty is an aspect of all real communication, and so instead of calling it "honest communication," it should just be called "communication." By definition, communication demands honesty. Therefore, with real communication, we maintain our integrity by keeping our behavior and internal state in accord. Integrity within our personal experience means that we have no conflict or inconsistencies between our internal state—what we think and feel, as well as our impulses and motives—and our behavior, expressions, and actions. If our goal is to be honest, and to keep our experience closely aligned with the truth, integrity is essential.

8:15　The more conscious we are, the closer we are to grasping what is true within our own experience. This means that our motives for doing anything become increasingly transparent and accessible to us. To maintain integrity and honesty, we're obliged to keep our communication and behavior consistent with our internal state.

8:16　As we grow in awareness, we will discover that our real motivations are of a different nature than we had assumed. Where we once acted out of ignorance or suppression, now we're called upon to operate in relation to a new understanding of our motives and internal state. What was previously the "best we could do" is no longer valid, and so communicating at that same level is no longer acceptable. Our integrity demands that we communicate and behave according to what we now recognize as true. Any time we become more deeply conscious regarding the nature of our experience, we must communicate and act in a way consistent with *that* experience, otherwise we will be lying.

8:17 For example, if my internal state is one of anger about something you said and my communication reflects this anger, at least I'm not deceiving you about my internal state. If I subsequently become conscious that my anger is actually an internal manipulation crafted to manage the hurt in response to what you said, then in order for me to maintain integrity, my communication would need to express the pain rather than the anger.

8:18 Whatever is true for you internally has to be reflected honestly in your expressions or you will compromise your integrity. Any lack of integrity will mean a proportionate split within your experience of self and life. Set aside any moral implications and simply consider it like the integrity of a porcelain vase: it's strong and fulfills its function when it is whole and unified. If there is a crack in the vase, a split between one part and another, the vase is weakened, likely to crack further, and can't hold water very well. If your experience is misrepresented in your expressions or communications, then your clarity and presence are diminished, your sense of authenticity is weakened, and you are pushed further from the truth. Honesty brings you back, but this business of being honest can also be misunderstood.

I'm honest to those who are honest,
I'm also honest to those who are not honest.
Thus I gain in honesty.
—Lao Tzu

Pre-Manipulation Communication

8:19 People often think they are honestly communicating when they're actually manipulating. This could be due to the fact that there are at least three layers to our experience that we may or may not be conscious of. We've seen that the first layer is what everyone knows as their experience—the impulse and motive to act or react in some way. The next layer in this case is simply being more conscious of what you're really up to or what's really true for you in your experience beneath the surface, and acknowledging these motives. That would be like grasping that you're hurt and relating from that emotion rather than allowing it to turn into anger and just acting out the anger. The deepest layer for our discussion is the original yet generally unconscious self-motivation that we're calling the bottom-line. Depending on one's depth of consciousness about their own experience, these last two layers could be called "pre-manipulation" communication.

8:20 Acting out an impulse via manipulation may seem legitimate since it is consistent with the impulse, but it still doesn't honestly express your experience. Instead, it is an attempt to *manage* your experience—to make it more closely conform to your needs. Communicating what's really there for you before you reactively turn it into a manipulation is an honest expression of your state rather than an attempt to *do* something about it.

8:21 Let's be clear: being angry and yelling that someone is an asshole isn't an expression of a pre-manipulation experience. It *is* a manipulation. This is true even if you thought that a different, more indirect expression would be more effective. In other words, you know you could've been more diplomatic, or chosen another expression that you may consciously think of as "manipulative," but instead chose to "honestly" express your "gut reaction." Yet all of those choices are manipulations and take place in the more superficial layer of experience. The pre-manipulation experience is what's true for you *before* the anger, what motivates the anger to arise in the first place, driving you to engage that manipulation.

8:22   When you angrily call someone an asshole, the goal is not to express your deeper drive—which is hurt—it is to manage your experience of feeling hurt. You want your expression to have some specific effect on the other person. When the manipulation is "anger," the desired effect is likely along the lines of wanting to make them feel bad. Maybe you want to get some small revenge for the pain you think they caused, or to have them change their behavior so you feel more secure. Basically, in some way you want to destroy the apparent cause for your hurt, so that you can eliminate the pain or danger. Your goal is *not* to have them experience the true internal state that drives you to want to manipulate in the first place—for example, feeling hurt and insecure as a person. Communicating the truth—that you are hurt and insecure—would be the "pre-manipulation" communication. Such communication can seem reckless, however, since it appears to expose your vulnerabilities rather than manage them. On the other hand, it is what's true.

8:23   This is only one example in a massive array of possibilities. Our internal emotional self-manipulations cover the whole spectrum— anger, fear, greed, desire, shame, irritation, boredom, shyness, frustration, gratitude, contempt, vanity, excitement, or any of a number of common emotions or charged internal impulses to feel or behave in some manner. Acting on emotional manipulations that occur in and *as* your internal state will manifest in various physical or objective manipulations such as yelling, convincing, cajoling, intimidating, seducing, lying, ignoring, scowling, smiling, frowning, hitting, crying, pouting, pestering, giving, and on and on. Remember, manipulation also applies to what we consider positive expressions, such as being nice, nurturing, comforting, complimenting, or flattering someone. These too are manipulations whenever the goal is to affect the other person to achieve some end for ourselves, rather than to simply share an experience. Whether positive or negative in nature, acknowledging what is behind these internal states and behavioral manipulations and then sharing *that* is pre-manipulation communication.

8:24 Such communication is still tricky, however, since in order for it to be a communication rather than a manipulation, it can't be expressed for the purpose of affecting the other's experience in order to manage your own—for example, eliciting sympathy, being felt sorry for, getting them to like you, or manipulating them in any other way. Although the subject matter might appear to be the same, using even your true internal state in order to elicit a reaction from another reduces it to just another form of manipulation.

8:25 Pre-manipulation communication requires that you communicate what's true for you only to get across what's true for you. When you increase understanding between yourself and another, your integrity is empowered rather than diminished. Communication also increases the effectiveness and the depth of connection you can experience with others, which is likely the reason you would brave such a course. Still, these are side effects of the task. Since pre-manipulation communication gets across your unaltered core experience, once shared, it's out of your control. The truth has been presented and what happens next is unknown. It's a bit like letting go of a bird that you hold in your hands. It will do whatever and go where it will, without you knowing where that's going to be. All you can predict is that the bird will be free.

8:26　I know this kind of communication is uncommon in our culture. Actions that do not serve the self's agenda are rarely seen as useful. But unless we become conscious of the original self-experience that sets our internal activities and automatic manipulations in motion, we will fail to be truly honest in our communications. Usually the domain of our true, primary experience is barely recognized internally, much less communicated to another person.

8:27　We've investigated the deeper layer of our experience enough by now to grasp that our core experience is based upon managing our fundamental self-identity—what we actually think is so about us. To briefly recap this dynamic: Our core experience exists for the purpose of generating, as well as looking after, the basic self or person that we think we are. In order to relate "this person" to everything else, interpretation creates an experience that automatically perceives *only* in the light of self-relativity. This is the "for-me" experience. In order to manage life and pursue self-survival, an internal reaction or feeling-state is immediately created to indicate what to do in relation to whatever is perceived. In this way, these feeling-states, known generally as emotions, are manipulations created to motivate the self to act or adopt certain dispositions. This internal manipulation then shows up as an attempted manipulation of one's self, others, or circumstance.

Out beyond ideas of wrongdoing and rightdoing there is a field.
I'll meet you there.
—Rumi

8:28 This brings us to the bottom-line depth of experience. When you deepen your conscious experience by realizing a bottom-line or source assumption, you discover what's behind the internal reaction that leads to a particular manipulative behavior. The bottom-line will be compensating for and managing some source assumption that's held as true about the nature of your fundamental self. The domain of such core experiences often reveals fundamental dispositions like believing you are helpless, unseen, worthless, unloved or unlovable, inauthentic, or incapable of life. Communicating this level of experience doesn't have anything to do with changing what's experienced. It *is* your self-experience before you try to *do* something about it.

8:29 This "true" or bottom-line experience can be tricky to discern. Such a distinction goes unnoticed by most people because the self-mind's job is primarily to manipulate, to create a feeling-state that pushes you toward some kind of action or reaction to manage or resolve the needs of the self. Your relationship to what's occurring in your own mind will depend on your degree of consciousness in the matter. The more conscious you are of the real source of your internal state, the more irrelevant you'll see your previous superficial manipulations.

8:30 In any case, communicating the most honest experience that you have—independent of trying to create an effect in others and regardless of possible consequences—develops a stronger sense of personal integrity and vitality, a deeper sense of being heard and understood, a growing sense of authenticity and self-acceptance, as well as increased clarity and decreased machinations, and so forth.

GETTING DOWN TO WORK

8:31   Such communication may not get you what you want, and might evoke outcomes that you don't want. It's certainly not the social norm. Yet if you concentrate on what really happens when you manipulate others, you will notice that you often don't get what you want anyway, and can still trigger unwanted reactions. The fact is that outcomes with others are unpredictable, whether you follow your usual path of manipulation or you take the risk of revealing your true experience. With the latter, however, there are several predictable outcomes: you will increase integrity, free up a huge amount of energy previously trapped in the struggles of manipulation, simplify and expand your sense of being, and increase both your presence and consciousness.

Suppressing Internal States Anchors Them to Self

8:32   One source of confusion about the difference between manipulation and the communication of an experience arises from our tendency to suppress socially undesirable reactions. When, on occasion, we summon the courage to communicate some previously suppressed internal reaction—maybe to admit that we are actually afraid all the time, or feel superior or inferior, or we feel inept or clueless, or inauthentic or perverted, ashamed or whatever—it might feel as though we're revealing something more central to our true selves, when actually we're not. Such an experience only *seems* to be coming from a place closer to our core because it has been suppressed.

8:33   Internal-state patterns that are buried or kept hidden tend to grow in power because we experience them as deeper, more intimate, and private parts of us, viewing them as personal aspects of our exclusive inner world. Because they are held within, we may develop an idea or unknowingly harbor an assumption that these aspects are nearer than they really are to the core of our self-experience. They may also seem significant because they hold a considerable charge due to their unacceptable social status. All these conclusions are mistaken, which becomes clear once we freely communicate these internal reactions. They immediately begin to lose that private and special status and eventually settle into the domain of self-mind aspects that we *do* share.

8:34 Unfortunately, as we've seen, anything shared is likely to be a manipulation because we're so accustomed to presenting our state in an altered form to help achieve some end. We may be unaware of it, but this means that our normal communications generally lack integrity. This unnoticed split creates the same dynamic as withholding some deliberately buried and hidden aspects of our self-experience. In both cases, we end up living within an experience of an inner world that doesn't match our outward presentation to others. Again because of its very privacy, this inner world gains significance and power, eventually becoming confused with our sense of "real self."

8:35 The greater the discrepancy between our expressions and our experience—the more we deceive, manipulate, pretend, and so on—the greater our sense of isolation and the stronger our sense that the isolated "one within" is our "true self." Obviously a side effect of this condition is that we will feel less heard or understood, and less connected or loved as a person. Our impulse to manipulate in the service of a mostly unconscious self-agenda is a dynamic that causes a cascade of overlooked consequences.

All forms of self-defeating behavior are unseen and unconscious, which is why their existence is denied.
—Vernon Howard

8:36   If you want to experience being loved, heard, and acknowledged, it should be clear that the only genuine way to do that is to engage in *real* communication. Take a manipulative or less honest course, and you'll find that whoever it is that is apparently being loved or acknowledged isn't what you experience as "you," and so deep down you still don't really feel loved, heard, or acknowledged. In order to have such an experience you must communicate your "real," unaltered self-experience.

8:37   Because everyone has very primal, negative, and selfish aspects, most people fear delving into their often hidden and suppressed, mostly uncognized self-experience. We don't want to acknowledge, much less experience, any disparity between ourselves and our self-image and ideals. We assume that if we keep those aspects unrecognized or ignored, we can pretend to be "better" than we really are. We may look upon these negative self-aspects as maladies that perhaps we can fix, but, until we become conscious of their source, there can be no remedy.

8:38   Another side to this is the fact that our resistance to examining negative personal aspects only exists because of the self-agenda. If we didn't have this monstrous mechanism of unconscious self-attachments and drives constantly trying to manage and manipulate life and circumstance in hope of some vague attainment or resolution, these negative aspects wouldn't exist. They are a function of the same dynamic that keeps you pursuing all sorts of experiences with the idea that they will provide something you want or need.

Cheese Chasing

8:39 You may remember from *The Book of Not Knowing* that I used an image of a mouse running in a wheel, chasing after cheese that is situated just out of reach. This image suggests that what motivates the mouse to run is something he will never get, but it does keep him running. The real purpose of this action remains unknown to the mouse but demands that the cheese seem both desirable and attainable so as to create the impulse and activity of pursuit, while also ensuring that the cheese is never reached.

8:40 This poor ignorant mouse seems an apt metaphor for the self-survival dynamic within which we are trapped. Without knowing it, we are drawn into chasing many forms of unattainable "cheese." One of these is found in the multidimensional domain of all those things we're drawn to try to attain, thinking they will complete us, resolve inner disquiet, or fulfill some need. While pursuing transformation, this dynamic needs attention and understanding. We need to find a way to stop acting out the many forms of cheese-chasing or we risk spinning forever in our own wheels rather than increasing consciousness or changing.

8:41 We've seen that our first steps toward transformation will be based on our ideals, or the ideals of a belief system. This obviously makes it difficult to avoid our wheel and further emphasizes the need to be clear that these beginning goals are only temporary—another application of our "Abdul camel." In the pursuit of transformation, it may be possible to utilize our cheese-chasing impulses to help us recognize "wheel-based" perceptions while at the same time working to transcend this closed-looped dynamic.

8:42   We know that giving up aspects of ourselves that we've held as necessary parts of our very person entails recognizing them as unnecessary and as not-us. Whatever *meaning* they may hold for us in our lives and for our survival has to be seen as either no longer needed or as actually meaningless. In either case, this work calls into question the meaning or meaningfulness of ourselves, our character, and our lives.

8:43   If our focus relative to transformation is on attaining some fantasy of a new and improved, more meaningful experience, we're merely chasing the cheese of self-improvement and are not likely to challenge the current meaning we attribute to ourselves and our lives. While we're aware that we're already programmed to avoid the negative and move toward the positive, we need to recognize that this also applies to our *meaningful* attempts at self-improvement. Basing transformation on these dynamics not only keeps us on the wheel, it restricts our efforts to the same domain of meaning that currently defines our self-survival. So although we may avoid the pain of confronting our inherent meaninglessness, we fail to approach any real transformation.

8:44   As long as any of our beliefs, assumptions, characteristics, or emotional patterns are considered meaningful to us, dropping them will be difficult. This domain of meaning will also keep us pursuing characteristic behaviors, since we will be pushed into reacting to the same negative and positive perspectives.

8:45   What's true is that self and life actually *are* meaningless, but it's difficult to make peace with this fact prior to reaching some degree of enlightened consciousness. Meaninglessness is seen as a negative whenever encountered by a self-mind because, by definition, it eliminates self-importance, takes away the idea of being special, having a destiny, attaining the final outcome of one's self-agenda, and any other *raison d'être* that exists as a background context for your particular self. Can you see that without meaning none of those could exist?

8:46　Absent the context of meaning, where is a self going to find the motivation to struggle in all the ways that we do to manage or manipulate life and circumstance? Where is our motivation to attain, to overcome hardship, to put up with our suffering? These actions appear as necessary when self has meaning, no matter what that meaning is, negative or positive. If self and life have no meaning, all these struggles would be seen as unnecessary.

8:47　Confronting the absence of meaning often turns into a systemic negative for a self, and can easily lead to depression. But notice: if coming face to face with something we call "meaninglessness" is regarded as negative, then *it has meaning!* By definition, such a perspective cannot actually be a consciousness of meaninglessness. Meaninglessness doesn't *mean* anything. It is not negative or bad, positive or good, since those distinctions are all founded on meaning.

8:48　To the self, meaninglessness is always seen as a negative because it deprives the self-mind of material for generating the concept of a "meaningful" future. Unless we find a way to transcend meaning, its lack will be seen as a downer. In fact, failure to conceive of a positive future is the conceptual cause of depression. Such depression won't serve your pursuit, so to counter it, I recommend creating and maintaining a strong concept of a positive future, even if it entails imagining that enlightened transformation will set you free and make you happy. Yes, this will be "meaningful," but it serves the function of avoiding a negative emotional spiral.

GETTING DOWN TO WORK

It can act as an inserted "camel" until it's no longer required—such as when you actually *are* free and happy.

---

*He who has a why to live,
can bear almost any how.*
—Friedrich Nietzsche

8:49   To be consistent with our transformation objective, it's useful to craft the various goals we may adopt so that they lead us outside of mere self-interest and instead reach toward more "selfless" qualities. Goals of this nature tend to create more satisfaction and sense of fulfillment, and so are also a tool for avoiding depression. It may be "cheese-chasing" but since it's known as such and used for a purpose that is aligned with our overall objective, it's unlikely to derail our efforts but will instead support change. As the transformation process matures, such goals tend to fall away naturally because they are no longer needed.

8:50   The domain of "cheese-chasing" is complicated and multidimensional, and is antithetical to transformation, and yet our imagined transformative objectives are likely to be some form of chasin' the cheese. This is another challenging trap that we need to take care to work with intelligently. Speaking of challenging traps, there is another balancing act we need to consider.

Orgy versus Attainment

8:51   Most people struggle daily with some form of choosing between immediate gratification and longer-term satisfaction. We see this dichotomy easily in things like food consumption. If you are someone who gains weight without really trying, you can either eat what makes you "happy" at the moment (gratification), or postpone much of it in order to lose weight and so be "happy" later on (satisfaction).

8:52 One of the qualities of gratification is that it is immediate but short-lived. As soon as the action that generates the pleasure stops, the pleasure goes away. Just so, acquiring a more constant or long-term sense of satisfaction—unfolding through a background commitment to an attainment not immediately accessible—requires overriding most of the myriad impulses that tend to arise in any given moment. In daily life, we constantly weigh one against the other.

If I deny myself I gain freedom but lose comfort.
If I indulge myself I gain comfort but lose freedom.
Indulge, deny, what is myself?

8:53 In our efforts to achieve transformation, the distinction can become a little more complex. Since we're driven to attain pleasure in many forms, the impulses to do so can be fairly constant. Some are quite subtle and some are very demanding.

8:54 For example, when we pursue some form of emotional pleasure—such as feeling accepted, loved, nurtured, safe, and so on—we are chasing after the idea of resolving some dilemma within our self-agenda. This dilemma can be felt as a lack, a sense of being unfulfilled or incomplete, a longing for something not clearly defined, and the like. Although resolution of this kind is more aptly characterized as a long-term or lifetime undertaking, its pursuit also shows up as an immediate driver of many of the behaviors and choices we make while attempting to alleviate this suffering or attain our emotional self-agenda needs in the short term.

8:55   We often take action that's related to current circumstances because we think we can somehow alleviate our long-term suffering, even if what's immediately available is clearly only a partial attainment toward that end—like trying to get approval for something done, or to be liked, or to feel good by engaging in some form of immediate pleasure like eating chocolate. Consistent with this pursuit is the "pleasure" of avoiding discomfort. We might feel good temporarily, but the driver to attain these quick fixes is the desire for a long-term resolution not particularly related to any of these accomplishments. By themselves, none of these are seen as a significant attainment, but they are still held as if they might be steps along the way toward resolving our sense of being incomplete or at least seen as the best we can do for now. These temporary but immediately available "quick fixes" exist as a nearly constant pursuit, representing a clear manifestation of our compulsion to fulfill our self-agenda.

8:56   The idea that we can somehow "have it all"—manage to realize some final attainment that will make us completely whole and happy—is often present in the background as a contrasting ideal to our current experience. Yet our attempts at short-term immediate gratification may well be driven by the same impulse as the desire to be complete, and so share in the same force, even if the outcome is admittedly temporary and insufficient. Since gratifications constantly fall away and fall short, we must endlessly repeat some form of these pursuits to assuage our ever-present self-agenda demands and distress. Can you see the relationship between repeated attempts at immediate gratification and your long-term background dissatisfaction or sense of being incomplete?

8:57   Any particular form of emotionally oriented gratification—food, drugs, sex, entertainment, fantasy, a pat on the back, social acceptance in the moment, winning, bullying, or what have you—will always be temporary and so pursuing them never ends. Whether or not we recognize this depends on our level of consciousness in the matter. If we shift from an unhealthy, damaging behavior to a healthier one, we may still be on the wheel, but at least this direction is more consistent with changing from indulging gratifying impulses to pursuing more long-term satisfaction.

8:58   In contrast to the "orgy" of immediate gratification is the discipline of "attainment." Any pursuit that requires discipline aims not for immediate pleasure but for a more systemic change that occurs over time and produces a deeper, more lasting effect. Instead of acting on an impulse for immediate gratification, we're looking for a more sustainable solution to our dissatisfaction. If the issue is, say, losing weight, we set our sights on a life change that will provide a more constant and deeper sense of satisfaction with our body image and, consequently, our self-image. This course is taken on largely because we recognize that the repeated pattern of immediate gratification has continually failed to bring any depth of personal satisfaction and is endlessly temporary. We learn to undertake more long-term "work" than that of simply gathering up grapes for the orgy.

8:59   Obviously, any progress in transformation will occur through the attainment approach, rather than self-gratification. Following our knee-jerk reactions to the impulses that drive us to manipulate outcomes isn't going to change anything—that's clearly not their purpose. Our own past shows the futility of hoping for a quick and easy resolution to our dissatisfaction, so we postulate that more discipline is required. This is likely true, but we also need to be cautious here not to confuse this effort with trying to realize ideals that we already hold. It's useful to remember that these ideals arise from the self that we experience now, not the self that we are attempting to become.

8:60 Another trap to watch for is allowing ourselves to fall into supposing that "long-term" connotes *later,* which too frequently means *never.* Although we need patience in order to dig in for the long haul, we shouldn't confuse that with waiting until a later time to make progress. Our intent needs to be to transform now, in the present, even though dramatic shifts may not occur right away. Transformation needs to be actively pursued, rather than held as something that might magically occur in the future.

*I never did anything worth doing entirely by accident . . .
my inventions . . . were achieved by having trained myself
to be analytical and to endure and tolerate hard work.*
—Thomas Edison

Confronting the Reality of Change

8:61 Many people who consider a pursuit like transformation mistakenly think that intellectually changing their minds will accomplish a real change. They seem to have no idea what it takes to change anything about themselves, or even to deeply learn something outside their current experience and beliefs. Even if they understand the concept, few people truly accept the reality that no matter how much effort is put into mental or emotional activities such as wishing, thinking, believing, and demanding, this will not get the job done.

Predictable Pitfalls

8:62 To create an image that might help you consider this matter, imagine that what's required to transform yourself is similar to what it might take to grow a new hand, or dissolve your foot just as an act of will. The first obstacle that occurs to us is that this is impossible. Just so. Holding that thought puts you in the proper frame of mind to confront the enormous challenge of real change.

8:63 Once we see that we can't *wish* it into reality, the next thing that arises is utter uncertainty about how to accomplish such change. Even though you can't imagine how to proceed, you have to start out anyway. Just as an act of will, try right now to seek out the kind of "reality" you'd need to create in order to actually grow a new aspect to your body, or dissolve an existing body part. You can see that this would have to go far beyond intellect and also beyond what you can currently conceive. Compare this to what you thought about transformation previously.

8:64 In this work, such an analogy should be taken seriously, but not literally. The work has to be done within the very nature and core of the "thing itself" which, in this case, is what you call "you" and your actual and fundamental experience of yourself. Consider that transformation and enlightenment are in no way superficial and can't be approached without delving right into the very heart and nature, the very truth and existence, of you and reality.

8:65 Looking at the various challenges and traps that are likely to arise creates the possibility of avoiding them or at least recognizing them more quickly if they do arise. A quick review of two points that have been covered earlier may help reinforce and clarify these basic traps.
- You need to keep a vigil on not fooling yourself. Change won't work if you keep fundamentally doing the same thing,

coming from the same "person" and self-agenda. Even if you make it look different, don't kid yourself into thinking that this is transforming.

- You also need to keep attention on the fact that your imagined goals will be based on your existing ideals. Since the end product of real transformation is unknown, you don't know what kind of experience or person it will produce. Although having an idea in mind may be necessary to begin, remember that it is only an "Abdul camel." Continue to challenge the image as you grow and mature so you can update your imagined objectives in relation to whatever is discovered to be "more true" as a result of increased consciousness.

More Misconceptions and Traps

Madness Is Not Enlightenment

8:66 Although there is a vast difference between an enlightenment experience and an episode of mental instability, having little understanding about this subject leads people to sometimes confuse a breakdown with a breakthrough. Without knowing what direct-consciousness is, people usually search for some kind of different "experience." Therefore a dramatic shift in mind and perception can be mistaken for a breakthrough and may be thought to be enlightenment. It is not. Only consciousness is enlightenment and only changing the self is transformation. Neither of these embraces insanity.

8:67 After very intense concentration and contemplation, some people can have a mental breakdown. I'm not talking about all those shifts of state or altered perceptive experiences that can accompany intense contemplation—these are normal and temporary. I'm referring here to a real mental crash. If you have such a breakdown and find it difficult to function, or feel that you have become ungrounded mentally or emotionally, or that you're losing your "grip on reality," then you are NOT enlightened. You are having a mental problem. Your mind or brain has been overloaded and has crashed in some way. This is also likely to be temporary. You will need to reconstruct a more stable and functional relationship to your mind and perceptions before you can proceed with life, and certainly before you attempt to pursue any efforts to transform or become enlightened.

An Acid Trip Is Not Enlightenment

8:68 While we're on this subject, don't confuse enlightenment with the use of mind-altering drugs. Such an experience might challenge your habits of perception for a while, but that's not the same thing as an increased consciousness. It is possible to have an enlightenment no matter what the circumstances, but drugs only provide an altered mind-state, and certainly not enlightenment.

Don't Act Out or Suppress

8:69 A good practice while working on transformation is to maintain a sort of "emotional objectivity," neither acting out nor suppressing whatever feelings come up. Acting out is letting an emotional impulse push you into manipulative reflexive behavior. This activity only reinforces the reaction by trying to fulfill some self-agenda stimulus. Since this need or fear is based on the *existing* self-framework, acting it out serves no transformative purpose. The same goes for suppression, which is overriding the tendency to act on some emotional impulse by burying it or ignoring it altogether.

GETTING DOWN TO WORK

Also being based on the self-agenda, suppression doesn't serve any more than acting out. It only withholds communication or behavior to avoid consequence.

8:70 Instead of either acting out or suppressing, I recommend that you fully feel whatever the emotion or reaction is and freely communicate what's there but without manipulating because of it. In this way you can more clearly see the purpose of the impulse as well as work to get to the bottom of it. You aren't denying or ignoring anything and you aren't just reflexively reacting, being dominated by your self-agenda. What you're doing is honestly investigating an aspect of your self and using it to reach greater clarity.

Avoid Dramatizing Discoveries

8:71 In a similar vein, but addressing a more difficult challenge: it's important not to over-dramatize core self-assumption discoveries. When you get deeply in touch with something true about yourself that has been long held beneath the surface, it can be quite shocking. This is likely to occur while unearthing those elements "close to your soul" that we talked about earlier. When looking into a core experience that is incomplete, trapped, inadequate, or what not—in a deep way that seems to be "intrinsic" to your very being—discoveries here can be quite intense, perhaps even shocking.

8:72 In order to get to the truth or source of these, it is important to avoid the trap of reacting to your discoveries by relating to them with emotional drama of some sort. Yes, they will seem very significant, but don't act them out or overdramatize what's so. Don't create a little internal or external soap opera about it for yourself. Stay with the real experience and remember that your purpose is to see what's true *beyond* your reactions.

8:73 Entering into a "drama" can be almost irresistible because this core self-assumption is so closely wed to the framework that evokes emotional dramas used reflexively to manipulate your own internal state. This core element will likely be a fundamental "truth" about yourself that you've been deliberately but unconsciously censoring from your awareness. This kind of avoidance is already responsible for many of the drives and impulses that push you to manipulate yourself or circumstance in the ways that you do. The intrinsic core aspects of your sense of being are at the base of all this and well worth discovering, but reacting by emotionally dramatizing your contact with them will only push you back to where you came from.

Stay on Track

8:74 Countless other barriers, pitfalls, and traps will arise, some personal, many universal. Keeping your efforts aimed at the pursuit of truth and freedom should provide the honesty and clarity necessary to recognize and move beyond them. With each stumble or failure, take some time to get clear about your objective and then make a point of recommitting to your goal and to the truth.

8:75 Certainly you'll need a clear-headed and rather unforgiving relationship to activities like breaking your word to yourself, or letting yourself off the hook too easily, since excuses and justifications are not what commitment is about, nor are they appropriate to transformation. On the other hand, forgiving yourself for your failures serves to put you in the most up-to-date place you can be with the observation that what you attempted didn't happen. Whether to be unforgiving or forgiving is determined by whatever is true, so find out. Ask: which action serves discovering the truth and supports getting free, and what's just more riding on the wheel? Work to become conscious of what's true and let this inform your self-evaluation.

8:76 The heart of this whole matter of self is survival or *life*. Whatever you identify with, it is wed to the life-principle and self-principle. This self-activity contains the force of life and will not give up, ever. It is the principle that drives every experience, and its persistence can make the Terminator look lazy. As long as your experiences are based on self and self-identity, this principle will orient all your experience and actions toward the survival of that self.

8:77 Although at this point you may be discouraged, I'd like to point out that this self-survival dilemma may not be as unassailable as it appears. It seems as if you *are* the self—in other words, what is identified within the field of experience as the self—and that this is just true and immutable. It's not. But you need to understand that the force of life will be applied to whatever you cling to, whatever you identify with, good or bad. This is not just another trap, it is *the* trap.

8:78 Understanding and transcending this "creative" but limiting principle is a cornerstone to effective transformation. We can make significant in-roads with this work by removing some of the fundamental scaffolding that constructs and buttresses the self-identity to which the powerful life-principle is applied. Toward that end, we'll next take a more personal detour to look into one of the most basic elements of self-identity: your life story.

CHAPTER NINE

Transcending Your Life Story

story[1] |stôrē| noun (pl. **stories**)
 1 an account of imaginary or real people and events told for entertainment: *an adventure story* | *I'm going to tell you a story.*
 • informal: a false statement or explanation; a lie: *Ellie never told stories—she had always believed in the truth.*
 2 an account of past events in someone's life or in the evolution of something: *the story of modern farming* | *the film is based on a true story.*

Living as a Story

9:1 If a new friend asked, "So, what's your story?" you'd probably convey some historical highlights from your past, focusing on pertinent topics that seem to relate to the social purpose for the conversation. But do you ever stop to think about the whole story that you *live,* the more complicated, unabridged version, both private and public, that you relate to as your life story? By this point you're probably aware that you walk around inside a mental construct that gives meaning and continuity to your perceptions and actions. If you look, you can notice it operating right now as a background context for your sense of "me."

9:2 What *is* the story of your life? Don't fret about every detail of your history, just bring to mind what comes up when considering your life so far. That's probably a collection of past experiences that seem to unfold behind you in time, a story of overlapping versions of yourself interacting with circumstances, people, and events. And there will probably be more than one thread or theme.

9:3 Of course, this story is subject to change over time as our memories morph for all sorts of reasons. However well we've managed to meet life's challenges, we'll tend to paint ourselves as favorably as we can, or in whatever way serves our reason for revisiting our memories. But no matter what character traits are highlighted and plot lines created, we should notice that they're more than just memories. They are selected and told for a reason, and the overall life story we're living has a lot to do with our experience of *who we are*.

9:4 Whether or not we share parts of our life story with anyone, it's apparent that in our own mind we're always weaving a tale in which we're the main character. This narrative isn't just history, nor is it there simply to help us avoid past mistakes. Instead, what we actually have is a functional back-story operating in the present to provide a "character" for ourselves to be, and so a specific perspective to determine our relationship to anything perceived. This means that the life story is the very substrate of self-identity.

Deciding . . . what to remember is how we decide who we are.
—Robert Pinsky

9:5 Significant personal change can be brought about simply by grasping and freeing ourselves from the scope and depth of this life story. This is why we're spending time to deepen our understanding of what this story domain is all about. What comes to mind with the words "life story" clearly relates to memories of our personal history, but we tend to miss the influence on what we're currently experiencing. To bridge this gap, observe how much one's internal state exists in the form of a story. It may not be seen as "life story" but it is in the domain of story-telling nevertheless, and it actually does relate to our history as well as our experience of life. Let's see if we can work our way toward discovering a link between present and past.

9:6 Our current experience of life has a rather constant internal component. For example, at one moment we might focus on trying to discern what's going on with some social intrigue that's playing out among the people around us. Our attention might then turn to a project we want to accomplish, visualizing our role and actions toward that end. Maybe we're just pondering what to do next, or perhaps we imagine ourselves playing some particular role while in conversation with another, or we might catch ourselves spinning an internal narrative that acts as a backdrop for our emotions and perhaps a justification for some related behavior. Each of these conceptual activities could be called a *story*.

9:7 This flow of drama and story goes unrecognized for what it is because it is taken for granted and simply held as a reflection on "reality" or "life." Each of these examples could easily be regarded as merely thinking, but what form does this thinking take? Little stories. Just so, you consider your history as being a collection of factual memories of the past. They might be memories, but again, notice how they take the form of stories. Each of these stories could be well developed or fragmented. It may be framed as a drama, just a plan, or perhaps a fantasy. The point is, our mental history of life is all narrative—it's a play, a movie, a scene, or perhaps a plethora of interwoven manuscripts, reports, and unedited notes and memos.

9:8 One way we can better see the connection between our ongoing story and life is to look at dreaming—which are stories that are acted out within our imagination as we sleep. We know that dreams are only figments of mind and not "real life" because they are strictly conceptual. But we experience each dream as a life-like drama unfolding usually with ourselves at the center. Then we wake up and realize "it was only a dream." What was there? We have to admit that there was nothing actually occurring except a story being acted out in our mind.

9:9 From time to time, we even think something that's happened in a dream has actually occurred in waking life, and occasionally we have to be a bit attentive to separate the dream occurrence from objective circumstance. We can see that it is only imagined, but when we're in a dream, the story or drama that is being acted out can appear as real as life. Except for the distinction we make of objective reality (realness), what is the difference between the dream and life? If a dream is nothing but story, then so is our experience of life. We can awaken from a dream and realize that the whole thing didn't really exist. Is it possible to awaken from life in some similar way? Yes, I am suggesting that our current experience of life is primarily a conceptual fabrication.

9:10 Another way you can see the influence that story-telling has on your experience is to watch your incessant internal dialogue. What is your internal dialogue but a form of story-telling? The story may change or ramble, and the subject matter may vary, but it always relates to you in some way—even if only in that you are both speaker and listener. Your interior voice is always unfolding a tale of some kind, even when it's just sentence fragments or a series of unrelated vignettes that don't add up to a cohesive whole. A badly told story is still a story.

Who are we but the stories we tell ourselves, about ourselves, and believe?
—Scott Turow

9:11   The real function of your internal dialogue probably remains unknown to you. Early in your development, long before you could speak, your mind created the context of language. From this leap in faculty, there arose a completely new domain that sprang from the dawning distinction of self and other as separate conscious entities. This self-differentiation and the need for a connection with the "existential other" became the foundation for your internal dialogue, and still serves the same function. The context for this activity is key in supporting the self-concept and so has more force to it than we imagine. The internal dialogue unfolding as a story isn't just a whim or even simply a forum for your observations. The sheer insistence that's apparent whenever you attempt to silence this voice should give some indication of its power.

Man acts as though he were the shaper and master of language, while in fact language remains the master of man.
—Martin Heidegger

9:12   These examples of imagining, thinking, dreaming, and talking to ourselves help illustrate the degree to which conceptual fabrications dominate our daily experience. They all occur as some kind of narrative, but the implications reach far beyond what we might call story-telling. There is a "mute" form of story that permeates our experience and goes unnoticed. In order to get at this depth of story, we need to shift our focus to the nature of experience itself.

9:13 Even though the only "place" experience can exist is in the present moment, notice that your "experience" of what's occurring is not just of this moment. It is actually a stretch of time that includes whatever is interpreted as actively influencing this moment. This will include the concepts of the past—frequently composed of what's occurred during the minutes or hours preceding the moment, as well as the more distant past. It also includes imagining where this story or process is going, creating an extrapolation into the future. These are automatically associated with your assessment of recent circumstances to give meaning to what's perceived. All of this is conceptual and dependent on an interpretative process rather than the occurring moment. Let's look more closely at this overlooked fact about the nature of experience.

Experience Always Degrades into Concept

9:14 We're going to return to the life story, but let's set it aside for now and notice that all experience immediately degrades into concept. What I mean is that experience can only occur *now*. It's what *is* experienced or perceived to be so in this moment. In the very next moment, relative to that experience, what remains is nothing more than a concept.

9:15 Whatever was experienced in the last moment is not being experienced now, so whatever's there regarding that experience is actually a concept and not an experience. We know this to be true in broad strokes—if we eat a sandwich for lunch, by dinner time we know that the "experience" of eating lunch is only a memory because we are not eating the sandwich now. Whenever something seems to be perceived that isn't occurring right now, it must be a concept.

9:16 There are at least two hurdles to overcome when attempting a direct experience of this fact. The first occurs when you can't make a precise distinction between what in your "experience" is concept and what is the actual experience. Simply having an idea of the distinction between concept and experience isn't enough to do the trick, but a good start is to notice that what you're experiencing now is loaded with and dominated by concept. Being able to distinguish between what in your awareness is conceptual and what is experience is necessary in order to know the difference.

9:17 For example, say I suddenly shout "Hey!" at you right now. Obviously you'll have an experience of the sound of me shouting. You'll also quickly discern whether the shout is a communication, if it represents an emotional upheaval in me, what it means to you in particular, your associations with previous shouts, and so on. All these are aspects of the conceptual domination of the experience of the shout but are not the sound itself. Therefore they are not the actual experience of the shout.

9:18 What's also true is that, in the next instant, the shout—no matter how real and present it seems or how strong the "reverberations" might be—is a concept. What's there in your so-called "experience" of the shout is actually a concept. The sound is no longer occurring, so what seems like an experience must be a concept the moment it has ended. When you can notice these differences between concept and experience, you see more clearly how concept dominates experience. In every moment, the presence of all this conceptual activity overwhelms whatever is this moment's experience. Since this is ongoing and repeated with each moment, it isn't hard to fathom that this would build over time and diminish to near extinction any unfettered and totally present experience of the moment of now.

9:19 The second hurdle is that it's hard to find the experience. Although we're pretty certain there's an experience in there somewhere, when we proceed to eliminate all that is conceptual or conceptually influenced, we find less and less that we can call experience. Add to that the fact that a "moment" isn't actually a span of time, but is only immediate and now, and we can see that anything about that moment which is prior to or past the moment itself is conceptual. So it begins to become clear just how difficult it is to locate an actual experience.

9:20 When we notice that it's *always* now, and so experience is always available or occurring, and yet—as we'll see later in the book—we can't locate this "now" in our experience, we begin to grasp that this conceptual dominance is overwhelming. If we go further and delve into the Absolute truth, we might become conscious that all of this so-called experience is actually more like a "matrix of mind," as if something superimposed upon the real Now, or Absolute truth. It's not accurate to say that it's superimposed, however, because that implies a division, one thing being placed over another. The truth is that they're *not* separate; we simply aren't conscious that this mind-matrix is what constitutes our experience of reality. The nature of this reality is then an "illusion," or perhaps we could say it's unreal because it's fabricated by this mind-matrix but is held as if it's objectively occurring.

9:21 Absolute Reality is what is absolutely true. Although difficult to grasp, it is Nothing and Now and All. What we recognize as the "all," however, exists solely in the domain of what we "experience" and "conceive," and this is only Mind. All of this conceptualizing and experiencing is related to the self, rather than to Now. Although there is more to this matter, the life story is essential in formulating this mind-matrix reality to relate to the self.

9:22 If this consideration becomes too abstract for you to continue contemplating, a common reaction is to become confused or grow bored with it and reject it as unimportant. This is because it *is* boring and it *is* unimportant . . . to a self. To your self, these facts are only of interest as an intellectual exercise or philosophical point made within your investigations. Past that, it is nonsensical and useless. However, when you recognize the fact that experience always degrades into concept, and that your "experience" of life is overwhelmingly conceptual, you are able to more deeply grasp the dominance of your life story in all this. As you study the *content* that results from this conceptualizing of your experience, you may get a sense of the possible *context* from which you generate the perceived "reality" within which you live.

9:23 We see that our experience is composed of a good deal of "story." Without this story-function, our lives wouldn't mean anything, or at least wouldn't mean what we think they mean now. Our stories are significant in that they contribute meaning to our lives, be it negative or positive. This meaning is always related to the self and to our place in the scheme of things. It provides us with the ability to respond to situations by knowing how to "be" and what to accomplish in order to persist as this particular self with that particular history. Detaching from one's life story goes a long way toward freeing consciousness from a confusion with this self-mind.

Life Story as Context

9:24 What's even more significant than any concept or internal chatter that might occur at any given time is the assumed "story context" that's constantly in the background of your self-experience. Notice that even without acknowledging its presence, there is an assumed concept and image of a "life" within which you live, and a "reality" and circumstance that surround you. Both are framed up as the backdrop of your story, and you could live your whole life within this context and never notice that, as much as any dream, it's a work of imagination.

9:25 According to a story I heard on NPR, David MacLean "woke up" one day on a train platform with amnesia. Although he was mentally functional, he had no idea who he was because he had no past and so no life story. At that moment, he says, he noticed a rather all-inclusive perception of his surroundings, yet one completely absent of any preference for one thing over another. Everything seemed on equal footing. This was a fine experience until he realized that he had no idea what to do next, and he panicked. If everything in his experience was equal, he had no way to discern how to proceed with life. He was immobilized.

9:26 Before long, a platform officer rendered assistance. He provided David with a possible scenario for his condition, which David immediately latched onto and found that he felt much better. The scenario was wrong and even negative, but it gave David a story in which to orient and anchor himself. He admits that even after

Transcending Your Life Story

he was told that this story was incorrect, he still held onto it for a long time. We can see from his account how the impact of losing even just the memory of his past life altered not only his sense of who he was, but his ability to relate to his surroundings. So lost was he that even the vaguely sketched and incorrect substitute scenario was enough to anchor a reality for him. This story helps reveal that the truth or facts are unnecessary in order for a life story to do its job of providing context.

9:27 When you reflect on the current circumstances of your life, what is it that comes to mind? You imagine a world "out there" and situations or activities that are being undertaken as they relate to you or your interests. All of this is imagination. Remember, anything that isn't an immediate perception of the objects around you is conceptual in nature. When you start to calculate how much of what you call your life actually consists of objects within your immediate perceptive field in any given moment, it probably doesn't add up to all that much. That means everything else about your life is conceptual. It's created by imagining circumstances that aren't present but instead consist of merely what you think *was* so, *is* so, and *will be* so. Not only is this all concept, it's related to your particular life story, which means that its nature and purpose will likely be biased, if not completely fabricated. Your life story and self-experience are being played out almost entirely within a conceptual domain.

9:28 Can you grasp the conceptual dominance of your daily experience and that it occurs primarily in the form of story? Let's look at a simple example: say you happen to be sitting in a lobby right now, listening to the sound of cars outside and idly looking at empty furniture. Even these objects will relate in some way to your life story as you connect them to past associations in order to create your interpretations to determine how you feel about them, what they mean to you, and so on. But what else is there besides the objects?

9:29 Say you're a bit early to meet up with a friend to go see a movie. That means you aren't just in a room, you're in a place to wait. Perhaps your thoughts turn to the evening to come. Your choice of movie will reflect the self that you are—including your history and self-interests—as well as your relationship with your friend. This current experience will be seen as an occasion fitting into the stream of your life. Maybe you were raised in a rural area and you struggle to live down the belief that you're a country bumpkin. So you've moved to NYC, work at being sophisticated, and therefore have chosen a foreign film for the night's entertainment. You can see how each thought and choice you make, no matter how small, is inextricably linked to and determined by your life story. This is so in every moment and every example of your entire experience of life.

9:30 We're not just looking at some wool-gathering tendency of an idle moment—it's the framework for your living. The story that persists as a background sense of your particular life constructs your self-concept and therefore relates to your self-survival and very much influences your current experience. Yet discovering the connection experientially isn't easy. Beyond the individual storylines that you may develop to guide your actions, try to grasp that there is a context for your individual experience of self that determines your thinking, self-image, actions, emotional reactions, and so on. This context shows up in what is called your "life," or more accurately, your personal life story.

9:31   What I'm talking about exists so much in the background that it requires a leap in perspective simply to notice it. Since we've made a distinction between concept and objective reality, we see that much of what we take to be objective is actually just conceptual or contains some conceptual application. Once we break through the assumption that everything we experience actually exists and is objectively real, we can recognize that most of what we "experience" as circumstance is actually conceptual, and a lot of that is imagination.

9:32   To progress toward grasping this, begin by mentally placing a "template" of this life-story idea over all your memories and your current experience. Make sure this template includes your "cosmology," which is your view of the universe and reality. When you superimpose this template upon your memories, it isn't hard to see that your memories are all concepts, and your recollection of them is formulated in a series of stories of what you say happened. These are strung together in what is called your past. The story of your past may not be accurate or complete; it may not even be true, but it doesn't need to be. As we've seen, it only has to be *imagined* as true. If you can see your memory of life as a fabricated "story" it's a bit easier to consider that your experience, as it currently unfolds, is also a story.

9:33   Once the template is superimposed onto your current experience, the thing that seems to contradict the idea of it being a story is the notion that your experience is "real" and "occurring," as opposed to conceptual and past. Yet by noticing that experience always degrades into concept, you also notice that even what you call "objective reality" in this moment is dominated by concept, and this puts it on the same footing as your memories.

GETTING DOWN TO WORK

9:34 When you look at your currently perceived environment through the filter of this template, you should be able to discern that your interpretations of objects also relate to and are influenced by your life story. By expanding this consideration to include your cosmology, you step into a more existential domain. You can now see that your life exists within a larger framework of an imagined reality. This whole domain is what I was referring to as the mind-matrix. Through all that we discover by comparing our template to our experience of life, we can see that it pretty much *is* our experience of life.

9:35 The context of our life story determines how we perceive self, life, and our present circumstances. The thing is, although it may seem as if life and circumstance just befall us, that isn't the whole truth. Perhaps there is a case to be made that circumstances arise independent of any interpretation or cosmological context that we might apply to give them meaning. Yet for us, circumstance *never* exists outside our interpretation, nor is it seen independent of ourselves and its relationship to our self-persistence. When the circumstances are viewed in relation to the self, a story is immediately formed. Without that interpretation, the circumstances have no meaning; they don't relate to our selves, and remain useless to our self-persistence.

9:36 With some deep contemplation, fueled by considerable observation of our self-experience, we can discern that every event and occurrence of our lives is part of a story woven since the original formation of our self-mind. It may be inevitable that we do this, but that doesn't make it true. If no "self" or self-identity can form without the stories that weave the disparate pieces of "experience" into an apparent whole, then we may have no choice but to create them. They may be necessary for constructing a self-identity, but

Transcending Your Life Story

a story is still a story. It is not the truth, and certainly not the Absolute truth.

9:37 What do I recommend? Get free of your life story.

Giving Up Your Life Story

9:38 After reading this, you probably have some idea just how much your life story dominates all your experiences. Still, it's not easy to grasp how thoroughly it's infused into all that you experience as your self and the world around you. Giving up your life story, just letting it go, is one of the more effective things that can be done to change your experience of self and life.

9:39 Your self-image, self-concept, and sense of self-esteem are all programmed aspects of your experience that are founded upon and consistent with your story and history. The excuses you use to justify your behavior, your character traits, and your limitations are all plucked from your life story. Check it out. Notice that every capacity or incapacity you attribute to yourself, your so-called "predisposition" toward others, your methods of dealing with life, your thinking, your beliefs, and your emotional patterns are all based on your life story and your interpretation of your history.

9:40 Letting go of your story dissolves all of this, or at least frees you from being bound to it. Of course, the story isn't likely to go all at once, just as you're unlikely to let go of every aspect of your self in this moment. But just in starting the process, much can be dropped, and this will have a significant effect that is likely to gain momentum over time. The more you clarify and transcend

GETTING DOWN TO WORK

your attachment to this life story, the more your self-patterns will dissolve. The moment any formerly entrenched piece of your self-identity is seen as imaginary and dropped, a space immediately opens up and there is the possibility of creating something else in its place, or nothing at all.

9:41 Much of your life story lives within you as your interpretations, agenda, and reactions and is not limited to the stories you tell. For example, the role your parents played in your life dominates much of your self-experience since they were the models you had with which to create an identity from the ground up. It's not only the way you remember your parents and your history with them that is at issue, but also the unrecognized aspects of your self-framework, which was created in trying to become a self—and survive as a self—in relation to your parents. This lives *in you*, independent of any thoughts about your parents and memories of past circumstance. In fact, an important part of divesting yourself of your life story is identifying these seemingly substantial pillars that support your self-idea.

9:42 A knee-jerk reaction to the idea of giving up your life story might be "but it makes me who I am." Well, yes, that's the point. You might fret that you wouldn't want to forget your past because it's precious to you, or perhaps was so traumatic that you never want to forgive and forget. This only shows how wed you are to this story. The only reason you don't want to drop it is that you experience being the one crafted by it, and so find much of yourself within it.

9:43 Let's be clear. Your life story isn't the same thing as your history—history is what *actually* took place in your life. But the story you tell yourself and others about your past isn't the same as an objective memory of what happened throughout your life. Your story is what you "live" that happened. What happened is what happened, and it is probably largely forgotten or was never completely known.

9:44 If you work hard and concentrate, you might find that it's possible to discern a nearly objective memory of what occurred *before* that circumstance was given meaning by you and biased by your subsequent reactions. (If you have an old journal, you might be surprised to look into it and see that much of what you now hold as part of your story was either not recorded or was presented differently at the time it occurred, and what you did record was biased by your reasons for choosing it.) As you work hard to discern what actually occurred, you may not remember everything, but what you do remember can be cleared of the additions that arose later in the telling, and the bias that occurred simply by choosing to add it to your life story. With such scrutiny, you may find events and perspectives that you left out of your uncontested story altogether. What actually happened is much different than your story.

9:45 To be sure, your life story, as a tale you tell yourself and others, may barely relate to what happened in your life. Even if it does, the reason for the telling serves a purpose so biased that facts are always of secondary importance. Some of your story is invention, some you bent and twisted so much that the story doesn't accurately represent your history anymore. What may seem accurate as a memory is still distorted by the meaning you give it now. Your reason for remembering it and placing it within your story is what gives it its current slant. It is *not* simply a memory but a function of your self-survival, and yet you hold it as if it's an accurate representation of your past.

GETTING DOWN TO WORK

9:46 If you're afraid that comprehending the fabricated nature of your life story will result in somehow losing memories, that's not how this works. You won't forget. As I often remind people: "Consciousness doesn't make you stupid." Anything you knew when ignorant doesn't suddenly become unknown when you increase your consciousness in some way. It might be seen differently and perhaps as useless and unnecessary, but you can still recall it. That being said, if you manage to drop your life story—if you stop letting it dominate your present experience and your sense of who you are, and stop using it as an excuse or justification for your reactions and behavior—I promise you won't miss it.

9:47 If you're sentimental about your life story, a more powerful and freeing relationship would be to view it as a kind of scrapbook. If nostalgic, you could pull it out every few years to have a look or share with friends but, other than that, this collection of selected memories should more appropriately end up on the closet shelf or in the attic, metaphorically gathering dust along with the rest of your scrapbooks. The point is, if you don't let it dominate your experience or life, your story serves no useful purpose. With that perspective in mind, perhaps you're ready to inspect and drop the conceptual fabric that is your life story.

9:48 ***Guided Contemplation*—Dropping Your Life Story**
Try to imagine what your experience of living might be like if you were to be completely free of your life story. Simply consider experiencing your self and life without the backdrop or even influence of *any* life history. Try dropping the whole idea that your story is in any way real or true, and resist the urge to replace it with some alternative story.

If it becomes difficult to focus on letting it all go, begin to work methodically at subtracting whatever comes to mind when you

Transcending Your Life Story

consider what your life was like. Concentrate on letting go of each aspect of what you've previously held as your history.

Erase your sense of the way your life has played out in general, and pause to completely expunge each and every one of the standout events that make up your past and helped form "you" as you currently experience yourself.

You'll know you're on the right track when you notice that doing so eliminates personality aspects such as your emotional dispositions, your character, your moods and reactivity, your self-concept and self-judgments, your self-esteem, self-image, and so on.

Drop your view of "life" as a story that you're living and acting out, and by extension let go of any sense of having a destiny to fulfill. Try to imagine that you are a bit like the man with amnesia. Create a sense of your self as a blank slate with no past and no future.

You have some idea about how the "universe" works and what "reality" is; this is your "cosmology." Let it all go—whatever you personally believe is true about the nature of the world and the nature of life.

Freeing yourself from your historical identity and attachments should give you plenty to do. Don't confuse any of this with suppression. Fully acknowledge what you experience at the deepest levels, yet truly grasp that the nature of both your history and story is not only conceptual, but also not true. Practice detaching from and dropping everything related to your life story. As you do, allow a new, unformed experience to arise. Try to avoid filling it in with another fantasy or imagination—just be open and *present*, and see what arises unbidden.

9:49 From even moderate success with this contemplation, you have a chance to face life as if for the first time. You'll find that you can no longer live as a "victim of past circumstances," because you have no personal history on which to base such a depiction. You'll recognize that you can no longer mope around as the long-suffering character you may have acted out in the past, or continue to preen as the special hero in your life story. You can't find any experience of being superior or arrogant, weak or cowardly. You no longer have any grounds to assess having habitual characteristics, whether it's being stubborn, flakey, self-righteous, seductive, aggressive, kindly, domineering, submissive, charming, opinionated, witty, naive, proud, wicked, noble, or any other characteristic emotional or behavioral pattern.

9:50 From such contemplations, you will have an experience of being free of these and more, or at least the ability to imagine and work toward such an experience. You may have a greater sense of being present and open within an experience that's informed only by the fact of being human, and not by a life story. All this will likely be temporary, since your self-mind will insist on returning to its familiar storyline. Persistent contemplation and investigation, however, will continue to dispel the story from your mind and so change your identity. Eventually perhaps, it can be dropped altogether. Freedom from your life story will open up a whole new perspective on what's possible in life and for you specifically. It will change the way you view yourself and your life because, regardless of what arises next, you will be holding the experience of yourself in a new context.

CHAPTER TEN

Breaking Free of Assumptions

The Closed Loop of Self-Referencing Perception

10:1 We've seen how our specific self-identity (our "shape," so to speak) determines and influences everything we perceive. Now I want to delve into a central dynamic that not only supports this self-referential perceptive influence but makes it almost impossible to detect. It may seem that we've completed our investigation of the way our experience of the world reflects our experience of ourselves, but we have yet to look into why it not only persists but remains invisible. While your mind may balk at covering ground it appears we've already addressed, understand that this is not mere repetition but is necessary for our task of making finer distinctions. Remember, we must continue to work to *experience* these distinctions rather than simply hear about them.

10:2 You've learned that your identity determines your interpretation of whatever you perceive. A core aspect of this dynamic is found in the fact that any *assumption* or *belief* you experience as yourself or as true of reality will not only influence your interpretations of everything encountered, it will determine your reactions and behavior. What's overlooked beyond this is that any consequential feedback you receive from your actions, as well as how you interpret this feedback, will always appear to confirm your assumption.

10:3 There is a feedback loop between your interpretive framework and your perception of reality. This "consistency illusion" is repeatedly reinforced by the feedback you get from taking actions based on your assumptions and beliefs—most of which go unnoticed as such since they are simply held as observations of reality. This loop seems to confirm the validity of these very assumptions and beliefs. In a real sense, much of what's perceived is not actually "there," it's in you. It is of your own making.

10:4 Let me clarify. First, any assumption you have about reality, others, or yourself will help formulate your perception of whatever you encounter. Any interpretation of what's there will be based upon your assumption, in effect altering and so "fabricating" what you perceive. Second, because your behavior and actions will be motivated by reacting to what's perceived, they will also be based on this same assumption. Third, any results that follow your behavior—such as another's reaction—will correspond with what you assume because the response is in relationship to your behavior, which was crafted by that assumption. Fourth, because the assumption continues to inform your interpretations, even this feedback will be viewed by you through the filter of what's assumed, confirming in your mind the assumption's validity, regardless of any objective inconsistency that might be the case. Can you see that, in this way, the whole "world" experienced by an individual will always appear self-consistent and objectively real even though it may not be?

10:5 Did you catch all that? I know trying to follow this may be headache-producing, so let's look at a very simple example. Say you assume that everyone lies. You will hear what Jack says as a lie no matter what he says, and you'll react to the "fact" that he's lying to you even though he may not be. An internal state will arise that's consistent with your assumption of "being lied to." His dishonesty may be seen as a threat to your social and perhaps physical survival, which will motivate you to adopt a disposition, facial expressions, posture, and other behaviors appropriate for relating to his lying.

10:6 Perhaps you call him names or treat him badly. This, in turn, will tend to evoke in Jack a reaction consistent with being called a liar, and he will relate to you accordingly. If he denies it, you will assume he is lying again. If he punches you in the face, you assume it's because you caught him in a lie. The feedback you get from Jack's behavior will appear consistent with your assumption because it is in reaction to your assumption-based behavior.

10:7 Can you see how your assumption is strengthened by your interpretation of the feedback? You interpret his reactions to your behavior from the same assumption that created your perception and motivated your actions to which he is reacting. In such a dynamic, the assumption will be reinforced over and over again, thus validating your perceived reality. It's very difficult to extricate yourself from such a loop because it is self-reinforcing. You will always view reality that way and it will consistently appear to be that way. In fact, it will seem obvious and you're unlikely to even question it.

10:8 Some of these assumptions are existential in nature and form the context in which the most basic aspects of your world are perceived. These are especially hard to discern. It is very difficult to conceive beyond such assumptions as: the nature of self is an object, or space is the same as distance, or perception is a direct reflection of what is received, or what the human mind grasps is the same as the truth of reality, or internal-state reactivity is caused by circumstances, and so on. To unearth these kinds of assumptions requires an increase in consciousness on a deeper level. Once discovered, however, it should be pretty obvious how they are reinforced within our perceptions.

10:9 Following this experientially is challenging, and even when you get a hit on it, it will tend to slip away. It's hard to grasp as an ongoing dynamic because your attention is automatically taken up by the pursuit of your self-agenda, which is what generates the dynamic in the first place. This self-consistency loop is burdensome to consider, and consciously focusing on it in real time interrupts your ability to manage life in your usual manner. I suggest you do it anyway. Choose a familiar life pattern and see if you can notice this dynamic occurring. Try to discover any assumption or belief that dominates and reinforces your perceptions, and how it creates a self-referencing loop that makes your conviction seem valid when it may not be.

10:10 What's being said here is that what you perceive as life is an illusion, and this illusion is self-reinforcing and thus very hard to detect. Such an idea may be intriguing as a philosophical or even scientific exercise, but without a focused effort, the reality is almost impossible to grasp as an experience. Recognizing that it dominates your experience from moment to moment is difficult and requires a real commitment to do so.

Life is more or less a lie, but then again,
that's exactly the way we want it to be.
—Bob Dylan

Revealing What's Invisible

10:11 It is the nature of this work to be difficult. After all, one of our goals is to reveal what is *hidden* in our selves, whether it's a common assumption or some deep mechanism that dominates us by operating continuously in the background. Discovering these can be problematic because even the reason for their existence isn't recognized. We often don't know how to begin or whether anything unrecognized really exists. Until some of these can be seen more directly, we can at least find ways to corroborate their existence.

10:12 One way to do this is by creating a practice to counter the above "illusion dynamic" through working to reveal any unconscious aspects that are influencing your experience. Any such practice is well-grounded when you begin by challenging your current assumptions, including viewpoints that you perceive as solid fact. You can apply this questioning to all sorts of domains. For example, what generates a particular social interpretation, such as a dislike or irritation? What founds your experience of gender— what do you assume is required in order to be a man or a woman? Do you have any assumptions that influence your experience of a family member? You could investigate what formulates your view of others in general, or what you assume are the components necessary for being you, or even what's involved in perceiving a tree. As with the practices of honest communication, non-judgment, and experiencing something for-itself, here too you are called on to refrain from knee-jerk reactions and instead challenge the validity of your perceptions.

GETTING DOWN TO WORK

> *We are enslaved by anything we do not consciously see.*
> *We are freed by conscious perception.*
> —Vernon Howard

10:13   In disrupting the interpretive process that we take for granted, we're bound to flail a bit as we bump up against our own preconceptions and uncover the unexpected. It's like tossing flour in what we imagine to be the general direction of an invisible man so we can begin to discern his shape. For example, in the case of the "lying Jack," we might question our assessment and instead consider the idea that he may be telling the truth. We can see how difficult this would be because it seems we're "perceiving" the lying, so it takes a deliberate and unusual act to bring to mind the question in the first place. Yet when we put our attention on the person rather than on our judgments, we find that we are free to listen to what he's actually communicating. By challenging our experience, we shift to the possibility of interpreting what he says in some other way. We also create an opening to further consider that his response to our actions doesn't necessarily mean what we imagine it does. In this way, we start to recognize something outside our assumption, which could lead to the possibility of seeing the whole "world" differently.

10:14   The first step of questioning the validity of your perceptions might be the hardest part, however, because it's difficult to recognize exactly what to challenge. When reality just seems to be some way, why would you create even the idea to question it? Where would you look to find stuff to question? You can start by looking right into anything that you're convinced is some particular way—what's true about you, or others, or about life. A prerequisite for discovering assumptions is confronting anything that appears to you as "just the way it is." Whenever you question the necessity or validity of something experienced, it immediately opens up alternative possibilities. It's useful to keep these possibilities open for a while, so that your mind doesn't rush to fill in the space with your ideals. In this way, you may be able to create a previously unimagined way of holding reality that is outside your loop, and yet one that works well for you.

10:15 As we try to sort out and discover what in our perceptive-experience is part of this feedback-loop of self-consistent interpretations, we begin to reveal the invisible man, and possibly free ourselves from beliefs long held. Our bottom-line contemplation method can help us unearth many of these unseen convictions. Tackling the loop, however, is best done in the middle of an ensuing reaction or perceived situation. This way, we not only interrupt the knee-jerk reaction to our perceptions, we challenge the necessity of the reaction and validity of the perception. In so doing, we bring attention to the matter, as well as reinforce the idea that *we* are the source of what we experience. Contemplating "on the run," in the middle of a reaction to an occurring circumstance, enables us to better make an experiential connection between assumption and perception. Yet all this takes discipline. Denying ourselves the luxury of using opinion and impulse to guide our actions is a hard row to hoe.

10:16 Speaking of discipline, according to the stories, Gautama Buddha lived for many years as an ascetic, purposefully depriving himself of any pleasures, rejecting all drives and impulses, and even embracing painful circumstance. Although he is said to have discovered that this would not lead to enlightenment—as had proven true of every method he'd tried—it does show his deep commitment. This ascetic practice was his last attempt in

GETTING DOWN TO WORK

a series of studies through which he learned that *all* "methods" are unsatisfactory. Once he decided that neither self-abuse nor self-indulgence were appropriate to his efforts, he embarked on his final sitting contemplation. Although asceticism itself may not produce an insight, it's interesting to note that this period of self-denial preceded the seven weeks of contemplation that ended with his complete enlightenment. It's possible that some form of challenging all self-motivating impulses is necessary before we can open up beyond a self-dominated experience and consciousness.

10:17 Although I'm not suggesting that our practices are on the same level as Gautama's, they are certainly based on the same principles and intent, which is to discover what's absolutely true. Yet, remember that it's not possible to grasp the whole story of self and the human condition—not to mention reality or existence itself—within the intellect. The Absolute truth may be beyond simple, but it is not simplistic. The mind always wants to oversimplify any practice so that it can be reduced to an intellectually manageable idea or image. But no matter what we might come up with, it cannot be accurate, and it's a disservice to our pursuit to remain there. When engaging in this work we must leave no stone unturned.

Everything should be made as simple as possible, but not simpler.
—Albert Einstein

How the Self Is, Is That the Self Is

10:18 Some assumptions are deeper than others, some invisibles are highly invisible. Continuing to challenge our perceptions and experience, let's look into deeply ingrained convictions generally shared by all humans and see if we can work our way into a couple of profoundly overlooked assumptions about the very nature and existence of the self. I recommend you go slowly and work carefully through what's said. It will take a while to unfold. The whole communication that follows should be held as a contemplation, experiencing each stage as you proceed.

10:19   We've already laid the groundwork for the following communication, but I want you to consider more deeply the existential reality that constitutes the experience of a self. Although many of the basic ideas have already been stated, the depths of experiential understanding of this communication often remain unfathomed. I want to again address the fact that the self finds its *selfness* in the very manner in which the self is formed, and I invite you to further consider some of the overlooked implications of this fact.

10:20   As we've seen, the self is known through the collection of characteristic emotional patterns, thinking, beliefs, opinions, moods, dispositions, judgments, and so on that form this self-experience. To say it more simply, it is the experience you're having of yourself right now. One way to begin an inquiry to clarify this self make-up is to deliberately create an experience completely unlike yourself—have different emotions than you normally would, think and believe in opposite ways than you do now, act unlike yourself—work on changing or being free of everything characteristic and familiar about yourself. Whether you're successful at this or not, it will help clarify exactly what it is that you identify with.

10:21   If you can experientially isolate the "stuff" that makes you "you" and then change it so that it's no longer seen as being self-consistent, even if only temporarily, then you have access to some real possibilities. One of these possibilities, already mentioned, is realizing that if you can change some familiar aspect that you hold to be yourself, it can't actually be *you*. If you experience an uncharacteristic feeling or thought, then obviously you are capable of creating such feelings and thoughts. Thought, feeling, and behavior may all be shared human functions, but you don't experience yourself as a generic human, only as a particular self. If you are capable of creating unfamiliar personal characteristics, it is possible that in reality you aren't the particular self you think you are.

10:22   A human self doesn't believe or experience that he or she *is* an emotion, or *is* a thought, or *is* a belief, but instead that he or she *has* or *does* these activities. Any self is distinguishable by the *kinds* of emotions it has, and how it feels and behaves while engaging these emotions. You know your own self by *what* you believe and the *kinds* of beliefs you have, as well as the way these are expressed or acted upon. Your self isn't known simply by the fact *that* you think, but instead by *what* you think and how well you think. These, along with every other perceived characteristic aspect, all form the self-experience that I've been calling the "shape" of self. The apparent "choices" of these activities collectively form a particular and unique experience that implies the existence of a self.

10:23   As we know, identifying with this "collection" constitutes an experience of self and determines your perception of the world. Yet it also creates the very sensation and experience called the "real" self. Any single aspect isn't enough to create a self-identity because any one aspect could be true of any human. Just as ice crystals themselves don't make a snowflake—it is the individual shape of the many crystals that make it unique and a snowflake—so it is with you.

10:24   It is the particular set of qualities and patterns you embrace that make you an individual. If you were exactly the same as everyone else, you wouldn't be discerned as a unique self—except by virtue of your body, which, if also the same, would only be unique because it is an object separate from other objects. There would be no unique experience to identify with. In this case, "self" could only be identified as the whole of human existence, not as an individual. This is not what you experience as you.

10:25   You experience that there is some characteristic way of *being* "you." You have certain talents, limitations, predispositions, abilities, flaws, strengths, weaknesses, patterns of emotion, moods, and reactivity, and many other attributes that are held as simply the way you *are*. This is what I'm calling "how you are" and is what makes it possible to have an experience and idea that you are an individual—it "shapes" you. It provides the distinction and so the *experience* of the particular self that you think you are. It is the experience you're having of yourself right now.

10:26   Try to imagine having no experience of any characteristic attributes, nothing that would create any sense of identity, no unique conglomerate of traits that you identify with or are attached to. Could you still experience being "you" like an identified self? The experience would certainly be radically different, wouldn't it? The only thing you might have left to identify with is the notion of being an entity supported by the idea of being the source or receiver of any activity of your perceptive faculties. This would not be similar in any way to your current experience of self. You may have a sense of "being" an organism, but this would not be the experience you have of yourself as a person and an individual.

GETTING DOWN TO WORK

10:27   Remember, whatever you identify as self will automatically become the focus of self-survival, because it is this "identified" self that you feel must exist and persist. The self-survival principle applies to whatever is experienced as the self, and to anything to which you're attached. Are you beginning to see the connection here? You aren't just persisting as anybody, or in any way, you're persisting exactly the way you are as "you." What you call *you* is the unique one that you experience being. This uniqueness is found in the "shape," and so the experience, that forms your particular self. It is this particular self that you strive to maintain, since if that dissolved, you would no longer be "you."

10:28   For example, if Johnny were given a severe lobotomy so that his characteristic behaviors—how he smiled, the way he argued, his opinions, charm, and so on—were no longer occurring, we might say something like "that's not Johnny anymore." Instead of being Johnny, he's been replaced by a bland, rather featureless creature. He still has a body and can walk and talk, but the special qualities we knew as that unique person have evaporated. Just so, as a unique identity, it is imperative that a self be both *unique* and *identified*.

10:29   Within this identified self, there must be a particular character and set of experiences that are distinct from others. To be clear, I don't just mean the peripheral experiences that you have or patterns that you observe about yourself, but every thought and sense and feeling and perception that occurs for you—everything you experience. These are unique because they are held within the context of being a self. There may be no element that is not in some way an aspect of all humans, but the way it's arranged and the quantity and quality of chosen elements are what make you a distinct individual. In the tinker toy box, all the pieces are the same for every

Breaking Free of Assumptions

child, but the ones that are chosen and how they are put together and come to be arranged—the "shape" that is constructed—is particular to each child. It is this shape that then must be protected and promoted in order to maintain its existence.

10:30   Except for the fundamental notion that you are an independent and invisible entity sourcing and receiving experience, in order to exist as a human any element can change and be replaced by something else—and then that becomes the self-shape. Usually this is a minor change, and brings a relatively minor change in experience. Yet even with these changes, you are always maintaining a collective and individual "shape" that is created by what you're attached to. This produces the constant and cohesive experience and sensation called you.

10:31   If you're following all this, then it's time to consider again in a deeper and more existential way: *how* self is, is *that* self is. What I'm saying here is that the very existence of your experience of self is found in the *way* that you are, *how* you are. It's what provides you an experience of being a self. No *how*, no *self*. This seems like it might be limited to identifying with unique characteristics, but it isn't. There is an overlooked assumption here attached to this distinction of self. Grasping the existential nature of what's been said, the possibility arises that the characteristics that bring you to be seen as a particular self are *not* an expression of a "source self" or "real self" that exists behind the scenes and manifests as these characteristics. This second possibility calls for more explanation.

10:32   A related assumption most people make is that their self-experience is an expression or manifestation of a source self, what people might refer to as the "real self," or "the man behind the curtain," or the "soul," or a "higher self," or some such—the innermost sense or assumption of an original source entity. This is often what people think I mean by *Being,* but that isn't accurate.

10:33 Take a look and see if you assume, as pretty much everyone does, that everything arising within your internal state (emotions, reactions, opinions, beliefs, moods, dispositions, etc.) comes from "you," even though this "source you" remains unseen. Now consider the matter further. Since you can change what appears as the content of yourself, then obviously the content doesn't necessarily arise as a function of "self" expression—as if the "real" self is simply responding or reacting to life as befits its "nature." If this is so, it suggests that none of what you identify with is really *you,* or is necessary as an expression of you.

10:34 This "real" or "source" self is only a reference or an idea, supported by the continuous *sense* of self that remains in the background as various experiences come and go. But consider that this self-sense is a function of the overall "hum" of the collective activity of self-persistence. Included in this is the constant sensation of the body, and the constant domain of feeling-sensation that is the base of emotions. These perceptive constants provide a sort of background hum or sensation that is taken to be the sense of the core or source self. But it isn't.

10:35 In enlightenment work, this "sense" of self is one of the assumptions most frequently overlooked as something to question, challenge, or transcend, because it is this core sense of self—anchoring the idea of the existence of a source self—that people tend to focus on. Once the contemplator gets past trying to discover his true self within all of his personal characteristics, when his intellectual attempts have all been exhausted and his internal chatter has quieted, he then tends to concentrate on this sense in an attempt to become directly conscious of its nature. It gives a place to focus on that seems very real, and the possibility that this isn't really him is overlooked.

10:36 My proposition here is two-fold. If the shape of your self-identity generates your sense of the individual self that you believe you are, then without this shape, this "you" can't exist. And since people generally hold that, although their experiences are something they "have" rather than "are," the fact that they emerge and express in the patterns that they do is believed to indicate a "source" self behind the scenes, one that is "choosing" or expressing these experiences and behaviors. The major assumption here is that this source self does so because it *IS* the self, or rather, that internal states and characteristic behaviors are done that way because the source self *demands* they be done that way in order to remain consistent with this existential "being" behind the scenes. Your characteristic self is unconsciously held as if it is an expression of your fundamental self. Without thinking about it, you assume this is why you are and have to be "that" way.

10:37 None of this is true, but are you following what I'm saying? It's as if this "invisible" source self is *seen* in the shape it takes within experience, and therefore this collection of familiar experiences and behavior is assumed to be revealing that self. But it is not. It's not easy to hear what's being said because we don't have much worked out in our culture or language to communicate what I'm trying to say. But if you study it carefully and contemplate the matter openly, it can be heard.

10:38 Another element in my proposition is revisiting the observation that if any aspect within the self-identity can change, it follows that *every* aspect can change. If every aspect changed, then obviously the self would not be the same self, and this would be a transformation. This would also reveal that none of those aspects, old or new, could actually be *you*. If truly realized, you grasp that you aren't any aspect, whether it is experienced as your self or not. Attaching yourself to some "piece of experience" is inconsistent with the effort to become free, since you then become fused with that experience, thinking it is you rather than something created by you or experienced by you.

10:39 This transformative possibility also implies that the very source self that we imagine exists behind our identities not only doesn't exist, it also doesn't demand any particular pattern to emerge or shape to be taken, thus providing a completely different way of holding both self and source. The paradoxical possibility arises that, although you *are you,* there is nothing there. You may have heard or thought something like this before, but don't be too quick to imagine that you understand correctly. An intellectual conclusion, or even some experience that matches the words, no matter what it is, isn't and can't be what I'm talking about. So stay open and continue to work to get it directly if you haven't already.

---

*Sometimes the questions are complicated
and the answers are simple.*
—Dr. Seuss

It's a Problem of Identity

10:40 The above assumptions lead us to another offshoot of confusion that arises when people tackle certain assertions about being the source of their experience. At first this is usually seen as just trying to be responsible for what one feels and does, but it goes further than that. If you say, "*I create my experience*," what is the "I" you're referring to, and does it really create experience? The only way you can understand what follows is by making some new distinctions—it also wouldn't hurt to become directly conscious of the true nature of you and reality while you're at it. I can say a few things that might help point you in a direction, but even so, the subject is likely to be heard as simply "philosophy." I have to lay things out one at a time, but they won't make sense until grasped all together, so hang in there.

10:41   Sometimes a claim is made that "you" create your experience and perhaps create reality. This is an interesting idea, but not one that seems reasonable. Nevertheless, it may be true even though it seems obviously untrue—especially the part about creating reality. You may recognize that you create your emotions and thinking, especially if you hold yourself as "the one behind the scenes." But that you create everything you experience seems a stretch, and certainly you have no experience of creating your body, or creating objective reality.

10:42   That said, let's more fully consider what we're talking about. Start with your body. Perhaps you can grasp that everything you experience of and as your body are distinctions that you make, and so interpretations that are created by you as the source, although you're likely to only get that intellectually rather than as real. Yet you probably don't experience creating the body itself, the is-ness of or existence of the body. First, however, let's acknowledge that you just did. You have made a distinction of the body-for-itself, or the body-independent-of-your-mind or experience. *That* is the distinction you're referring to when you say you don't create your body. Isn't it? Who made that distinction?

GETTING DOWN TO WORK

10:43   Still, you will probably have the conviction that your body existed before "you," as the one behind the scenes, or before you realized any ability to perceive or "make distinctions." So how could "you" make the distinction of the is-ness of the body? There is a bigger problem here that stems from the limitations inherent in the distinction that you call "you," but we'll get to that in a bit. Right now, ask yourself, "Where does the 'is-ness' of anything exist?" Only in your experience. No matter how much you may insist that it's outside your experience, the very insistence that objective reality exists apart from your experience is something that exists *in your experience*.

10:44   Now I can imagine that many will be hearing this as abstract metaphysics or just plain silly, and their concern is valid. But I'm not talking about what you likely think I'm talking about. The demand for the context and distinction of an objective reality, something that cannot be fooled with, is very real and needed by self and life. It's the foundation in which you get to exist, so you certainly don't want to monkey around with it.

10:45   In other words, you don't want reality to be in your own hands or a function of your own mind, because you know you're ignorant and have no idea how to "create" yourself, much less reality. But before we go on to the next point, can you see that this is still a distinction you make? It may be etched in stone, but it *is* you who makes the distinction. The is-ness of which you speak is *in your experience* (ta da!)—therefore it is a distinction being made by you. It's not elsewhere for you; even the idea that there is an elsewhere exists solely in your experience. The whole domain of "not-you" is a distinction you make, and this includes the distinction (experience) that it is independent of you.

Breaking Free of Assumptions

10:46   You might say that existence "as-itself," which is its true nature, isn't something you create. But let me ask, what experience do you have of existence *as-itself*? That's right. Absolutely nothing! You don't have any experience of as-itself except as an idea that there is such a thing and you don't know what it is—but in the back of your mind, you'll probably assume that the as-itself is really the same as the for-me or for-itself experience that you have. Perhaps it seems as if somehow the experience of as-itself is just behind the experience you can have of for-itself, like a foundation of what you experience or perceive. Since this is the process that occurs when you shift from a for-me experience to a for-itself experience, it seems like the same would apply moving from for-itself to as-itself.

10:47   This is incorrect. What you actually have is nothing. You have no experience of anything as-itself. So why insist that as-itself—or simply the Absolute truth—is of the same nature as the experience that you call its is-ness? The distinction you make of is-ness is the distinction you make. Get it? I know this may not be easy to swallow but, nevertheless, it's true.

10:48   Now regarding my main point: many misunderstandings arise when grappling with the notion that "I create reality." These are generated by the fact that you identify "you" in a certain way. In other words, when you talk about "you creating this" and "you creating that," there's a *problem of identity*.

10:49   What you call you—primarily your identified self and cognized mind—may not be the creator of all this. "You" as a self and an experience is itself a distinction. So, if you don't know what *you* are, or what the Absolute truth is in this matter, you need to give some space when talking about what "you" create. Whatever *is*

True *does* create it all, or perhaps more accurately *is* everything, including the *experience* called "you." Not being in touch with that reduces the conversation to the mind, and this is not what I'm speaking about here.

10:50 If you identify with being a self-identity, then you only experience being responsible for what you can create as an act of will—whatever you experience as activities willfully generated by your intent. You will only have access to whatever you are conscious of creating. Perhaps you experience generating a thought or emotion, creating a perspective, or producing an imagination. Perhaps you can even catch yourself being responsible for the creation of the foundation framework that acts as a context for your mind and perceptive-experience. If you identify with the Absolute, or what *is* reality and *is* the source of the experience called reality, then you could say that *you* create all experience as well as reality. If not, then this statement would have to stop with whatever the "you"-that-you-identify-with genuinely experiences creating or generating or being the source of. Yet, as we can see here, you create your experience to some degree no matter which way you slice it. Thanks for playing!

CHAPTER ELEVEN

Transforming

11:1 Soon we'll take a look at what we've touched on so far as a possible practice for pursuing transformation and increasing consciousness. Before we consider what such a practice might look like, I want to underscore three actions that will help us more effectively take on our practice while also grounding it in the reality in which we live: increasing our awareness of the limiting nature of our preconceptions, learning a new way to deal with suffering, and growing out of our childhood programming.

The real voyage of discovery consists not in seeking new landscapes but in having new eyes.
—Marcel Proust

Dropping Preconceptions

11:2 One easily overlooked impediment to pursuing any practice is our relationship to our own opinions and conjectures. It's natural to project a course of action for a new endeavor by basing it on past experience, but this limits us to what we assume is the "right" approach to our objective. What we often fail to take into account is that if our objective is new—as in the case of transforming or pursuing consciousness—the methods that we use to reach it will probably also have to be new. Often without our awareness, we entertain opinions and beliefs about how things work, and these will push us down preconceived avenues, restricting the open-mindedness we need for considering unfamiliar approaches. We need to take care not to unknowingly insert our presumptions onto methods we imagine will achieve our objectives.

11:3 If you yourself haven't yet *done* it—whatever "it" is—your opinions and beliefs about the matter are likely inaccurate, and they should be discarded. While this might leave you uncertain about your next step, it also allows you to approach the task with an open mind, making you more likely to consider avenues or methods that would have been omitted if you only heeded your opinions. In this light, honestly look into what you think you need to do in order to become directly conscious or to transform. Really examine what you hold as *the* way to transform yourself, or the "best" direction in which to pursue increasing consciousness. Uncover any overlooked presumptions that might hamper your ability to open up to new possibilities.

The greatest deception men suffer is from their own opinions.
—Leonardo da Vinci

11:4 An attachment to opinions can hinder even those who've had a direct experience. If you've had some insight, you'll tend to extrapolate from that experience to arrive at new conclusions, as well as get stuck in methods that seemed effective in the past. Sometimes this can be like a baseball player's lucky socks—just an association amounting to no more than superstition. You may have noticed that contemplators are always drawn to invent their own internal methods attempting to accomplish a breakthrough, and some of them may be very subtle and go unnoticed. These inner gymnastics will keep changing as your mind struggles to find a way through, but remember, they won't actually work. The nature of direct-consciousness defies all methods, and your previous efforts are completely irrelevant to the task of becoming conscious of whatever ignorance still remains. If some internal state or personal method happened to precede a past breakthrough, you might assume that it had something to do with success. Chances are it did not, but even if it did, the next breakthrough is totally up in the air. So it's best to approach your contemplation with complete openness each time, letting go of any presumptions about how a breakthrough might come about.

11:5 Regardless of your experience level, notice how many of your opinions are quickly eliminated by such an examination. The most important point here is that critically challenging your beliefs and positions about this work creates the space for real openness. Be skeptical of any direction that seems overly comfortable for you. Rather than clinging to some predetermined course, approach the matter with an "uncluttered" mind.

Learning to Enjoy Suffering (or at least get through it)

11:6 A central player in all this that deserves more attention is suffering. Without some discomfort or dissatisfaction, why would it occur to anyone to change their self or their experience? Probably because we spend most of our time running from pain, we don't notice it is a constant motivating factor that affects everything we do or consider doing in life. In contrast to this constant background angst, the idea of self-transformation represents a hopeful

GETTING DOWN TO WORK

possibility in which to attain one's lifelong personal ideals, which naturally implies an experience of feeling satisfied, whole, and comfortable in one's own skin. But for reasons already discussed, we know that any attempt to realize our ideals is a futile exercise of chasing after unobtainable cheese while merely spinning our wheels. One unmentioned element of our wheel is that we're not just chasing the cheese, we are also running from the ever-present threat of the "cat" behind us—pain. Our fear of pain is actually part of the same activity that is our desire for pleasure.

11:7   In one way or another, the underlying motivation for our pursuit of anything is to avoid suffering. While avoiding suffering sounds like a reasonable course of action, it may in fact get in the way of freedom, happiness, and transformation. If this is so, perhaps we could learn how to enjoy our suffering. I'm not talking about some kind of masochistic pleasure but rather a transcendent, inclusive relationship to suffering. To "enjoy suffering" sounds like an unreasonable contradiction, since enjoyment is pretty much seen as the *opposite* of suffering. But if we continually turn away from pain, which is bound to arise for us in varying degrees of intensity, how can we ever address it in any conscious way? If suffering is indeed at the heart of the motive to transform, then we need to *know* this heart and, as it turns out, transcend this motive.

... one of the strongest motives that leads men to art and science is escape from everyday life with its painful crudity and hopeless dreariness, from the fetters of one's own ever-shifting desires. A finely tempered nature longs to escape from the personal life into the world of objective perception and thought.
—Albert Einstein

11:8 Consider how you might feel if, rather than automatically reacting to evade, resist, or suppress your suffering, you could shift your perception of it such that you appreciate or even embrace your pain. Allowing yourself to fully face suffering as it arises would dramatically alter your relationship to it. After a lifetime of chasing after pleasure and resisting pain (if not flat-out running from it), making an intentional shift toward the enjoyment of suffering effectively spins you around to face it—a complete reversal! But in our culture especially, this way of relating to suffering just sounds absurd.

11:9 Think about it though: if you could somehow enjoy your suffering or at least embrace it, how could the avoidance of it remain such a great motivator? The definition of negative internal states would be turned on its head. If pain became something appreciated and not resisted, imagine how much less control it would have over you. To whatever degree pain loses power over you, that is the degree to which you will be freed of its dominance and influence.

11:10 At first this may not sound as significant as it is, but that's because you're likely stuck in considering the matter intellectually, as an abstraction separate from the whole. Instead, I invite you to come at it *experientially*. Remember that your experience of everything is always "for-me," meaning that it's always divided into positive and negative so that you can manage your relationship to life. Even without dismantling this whole for-me perceptive dynamic, simply transforming your experience of suffering in this way would take away or mollify most of your major reactions and change the course of your life experience.

11:11 This change would extend beyond the way that you currently relate to the presence of pain. It would also apply to your experience of the "world" in which you live, and include a shift in the criteria

GETTING DOWN TO WORK

by which you make decisions regarding possible actions. Without pain as the predominant consideration, your range of choices, big and small, would greatly exceed your present options. You would no longer avoid challenges on the sole basis of fear. In time, you would enjoy greater autonomy relative to self-survival since, while it isn't always apparent, you unconsciously evaluate *all* incoming information in light of its threat or use to you. If your brain weren't so thoroughly engaged with a fear of suffering, these automatic assessments would be far more balanced and open. Basing your decisions on unbiased information would constitute a whole new level of freedom to act, and your behavior would obviously also change.

11:12   For example, it's pretty clear that there is a great deal of suffering when you get your heart broken. If you've never had a broken heart, then you've probably suffered the loss of a loved one or some other painful episode in life. What happens when such unmitigated suffering arises? Well, you feel awful, sometimes so terrible that you honestly don't know how you can make it though such pain. You try to deal with it and find some way—*any* way—to make it stop. You may scream and cry or try to distract yourself, or get angry, plead, rationalize, or any number of activities desperately trying to manage this suffering.

11:13   You can see that your life becomes dominated by the pain. Your every thought and mood, indeed your entire perspective is influenced by this hurt, and the world can seem a very dark place. The central ingredient to all suffering is pain, and pain suggests certain reactions—running away, ignoring, suppressing, resisting, destroying the cause, etc. What all these have in common is getting "away" from it. You enter into a struggle to somehow deal with it, mostly attempting to eliminate your pain.

Transforming

11:14 So I'm asking you to wonder: what if instead of automatically struggling to get away from it, you moved "toward" your pain and embraced the feelings that are there? Just as you can embrace a person, or lean your body into the wind, or savor a delicious food, you can do something similar with your feelings and attention in regard to suffering. You can move your feeling-attention to fully inhabit any experience at hand. You'll find that turning your attention toward something changes your disposition about it, and also changes your experience such that the pain diminishes.

11:15 The dynamics behind this are unimportant; what matters is making a radical shift in your relationship to painful experiences. By turning to face and embrace them without resistance, they tend to cease being so painful and may even disappear. Yet whether or not they are still experienced as painful, you are no longer in a position of *struggling* with the experience or resisting it, and can fully feel and let it be.

11:16 Once this occurs, it isn't necessarily felt as suffering anymore, since suffering is "putting up with an unwanted experience," and you aren't "putting up" with it anymore. Instead, by turning toward the pain and embracing it, you are treating it more like a "wanted" experience, eliminating the element of resistance and struggle. Contrary to common sense, the very act of mentally resisting or moving away from pain adds new layers of suffering, fear, and helplessness, as well as amplifies the pain. These additional layers are done away with the moment the pain is embraced, and the pain that does remain is diminished.

11:17 More important than lessening pain, the possibility opens up that you can actually experience the heartache—or whatever—without it being painful. You might even "enjoy" the experience. This kind of enjoyment isn't necessarily like enjoying pleasure; it's perhaps more like the satisfaction we feel when scratching an itch. A strange comparison perhaps, but we don't have much to compare it to because this kind of experience is not common and so hasn't made it into our cultural lexicon.

11:18 Once you eliminate the foundation assumption that the pain should be avoided, it becomes possible to view and feel the experience more for what it is, and simply as an *experience*. You then shift to a position from which you can inquire more deeply into the matter: What is this experience? What does this pain serve? Contemplating such questions in earnest puts you in a different, more proactive relationship to suffering. Instead of struggling in vain, you recast your unwanted emotion as a potentially useful avenue of investigation. Contemplation also requires that you keep moving your attention *toward* the subject, openly delving into your experience to discover its existential nature.

11:19 Discovering the purpose that some specific experience serves—why it seemed necessary to have it arise—allows the possibility of taking action to modify or eliminate your need for this service. For example, suppose you learned that your heartache exists to compel you to manipulate self and life, urging you to take action in relation to a thwarted need, one that you assume is essential for your emotional well-being. Suddenly your pain exists for a reason, and you appear to have some options. You can actively choose to give up the assumption about your emotional needs and re-form what you're attached to, or you can take steps to provide for those needs yourself rather than attempting to fulfill them through some external means.

11:20   It's feasible that you could pass through this transition without suffering, or at least an incredibly shortened period of pain—lasting only however long it takes you to accomplish it. Even this transition is far less painful because it is now an embraced experience that you're contemplating rather than a resisted experience that you're suffering. If the nature of this activity comes to be seen as a natural and healthy occurrence, like burping when you have too much gas in your stomach, it could even be enjoyed.

11:21   Let's be clear, when I speak of suffering I'm not just talking about the obviously painful times such as getting your heart broken, or losing a loved one, or dealing with a painful disease or injury. Also consider the suffering you experience and may sometimes overlook in common feelings such as loneliness, jealousy, boredom, confusion, fear, despair, sadness, anxiety, embarrassment, bitterness, stress, anger, shame, and many other feelings subtle and gross. Try to grasp how suffering is always found in "relational" dispositions such as feeling superior or inferior, being a bully, needing to be right, being controlling, playing the victim, being a drama queen (or king), needing to be witty, needing or fearing any particular outcome, big or small—these are all occasions that inherently engender suffering.

11:22   Now imagine this whole domain of experience—comprising much of what occurs for you every day—being changed into a sort of "enjoyable" domain, or at least one in which you can let "unpleasant" experiences *be* without resisting their presence. If that were true, then most of the above-mentioned activities and dispositions would become far less necessary and useful to you, and would eventually no longer arise. Can you conceive of the remarkable shift, not only in how you'd experience these things, but in how you'd experience your self, life, and others? It's worth a try, isn't it?

11:23   If you want to engage in the pursuit of transformation, I think learning to embrace pain is one of the key elements to include in your practice. It isn't likely to occur overnight because suffering is a foundational aspect of self-survival. Being a self demands that we manage life by producing an experiential field of positive and negative charge—ergo pleasure and pain. Yet choosing to embrace and possibly even enjoy your suffering *is* something that can happen overnight.

11:24   If you grasp the transformative possibilities available in this shift, all that remains is to undertake a regular practice of turning to embrace your suffering. Each time you notice something causing you pain, even if minor, turn toward it and fully feel whatever is there without assuming it has to be bad. Then contemplate the experience. Try to get to the bottom-line or assumptive source that generates it, as well as uncover why suffering seems to be needed by you. What does it serve in this case, what is it doing?

A student, filled with emotion and crying, implored,
"Why is there so much suffering?"
The Zen Roshi replied, "No reason."
—Shunryu Suzuki

11:25   Over time, you will discover that many of the reactions you suffer are unnecessary and disempowering. Perhaps all of them are, but this is something you will need to discover for yourself. The first harmful feelings to drop are those associated with jealousy, arrogance, shame, sarcasm, animosity—any negative, superficially protective, socially based emotions that don't serve you in creating empowering relationships. They aren't needed, and only add to your suffering. As you begin to grasp the nature of pain, a new relationship with suffering can emerge, and transforming your self becomes a more realistic possibility.

Putting Away Childish Things

11:26   Beyond any specific emotional suffering we may encounter, we also need to address the background suffering that drives our self-agenda—the general sense of being somehow incomplete as a person, and dissatisfied with our experience of life. This sense of deficiency relates to the idea of being less than our ideals. Because of this, our self-agenda dominates our sense of future, which is charged with alleviating this distress.

11:27   You need to connect the dots by noticing that your self-agenda—what drives you through life as a person—is based on a background sense of suffering that could be called *dissatisfaction*. If you felt whole and complete, satisfied and joyful, totally realized and actualized as a person, do you think you would still be so strongly driven by your needs and fears? Would you still *need* to be right, or to get approval? Would you still long to remain hidden, or strive to be liked, or desire to get people off your back, or loudly demand respect, or do whatever else you require in relation to others? Would you need so many distractions, or fear so many outcomes? If you weren't suffering this deep sense of discontent, would you still be compelled to judge yourself so negatively? Of course not. All these "needs" are based on a sense of incompletion. It controls the flow of your life by generating the personal suffering that drives your particular self-agenda. Sobering thought, isn't it?

GETTING DOWN TO WORK

11:28   Once again, this domain of suffering isn't always recognized as such because it remains unseen and in the background. If considered at all, the sense of being incomplete that both arises from and drives your unresolved self-agenda is simply held as your normal experience. It's as if an invisible force has been there from birth, providing your natural inclinations, your likes and dislikes, your innate personality, and, for reasons unknown, some form of personal defect or deficiency. People accommodate and live with this sense without ever thinking about it, the same way they live with gravity or breathing. It's considered an inherent aspect of the human condition, but actually it's only an inherent aspect of an individual's self-survival. To get at the Truth of your self, you need to become conscious of existence outside your self-referential framework.

11:29   Such a breakthrough requires that both self and experience be viewed from a base of Nothing—from a complete openness that's free of any assumptions about the way reality works. These assumptions will always force your mind down the same roads, and you will inevitably draw the same taken-for-granted conclusions. But before we go on to further consider our more primal experience, let's quickly review some of the basics of how a self comes about. So one more time into the breach, and then onward.

First things first, but not necessarily in that order.
—Doctor Who

11:30   In order for an entity to "exist," something has to "be there" or become formed. In order for this form to persist, it must engage in activities and deploy mechanisms that can carry out the functions that allow for continued existence, aka survival. In the case

Transforming

of ourselves, these activities collectively create what's called *experience*—perception + interpretation + meaning + reaction, and then behavior to manage resultant impulses. These activities both shape and are shaped by the beliefs and assumptions that dominate the self-mind. As these beliefs become reinforced through repeated engagement, a self's attachment to them grows. Patterns emerge and are in turn strengthened, eventually becoming part of the overall form of a self's identity. Although this is stated abstractly, the reality is grounded in your ordinary daily experience.

11:31 Your formation as a person occurs from the very beginning, from the moment you exist as a self. You can see that this experience has been influenced from the outset by the details of your entire life history. The person you are now was developed throughout childhood—by learning and growing, reacting and surviving, attaining and maintaining. The demands of adulthood may continue to make the child formation more sophisticated, but you don't really transcend it—which you can easily see in your childish emotional reactions, which happen to be based on your sense of being incomplete. But the very pursuit of consciousness and transformation demands as well as offers you a way to finally grow up—to let go of your childish needs, to transcend your emotional reactions and their roots, and to let go of your personal dramas and agendas.

11:32 You obviously have some notion of *wanting* to grow up. You wouldn't be reading this if you weren't tired of clinging to childish formations and historical identities—both of which have long outlived their usefulness. Think about it: the very activities that were created to "serve" the self have *become* the self! This build-up of what is experienced as your self includes many unnecessary characteristics and beliefs that are inappropriate childish or adolescent adaptations from times past. Honestly consider your experience in this light. How many emotional reactions, limitations, and behaviors are really just an altered form of the same kinds of things you did as a child or teen? No reason to stop there. How many childish behaviors and feelings have you created since you've been an adult?

11:33 I suspect that almost everyone feels that he or she will eventually grow up and become a "real" and whole person . . . some day. In contrast to your current, seemingly inherent sense that you're somehow defective or incomplete, don't you imagine that in the future somewhere ahead you'll be an authentic, complete, and whole person? The one that you feel you're not—yet? But you're still waiting, unaware that you continue to act out an unresolvable self-agenda, most of which was constructed while you were a child. If not now, when exactly are you going to grow up?

11:34 By this point, you may see that you're caught up in self-referential loops, endlessly struggling to resolve unexamined underlying drives. But just becoming aware of this possibility won't free you. You need to experience these dynamics *as they occur* for you, committing to a deliberate practice of inquiry to see firsthand how these dynamics are built-in and *self-perpetuating*. This loop is difficult to interrupt because, by design, it goes largely undetected and its workings are almost incomprehensible. The sooner you grasp the nature of this whole "world" in which you're trapped, the sooner you can break free.

11:35 But make no mistake, self-survival is a force to be reckoned with. Before taking up a practice toward getting free of the ensuing dynamics that create this "perceived" world, you should consider that if you aren't committed to taking it on without being led by the hand and given step-by-step exercises or instructions, you're not ready for this work. If, however, you're ready to grasp the truth of any matter you tackle, find a way to understand what's being communicated and see it manifesting in your own life and experience, to prove to yourself the assertions made here and validate what's true without bias or alteration, then you're ready to really make use of this book.

Creating a Practice

11:36   Having moved through a lot of material about consciousness and transformation, perhaps it's time to touch on some of the main points that have been made. Looking deeply into your self-experience—going beyond the fantasies and beliefs you have about yourself as discussed in Chapters One and Two—is the first step toward changing it. This is not done in the rarified atmosphere of a mountaintop, but in your daily life as you live it. None of this communication will make a difference unless you create it as real and "alive" in your own experience.

Practicing Contemplation and Consciousness

11:37   Our ultimate goal is to become deeply conscious. We've seen right from the beginning of our investigation that pursuing consciousness is not the same as pursuing transformation. Consciousness is about what "is," transformation is about changing what we experience and identify with. Yet we also see that once we get past the superficial relationship of mere self-improvement and instead entertain a significant transformation of our very selves, consciousness becomes not only a central requirement, but a byproduct of the effort to change.

11:38 Our primary "method" to increase consciousness is contemplation. Contemplating our true nature is a direct enterprise, repeatedly and steadfastly setting out to become directly conscious of who and what we really are—existentially. Such work stands on its own. The kind of pure contemplation that is used to pursue direct-consciousness requires a focus that's free of presumptions, and an openness detached from self-concerns and life management. We've learned that clarifying our real nature—what we actually are—is necessary in order to recognize all that we're not. To experience firsthand that our self-identity is indeed not *us* is required whether we want to change it or let it go. Whatever our goals, this kind of contemplation should be a part of our practice to transform.

11:39 As we attempt such a change, however, we run into stubborn core characteristics that seem like they are just natural and inextricable parts of our person. This reveals a need for increased consciousness once again in order to uncover the source domain of mind that keeps us stuck. Our method in this case is the same as for pursuing our true nature, yet this contemplation is focused on our personal experience and unearthing what is lived and assumed to be true, rather than what is absolutely true. Here we contemplate to discover an Uncognized Matrix of Mind, the contents of which are existential-appearing assumptions and beliefs that are the foundation of our character and experience.

11:40 We also use transformation to provide feedback about limitations in our consciousness. If we're unable to let go of some aspect of ourselves, as we were invited to do in Chapter Five, or if we experience suffering in some area of life, these are indications that we are still ignorant of something. This is a good way to create a "reality check." When we start feeling cocky and begin to hold our level of self-awareness as more or deeper than it really is, challenging ourselves to change or to become conscious of that of which we are still ignorant helps bring us back down to earth.

11:41 There are many serious people engaged in various forms of contemplative efforts. Frequently, however, they become trapped within adopted methods, which may have served them to begin with but have devolved into a limitation. Remaining within the safe confines of a meditative community, rituals, or even isolating yourself in solo contemplation are unwise as end goals. They may be useful to assist in getting a foot in the door, supporting you in focusing attention on your task, and perhaps reducing distractions. But once you become accustomed to a method, and have adopted a set of ideas and assumptions, you're bound to discover a certain complacency and even pretense creeping in. You may find that rather than confronting your remaining ignorance and challenging overlooked beliefs, you're reluctant to "rock the boat." At this point, you may instead prefer to imagine your accomplishments to be more than they actually are. This is true of any practice or pursuit that you become good at or even master. In such a case, I recommend boldly stepping outside your comfort zone and taking up a pursuit that challenges whatever understanding you've reached. An endeavor you find difficult to engage helps reveal your limitations and provides feedback that points to overlooked assumptions, beliefs, and ignorance, thus leading you to a deeper consciousness.

> *I have been impressed with the urgency of doing. Knowing is not enough; we must apply. Being willing is not enough; we must do.*
> —Leonardo da Vinci

11:42   Contemplation, whether going straight for the Absolute truth or uncovering bottom-line assumptions, is about increasing consciousness and must be the strongest pillar in our practice. Properly understood, contemplation and transformation can serve as invaluable tools in becoming more and more conscious. Yet transformation requires further attention all on its own.

A Transformation Practice

11:43   In creating a transformative practice for yourself, you'll need to incorporate the principles and understanding you've gleaned throughout the book. Any such practice must be personally developed and crafted, yet it's wise to base this practice on principles that draw you out of your assumptions and ideals, and push you to discover the truth about being human and being a self. As suggested right off the mark, it's ill-advised to merely pursue positive experiences, and you need to be vigilant against simply pretending. If you incorporate images and methods developed by others, or even by yourself, remember that any model or schematic will be limited and often misleading. What's true is what's true; trying to pigeon-hole that into a conceptual representation of any kind will always fall short.

11:44   In Chapter Four, I proposed that you create a "transformation objective," a specific idea of a "you" that's worth being. By this I mean an imagined new self, deliberately crafted for use as a temporary goal to begin the process of discovery and change. For example, if shyness is a specific characteristic of yours, you might include qualities of being outgoing and communicative, perhaps further imagining an experience of being fearless in your encounters with others. More generally, included in your objective you may imagine an internal state that is fully sensitive and aware but free of reactions and turmoil. If your image also includes the notion of being real and complete, you'd want to create the most genuine experience you can of what that might be like. It's useful for just about anyone to create for themselves a realistic sense of what it would be like to experience an open mind that is not prone to generating disempowering concepts, and then work to inhabit that sense.

11:45 Remember, for it to be powerful and effective, in designing this transformation objective you should adhere to the simple principles laid out in Chapter Four. You'll want to press your mind toward the truth by continually pursuing an increased depth of *honesty;* your aim should be *far-reaching,* in that it's personally difficult to attain and also demands changing what's experienced as you now; your goals must be *grounded and healthy* enough to provide realistic sustainability as a practice; and even when it becomes challenging, you must maintain the intent that your objective demands moving in the direction of getting *free* of self-limitations and self-identity.

11:46 Whatever you come up with for your objective should challenge your existing experience as a self. In time, this will lead to a deeper awareness of what's personally and unconsciously true of you, offering the opportunity to identify and thus eradicate whatever you find. For example, if shyness is one or your behavioral characteristics, being boldly overt could well be quite challenging, helping reveal deeply held beliefs about yourself as well as offering an alternative experience. This might be one goal within your objective that is far-reaching for you, rather than, say, being nice to people, which may not be much of a stretch for you.

11:47 Whatever your specific objectives, careful attention and honest introspection need to be fairly constant. Consider the real motives beneath your feelings and behaviors, and remember that your objectives must remain aligned with whatever you discover. Perhaps you tend to be grumpy and are quick to anger and you decide that being kinder and more social is a far-reaching goal. Once you get into your initial awkward foray of pretending at kindness, however, you may realize that your temper is more protective than anything else, because you use it to manage your fear of disapproval. A more appropriate goal to adopt would be to open up and be more vulnerable and exposed. If you remain honest and flexible, the goals of your objective will evolve right along with your self-awareness.

11:48 Working to achieve change consistent with your transformation objective will demand becoming conscious of the source of your drives. Discovering what holds you back from such change means unearthing your personal bottom-line convictions and existential assumptions. Grasping the nature of these reveals that they are activities of your own mind. If you're doing them, it means you can stop doing them and free your consciousness from this constriction. For example, perhaps the shy person discovers she has a core assumption that she's really worthless. Experientially grasping that this is only a previously unrecognized concept, she can eliminate this belief. The shyness will no longer be a characteristic behavior for her because the foundation conviction that drove the shyness is now gone.

11:49 Becoming more aware of your core operating beliefs and assumptions also creates a whole new domain of honesty. As we discussed in Chapter Eight, honest "pre-manipulation" communication—openly and directly relating from your bottom-line awareness without alteration or manipulation—will change your relationship to your internal state, as well as radically reduce your manipulations of others and yourself. Such action can only take place, however, with a deepening level of consciousness about what you're really up to—what you unconsciously struggle to maintain or resolve.

11:50 Can you imagine the difference in experience that our above angry man would have if instead of feeling and acting from his anger, he shifted to an internal state—and thus also behavior and communications—consistent with being vulnerable and exposed in relation to others? It's not so much that he needs to go around telling everyone he feels vulnerable, but that he allows this feeling to be acknowledged as his deeper motivating sense rather than turning it into anger as he attempts to manipulate and control his fear. Instead, if he operates from the principle of being honest with himself about his true experience, he will be much more authentic and present in his relationship to others.

11:51 Acknowledging and exposing the bottom-line self-convictions that motivate you to manipulate, and then either consciously transcending them or at least being straight about them, makes a huge difference in your sense of integrity and authenticity. Honest pre-manipulation communication will seriously interrupt your self-agenda, but you can't really engage this practice without deep introspection and contemplation to better discern what's fundamentally true for you. Such practices will have a profound impact on your experience of both self and life.

A lie will easily get you out of a scrape,
and yet strangely and beautifully,
rapture possesses you when you have taken the scrape
and left out the lie.
—C. E. Montague

GETTING DOWN TO WORK

11:52   It may seem that there's so much to tackle, you don't know where to begin. Don't worry, start with the most obvious experience that you want to eliminate. Pulling on that thread will begin to unravel all the rest. In Chapter Four we saw that eliminating the negative aspects of yourself or your experience will also transform your positive attachments, since not only will you discover that many negative consequences are, in fact, the result of something held as positive, you'll find that positive and negative are inseparable, so eliminating one will eliminate the other. Eventually you will have less and less self. Keep working hard to move in the direction of not being confused with your particular self-identity, and perhaps not being confused with *any* self-identity at all. Freeing yourself from anything, at least to some degree, assists you in becoming a bit more conscious of what's true beyond the self-experience.

11:53   As revealed in Chapter Nine, dropping your life story and related historical programs should be one of your first goals, because it's the most immediately effective way to create significant personal change in your self-context. Your excuses for being the way you are immediately dissolve. Because they are based on past patterns and the meaning assigned by you, your judgments about yourself begin to fade away, along with most of your characteristics and much of what you identify with. All of these are currently held together by your life story.

11:54   Although detaching from your life story to any degree will diminish the effects of both your self-beliefs and programmed self-agenda, you're still not out of the woods. Your core attributes will continue to seem like personal characteristics because this programming is ingrained within your *self* concept. Your needs and fears will seem necessary, and your views will simply appear to reflect the way things are. Any personal mental or behavioral activities generated from these "characteristics" will help maintain and reinforce their validity, which increases the difficulty of seeing them, let alone dropping them. Repeatedly contemplating and confronting your core self-assumptions will help you free yourself from this persistent self-referencing identity.

11:55 Another grounded addition to help focus your practice is working to free yourself from being at the effect of the many circumstances that stimulate your predictable reactions. Continue to revisit the practice of shifting your automatic for-me interpretations to for-itself interpretations. At the same time, you should also practice not judging others or yourself, even if all you can manage at first is entering a state of non-judgment for a short time. Your automatic "for-me" interpretations will be interrupted, providing an alternative experience and reinforcing the possibility of living and relating from a different awareness.

11:56 Even as you work to experience everything for-itself and change your relationship to suffering, at times you'll probably be knocked off course by suffering itself. Experiences that are interpreted as painful are more likely to produce reactions of aversion and rejection than they are to invite introspection. Because pain is more "real" to a self than any "philosophical" considerations, it's extremely important that your practice be grounded in genuine experience. If you try to do this by intellect alone, you will drift into abstract notions and your investigation and contemplation will take a back seat whenever something hurts or life difficulties arise. From a self's perspective, pain *means* "stop" and you'll tend to do that. If you want to understand your own condition, however, you need to use pain as an opportunity to delve more deeply into real consciousness, instead of being defeated by what dominates you already.

11:57 As you engage in your practice, ups and downs will be natural and maybe even commonplace. When you run into pitfalls and failures, keep renewing your commitment to the practice and to the truth. Observe your communications with both yourself and others. Remain aligned with the results of your bottom-line investigations, and practice hitting the "pause button" whenever it's required to keep you from engaging in self-agenda manipulations. The more emotionally fraught your interaction is, the harder you must strive to reach your goal of pre-manipulation communication. If you can detach from identifying with whatever seems so important as to require such a struggle, the whole struggle and turmoil will disappear quickly and your efforts will lose necessity. If you can manage it, this is certainly the best course to take. But take care not to chase the cheese of idealized experiences or just indulge in the orgy of gratification rather than growth. Although you'll run into that closed loop of assumptions that endlessly reinforce themselves, this can be overcome with enough attention and contemplation.

11:58 A transformation practice can be very challenging and complex. You might want to change or become more conscious, but if the nature of self and experience eludes you, you don't really know what it is that you're trying to change or become conscious *of*. This isn't an insurmountable obstacle, however. The main relationship to the challenge of ignorance should be to steadily question. Genuinely wondering from a state of not-knowing creates openness to learning whatever it is you do not already know. What can you learn just by asserting what you already know? Not a thing. So whatever form your practice takes, you must persistently work to become conscious of every aspect of yourself, including all that makes up your entire experience of you and reality.

The "Do It Now" Principle

11:59 One principle that can easily be overlooked in any pursuit is the necessity of *doing it now*. Adopting a practice for transformation or enlightenment assumes a process. Process implies something unfolding and so suggests that the results of the practice will come *later*. When we take on a practice with the idea that we'll transform or become conscious later, this usually turns into never. "Always creeping toward and never attaining" becomes another form of running on the wheel. It is important for several reasons to attempt the accomplishment right now.

11:60 For one thing, trying to transform in this moment puts you up against the reality of your experience and presses home the very "place" where this transformation needs to occur. "Later" always remains a concept, and this isn't the reality where transformation can take place. When you clarify your transformation objective, your Abdul's camel, you should force yourself into that very present experience. Not only will you find it possible (although you may also find it difficult), you will create an experience in your occurring awareness that moments before was only a thought. This grounds the experience and makes it real. It also shows you that it is possible and not just a fantasy.

11:61 It is likely that experiencing your objective will be temporary and require discipline to maintain, but it will reveal far more clearly the reality of this possibility and the self-aspects that contradict such an experience. Forcing yourself to enter this experience helps you see contrary self-aspects that suggest you might be pretending, and others that resist the change, allowing you to experientially follow these self-convictions back to their root bottom. It's a bit like trying to pull up a tent when it's time to leave the campsite. If some unnoticed stakes still remain, pulling on the tent will tighten the fabric and allow you to feel exactly where they are and pull them up.

11:62   Repeating this regularly—shifting to an experience consistent with your transformation objective in present time—forces you to find and pull up all the "stakes" that keep you pinned to your old experience. In this way, you aren't waiting for "later" to transform; you are actively taking it on now.

11:63   As a temporary shift, it is only a first step, but an important and powerful one that provides the perspective necessary for transformation to truly be your goal and not just a fantasy. Not all of this will be apparent until shifting into your objective has become a familiar and recurring experience. By then, you will have released your being from so many attachments that a new perspective and consciousness will already be emerging.

11:64   This expanded consciousness will assist you in updating your objective and making it even more real and honest. As you proceed with this "doing it now" practice, you'll be attached to fewer identifications, and be less cluttered with various reactions, and other unnecessary inventions of the self. The open and present experience that begins to emerge will be more conducive to an even more powerful contemplation, leading to deepening enlightenments. The more enlightened you become, the freer you become. Eventually you won't need to pursue any transformation at all since there'll be nothing left to change—this is when "form" becomes the same as Nothing.

Summary Review

11:65 Here's a simple review of the main points made in our pursuit of transformation and enlightenment:

1. Commit to transforming yourself, and create a temporary imagined-experience of a transformation objective to serve as a contrast to your present self-experience and provide a direction for action. Make this objective far-reaching, based on honesty, and challenging to obtain. Then choose realistic goals toward that end that you can pursue immediately and in your present experience.

2. Get to the source of every characteristic reaction or emotional struggle via bottom-line contemplation and investigation. Start with your most unwanted and dominant reactions. As these become experientially known for what they are and you free yourself from them, a new set of unwanted experience will become apparent. Apply yourself to these, and continue in this way until every aspect of your self and your experience is uncovered and understood.

3. To support this effort, include the following in your daily practice:
   - Honest "pre-manipulation" communication.
   - Experiencing others and things for-themselves rather than how they affect you.
   - Engaging in non-judgment of self and others as much as possible.
   - Detaching from your life story.
   - Discovering the self-reinforcing dynamic that validates your assumptions.
   - Embracing your suffering.

4. Simultaneously pursue enlightenment. Contemplate to become directly conscious of who you are. When this is clear for you, then work on becoming conscious of your true nature, the true nature of others, life, objects, existence, and reality. After many deepening enlightenments, tackle anything and everything that remains unknown or unconscious. The ultimate goal is complete enlightenment and absolute freedom.
5. As you pursue these practices, use each to empower the other. As you become more and more conscious, keep updating your transformation objectives, and use any challenges in your transformation efforts as feedback about your level of consciousness as well as indications of areas of ignorance that need more attention. Eventually, you won't need any imagined transformation objectives since complete freedom will become the only goal.
6. Be increasingly honest, and live life as an open and constant question and contemplation.

11:66 All of this is a lot to absorb. At first it is likely to seem confusing and complex, but as you struggle to comprehend what the pursuit is really all about and begin to grasp the underlying principle and intent, it should become increasingly organic and singular—your pursuit is the Truth. From this evolution, your practice will also mature and deepen.

PART THREE

The Absolute and Beyond

CHAPTER TWELVE

Enlightenment: Some Nothing from Which to Come

The Opening Power of Enlightenment

12:1 How should one regard the prospect of a first enlightenment? Prior to having such a direct-experience for oneself, it's difficult to avoid seeing it as an end goal. That said, it's also often held as something unattainable—due in no small part to the way this consciousness is portrayed in our culture. As enlightenment is often depicted, you'd think direct-consciousness results in going from being unenlightened to becoming an instant Buddha. In reality, there are many degrees of direct-consciousness attainable without getting to "complete" enlightenment, and they don't demand a lifetime in a Zen monastery, simply a commitment to the truth.

12:2 To be sure, becoming completely enlightened might well entail decades of contemplative work and countless enlightenments, since an ever-deepening direct-consciousness must emerge until there is no unconsciousness remaining. Very few people have the diligence for such an endeavor, so it's not particularly useful to compare oneself with this ideal result. Consider instead someone with a goal such as playing the piano. Should the music lover learn to play *only* if he or she plans to become a virtuoso? Enlightenment should not be put on a pedestal or held as unattainable when the truth is that virtually anyone can achieve greater consciousness. Some may have challenges with the discipline and focus it might take to get there, but everyone can become conscious of who they are, even what they are. It *is* YOU—how could you be unattainable to you?

12:3   Don't succumb to misinformation that might lead you to put it off—in fact, grasp your true nature right now. It will provide you with a whole new context in which to relate to self and reality, a new beginning that emerges at the moment of your first enlightenment. From here you might grasp that this new context is *no context*, which means you'll finally have "some Nothing from which to come." Such an opening gives you a platform, so to speak, to stand upon—or, more accurately, a "non-platform" to view from. This not only takes your consciousness work to a new level, it greatly increases the depth from which you can approach any endeavor.

12:4   People study with me to increase consciousness, but many also have secondary goals in mind. One mathematician even received a grant to set aside his research at MIT for an eight-month sabbatical as an apprentice. (Since you're likely to wonder: yes, he *did* subsequently have a breakthrough in his work.) While I admire and love every student, I must confess that in some ways I can't always relate to the world that is commonly perceived. So, I can only speculate about the power that direct-consciousness will contribute to your ability to think openly and beyond the norm, and to be able to consider and investigate outside cultural assumptions. Having lived my entire adult life post-enlightenment (which began at age twenty-one), it's sometimes difficult to recall the rather insular perceptive-experience that's normally accepted as human reality, or even to say with any real certainty how much of my development or achievements were assisted or made possible by those early awakenings.

12:5 I can say, however, that nothing I've done—certainly nothing I've mastered—would have occurred the way it did without enlightenment. I would not have been able to discover or create all that is best about the Cheng Hsin work, nor facilitated others in deepening their own consciousness. I've also seen students whose relatively minor breakthroughs have opened them up to a sudden comprehension about the nature of self and mind, and led them to discover new depths in many other aspects of their lives. To be clear, such a *kensho* ("first glimpse") usually doesn't change the basic framework of the self-mind all that much, but it does open a window in what was previously thought to be a brick wall, and with that, so much more becomes possible.

12:6 One thing that any degree of enlightenment provides, beyond a direct-consciousness, is a much more real sense of *openness*, which greatly empowers the principles and mind-states that enhance learning, discovery, and creativity. My own interest in discovering the truth about so many things—like time, for instance, and selfhood, and the principles that lead to effective and effortless use of the body, as well as effectiveness in *any* activity or interaction—has largely been generated from the open "platform" afforded by enlightenment. Coming from "nothing" allowed me to seriously and fruitfully question the nature of mind, emotion, perception, and insight, the principles underlying skill and communication, as well as many of life's more "imperceptible" matters, and to probe deeply into the human condition. None of this would have unfolded the way it did without the platform of direct-consciousness.

such a thing, it's obvious that he had a strong mind and determined focus. In that light, consider his response to his friends' attempts to contact him during his self-imposed isolation:

> *I am persuaded by this natural instinct of mine that I must take heed if I wish that the threads which the Fates spin so thin and weak in my case to be spun to any length. My great thanks, to my well-wishers and friends, who think so kindly of me as to undertake my welfare, but at the same time a most humble request to protect me in my current condition from any disturbance.*

12:13 It's not difficult to imagine that he entered a state of earnest and open contemplation during those years. Remember, it is not necessary to call it by any special name, or burn incense, or to sit or breathe in any particular way in order to contemplate. What you need is a resolute desire to know the truth, and to be open and remain strong with your intention to become directly conscious of whatever *is* true.

12:14 Kant apparently did this for a decade. He transformed the entire field of philosophy because he realized and then asserted that the mind so dominates our perceptions that what we experience simply cannot be trusted to be the truth. This set philosophy on a new footing. I think he must have had an enlightenment of some kind, if not several, since I can't imagine grasping such a thing, unheard of and unknown at the time, without such a breakthrough.

12:15 In any case, he wrote *The Critique of Pure Reason*, trying to share his insights, yet it was and still is difficult for people to grasp. In his preface, he wrote:

> *Human reason, in one sphere of its cognition, is called upon to consider questions which it cannot decline, as they are presented by their own nature, but which it cannot answer, as they transcend every faculty of mind.*

12:16   Such an insight certainly points to a direct-consciousness of some kind. His fundamental breakthrough about mind is probably what opened the possibility in human thought that allowed Freud to go on to invent the "unconscious mind" and create the science of psychology. I've no intention of trying to substantiate that idea; the point is that from one discovery come many more. Understanding even a single foundation principle or truth about reality leads to more and deeper questioning and further possibilities for understanding.

> *Dare to be wise!*
> —Immanuel Kant

12:17   Of course, we know that people like Gautama Buddha and Lao Tzu founded their communications on enlightenment, but perhaps also Sun Tzu, and Socrates, maybe even Isaac Newton. Direct-consciousness is not limited to any particular culture or profession (nor age, gender, religion, or *any* beliefs). A direct-experience could be shallow or deep, but it will influence and awaken the mind in some way, and set the stage for insights in whatever endeavor to which the mind is applied.

12:18   Much can open up simply from questioning the truth of any aspect of "reality." This is the job of contemplation and enlightenment. Yet "enlightenment" shouldn't be the only focus. When it is, one's "view" and pursuit are likely to fall into a particular context determined by the thinking and assumptions surrounding whatever one imagines as that endeavor. Such a narrow perspective could easily become mindlessly ritualized, or succumb to dogma or fantasy. But even if it doesn't, it's hard to remain open and fully challenged when the mind is fixed on a single image of the goal. So remember to "step outside" your practice and have a look around rather frequently. Work to leave no stone unturned—even if it clashes with your beliefs and images of enlightenment.

The Need for Openness and Not-Knowing

12:19   For those who operate from an unexamined assumption that their experience—and so what they "know"—is all there is, the possibility of enlightenment is hard to grasp. Although their idea of this "all" will likely include a reasonable awareness that there are things unknown, this is still a form of knowing. It is a "known" unknown, or a conceptual placeholder for what's unknown. This isn't true not-knowing, which is misunderstood in this case, and unfortunately so, since not-knowing is essential for any true investigation. It is the first ingredient for openness, questioning, learning, and direct insight. No real contemplation can occur without an experiential base of true not-knowing.

12:20   The tricky part is that pretty much everyone confuses their *idea* that something is unknown with an experience of not-knowing. These two are not at all the same. If this idea of the unknown is all that exists for someone, then the real principle of not-knowing remains inactive, and so the *experience* of not-knowing cannot blossom. One can sit in contemplation for hours or for years and still fail to open up.

> *Zen has nothing to grab onto.*
> *When people who study Zen don't see it,*
> *that is because they approach too eagerly.*
> —Ying-An

12:21 If you do not have openness in the matter, how can you make any leap outside of what's known or planned or predicted? Your contemplation becomes simply waiting for some new "experience" to arise, rather than grasping the truth. This is not contemplation nor does it lead to direct-consciousness. Waiting and hoping or even fervently believing in enlightenment is inappropriate to the task. Although there is what might appear to be a lot of waiting involved with contemplation, and it may be quite human to hope and believe, these are beside the point. Dealing with them is best done by repeatedly tossing them out, and at the same time being impatiently patient.

12:22 If there is no experiential not-knowing, there is no real openness. If there is no openness, there is only "knowing" or "experience" in one form or another. This is then seen *as* reality, in which the search for truth is limited and located within what's "known" and "experienced." (That is as clear and as short as this explanation gets, so re-read it if necessary.)

> *If we will repeatedly suffer the humiliation of admitting that we really do not know what we're talking about, eventually we will.*
> —Vernon Howard

12:23 The Absolute truth cannot be found within experience. This should be obvious, unless we believe that what we currently experience is the Absolute truth, which is exactly what is assumed in the absence of experiential not-knowing and openness. If we base our search on this assumption, it makes sense that what is experienced, perceived, and known will be seen as true and as reality. How else could it be seen? Searching for some unknown "absolute truth" would naturally be done within these same parameters since these parameters would exist as "all there is."

12:24 What's missed here is that this very experience and perceived reality are themselves not known in any absolute sense. If you can manage to look with a bit of openness, it starts to become more clear that you don't really know *what* experience is as-itself. You only know it as a tool for grasping the "object" of experience, which is not the same as experience itself. When you study the matter, it also becomes apparent that all perception and all thought are indirect forms of "knowing," and are therefore *not* a direct or absolute knowing of what is. This distinction can easily be missed, or grasped and lost again a few times before retention. You must truly recognize that your entire experience of everything right now, your current perception of reality, is not a direct-consciousness of what is as-itself—in other words, is not what actually exists as an absolute—otherwise there is no real possibility of contemplating the true nature of anything. On the other hand, if you can create for yourself true not-knowing, and so true openness, this obstacle is overcome.

12:25 When such openness is not present, people are likely to remain stuck in the domain of perceptive-experience. Although essential, the mere desire to be free is not enough. Genuine intent and a steadily maintained openness are indispensable in this work because our purpose is either to grasp the truth or to accomplish a change, and by nature both of these exist as *unknown*. The "how

Enlightenment: Some Nothing from Which to Come

to" also remains unknown and must be discovered for oneself. Without contemplation and openness, such discovery is unlikely.

The aspects of things that are most important for us are hidden because of their simplicity and familiarity.
—Ludwig Wittgenstein

The Koan of Now

12:26   Whatever *is*—absolute reality—is true right now, in this moment. The *when* of existence is *now*. *Is* and *now* have something in common—they share the same "place," so to speak. When we speak of *now*, however, we fall into the trap of thinking of it as a moment in time—as though now is just one bead among many on the string of time. In this work, we cannot afford to hang on to such an assumption.

12:27   Have you ever noticed that it is always now? It is *always* now. We think we go through many nows as we travel through time, but fail to notice that we never leave now at all. We might imagine that we'll "get into" the future, as though it's some other place, but when we get there, it turns out to still be now. The past is experience that we say *was*, but this experience is a concept called a *memory*, and the memory is occurring now. "Past" and "future" are always only occurring now.

12:28   In the context of time, *now* seems to be a moment in a series of moments, as if on an infinite line. Yet if you work hard to discern the moment, you can't actually find it in your experience. What you find is a process, one of recognizing distinctions being made—this is perhaps a very short process, but a process nevertheless. This isn't now, since, within this process, how many nows are there?

12:29 You could say that the real moment of now is infinitely small, but what are you saying with that? First of all, you can't conceive of infinity, so that takes it out of bounds of your discernment, making it a cop-out in your contemplations. If I'm to be believed, infinity and absolute nothing share the same nature. That would seem to suggest that *now* doesn't really exist. But I'm not inviting you to believe anything I say. I'm inviting you to grasp for yourself what's true in this matter. At this point, perhaps you are mulling over some idea of an extremely short—perhaps quantumly small—span of time. Drop that and try to stay with my assertion that *now* cannot be a span of time; it cannot be more than it is, nor can it be mixed with what it is not.

12:30 So what is *now*? Where is *now*? When is *now*?

12:31 Let's back up a bit. Whenever we set out to experience something for-itself, we must acknowledge that this directs us toward a more genuine experience of what's there. Experiencing anything for-itself eliminates the personal and "functional" interpretations that are necessary for self-survival—such as meaning, use, charge, association, etc.—revealing a clearer perception of what's there. In this way, we are able to recognize that there are a great many conceptual additions overlying our perceptions and these are not the thing for-itself. This is covered quite thoroughly in *The Book of Not Knowing*.

12:32 So when searching for absolute *Now*, your first task might be to focus on what you perceive as the present, and work hard to

Enlightenment: Some Nothing from Which to Come

experience it for-itself. That would require eliminating from your experience of now everything you can discern as a function of the self-principle. Whatever the self-principle generates in your perceptive-experience is there solely for the purpose of creating a functional interpretation, and therefore has no use for an experience of what is simply *so*. The "for-me perception" is only superimposed upon what's there—occurring as if a "figment of mind," and not as what's true. Since this "for-me" fabrication appears as if it is reality, and arises for a purpose incompatible with experiencing what's true, it completely obscures any consciousness of the true nature of *now*.

12:33 Eliminating all that is "for-me" from your perceptive-experience leaves you with a rather basic sense of perception. This perception might include your immediate physical surroundings and internal state, but minus the usual additions of meaning, association, function, or charge. It feels quite present and *here*, yet also a bit "ill-defined" and thus incomprehensible.

If you are in the future, then ego seems to be very substantial.
If you are in the present the ego is a mirage, it starts disappearing.
—Osho

12:34 Going beyond experiencing the present moment for-itself, your attempt to grasp true *now* pushes your attention toward the very moment that is *not* "a span of time." Because of this, you must realize you can have no thought about it, or interpretation, or even perception, since all of those take time no matter how small the amount. They are also indirect and not the thing-itself. Since you can't "do" anything with it, not even perceive it much less think about it, you might be left with a sense of presence and not much else. If you aren't confronting all of this experientially, having insights as we proceed, I recommend doing so. It makes a vast difference to experientially work it to the best of your ability rather than just hear about it and intellectually understand.

12:35   You'll find that any attempt to experience absolute *Now* will fail to be this very moment because experience is *processed* and so cannot be *now*. Recall the earlier work you did noticing that experience always becomes concept. One instant past the moment of experience, all that remains of that experience *must* be a concept because it isn't occurring now, and now is the only time experience can be an "is."

12:36   In our normal relationship to this matter, we allow "experience" to be what appears as the occurring circumstance, and distinguish that experience from the concepts that we use to retain it in our awareness once it's past. But we can't actually find the very *now* that we say we experience because what we recognize and know *as* experience will necessarily be some conceptually dominated process that has spanned time.

Everything we hear is an opinion, not a fact.
Everything we see is a perspective, not the truth.
—Marcus Aurelius

12:37   If you become more rigorous in your investigation, and grasp the fact that true Now is only *now* and does not span time, you will notice that you fail to find *anything* in your experience that isn't process. In this way, you grasp that you don't experience *now* at all. And yet there seems to be experience, and something seems to exist. Don't throw up your hands and give up just yet, or try to make an intellectual conclusion. Stay with the questioning.

12:38 We appear to be getting closer to the nature of *now*, but we still need a healthy dose of not-knowing and openness. We need to come to grips with the fact that absolute *Now* cannot be experienced or conceptualized. That's hard to do when concept and experience are all we have access to. We're loath to give them up, or perhaps—since we have no other place to put our attention—we *can't* give them up. Yet, if we can only recognize and "experience" something by going through a process, then we can't actually experience *now*. What we can do is become directly-conscious of it. Believe it or not, becoming directly-conscious is not dependent on process or experience.

> *There are more things in heaven and earth, Horatio,*
> *than are dreamt of in your philosophy.*
> —William Shakespeare

12:39 Humans assume that the only way we can be conscious of something is by undergoing mind processes to recognize an experience or perception. I'm asserting that there's more to consciousness than recognizing "experience." But the question people often ask at this point is "then *how* do I do it?" The problem with the question, although reasonable, is that the "how-to" is about process. Essentially you end up asking, "By what process do I become directly-conscious?" There *is* no process to get you to this level of consciousness. You must, as they say, "make a leap" (but leave out the leaping part).

12:40 Another way to talk about this is to say that you are already *being now*. This is the "process," so to speak, for getting it. Put attention on the matter. Notice all that is not *now*, and instead, dwell on the moment. Keep your attention on *now* beyond what is apparent and beyond experience, but not beyond what is true. Stay here until you become conscious of absolute Now.

12:41   It's not impossible to become conscious of Now, but it takes a direct-consciousness—what some might call an enlightenment. I wouldn't know what else to call it. Direct-consciousness is as close as I can come, since it is conscious and it is direct. And by direct, remember, I mean there is NO separation—no distance, no process, no difference between the Truth and *you*.

12:42   Within the context of time, now appears as a moment in a sequence of moments. But within the context of Now, time is an invention. Time actually exists in the context of Now, not vice versa—except as a convention, which is what our experience assumes is the end of the matter. Now is always the case. Now is actually an absolute. Absolutes don't lend themselves well to any kind of model, or understanding. They also don't "play by the rules" of logic, experience, or objective conditions. As an absolute, it is also infinite, has no location, and isn't elsewhere. It *is* Now! Which means it *is* existence. It's everywhere and nowhere at the same time because these two aren't actually different.

12:43   So I'm sounding goofy again, I know. But when it comes to Absolute truth, there is no way to avoid sounding goofy. We can't help but hear such communication from the self-perspective. Since self needs to perceive a relative and solid pragmatic reality in order to manage life, our normal perspective has no place for absolutes. Absolutes are generally viewed as mere abstractions, and worthless except perhaps as a pleasant philosophical diversion, or as mystical silliness. At times, they can even evoke a sense of threat, because survival can't take place within absolutes alone. We need consistent and objectified perceptive-experiences

Enlightenment: Some Nothing from Which to Come

in order to remain cohesive as a self-structure and to successfully stay alive.

12:44 But don't worry, absolutes, like absolute Now, are *already the case*, and we're doing just fine—whether we look into them or not. Now forms the base or source of the reality within which we already live. We are simply ignorant of this truth because it has no use or place within our survival interpretations. That doesn't make it any less true.

12:45 There is a relationship between Now and enlightenment. Enlightenment is about what's True, and what's True is true Now. If you want to become conscious of what you are, for example, it is what you *are*, and that means *now*. You're not attempting to imagine what you will be or were, but to be conscious of what you *are*. So the *are* of you is only *now*. See how that works? There is no other place to look for *you* or the Truth. It has to be what *IS*. Yet when we try to address what-is, our first impression is so clouded over by what-isn't that what-is in this moment isn't just obscure but unseen and unknown.

The Overlay of Perception

12:46 Our look at *now* brings to the fore once again the fact that our perception is dominated by so much that is not this moment. The very absolute condition or real Now—what's really true about existence in this moment—is buried beneath a plethora of concept and experience that is not the moment.

12:47 We've covered this aspect somewhat in this book and more in *The Book of Not Knowing*. The reality of it, however, probably remains only a notion or idea, rather than a present experience occurring *as* life. For that reason, we'll take it on in small bites, but do try to get this experientially. We've seen that one of the most dominant overlays upon the present—one that determines a great deal of how a person's self and life is lived—is that of having a life story.

12:48　The very context of having a "life" overlies and influences each moment, because each moment is seen in relation to every other moment that comprises the past, as well as an extrapolation of the future persistence of this same life. We are distracted from the real moment by our ambition to actualize some story plot, be it minor or major. This is a departure from what's true in favor of what's "planned."

As long as we have some definite idea or hope about the future, we cannot really be serious with the moment that exists right now.
—Suzuki Roshi

12:49　As I've suggested, removing the life story is taking a large step toward freeing the consciousness that you *are* from the story to which you adhere. Yet even when you're rather present with your attention, and free from attachment to a life story, there is still a great deal that remains between you and real *now*.

12:50　Perspective, thought, feeling, and interpretation all dominate and overshadow your encounter of the present. *Now* is not limited to or reflected within any of those activities. This moment is not a view of, or notion about, or a reaction to, anything. It is not found even as a "sense" of now. Yet a basic sense of existing or existence in this moment—free from as much overlay as you can manage, left undefined, without trying to draw conclusions or pin it down—is about as close to this very moment as your experience can get.

12:51　So where should you focus your attention to look into this moment of existence? Let's do an exercise to see if you can move toward real Now, or what we might call absolute Existence. Try to make this as real as possible. Imagine that an ultimate Big Bang in reverse, a sort of anti-Big Bang, suddenly blows up all existence. Absolutely everything that could possibly be experienced is gone. Add to that: time has also been blown away, and space is non-existent. So there is really nothing at all left.

12:52　Has *Being* ceased to be? Has *existence* disappeared or diminished in any way? No. Not at all. We confuse being some *thing* with Being. We confuse experience with what *is*. Notice that with nothing at all, *existence* still *is*. It just isn't any thing. It doesn't exist in or as space or time, and so not as process or experience. In other words, *is* can't come or go, it can only *is*.

12:53　Focus on *is* for a moment. The nature of *is* still "is" even if nothing exists. If everything is destroyed, *is* remains. How can *is* go anywhere? There is nowhere to go. The nature of *is* is Nothing. The nature of *is* is absolute. If you identify with *is* then nothing can come or go. There is nothing that needs to be or not be.

12:54　People can have a hard time with this assertion even as an exercise or contemplation since it requires attempting a consciousness that can't be thought, sensed, felt, perceived, or experienced in any way. Irritating, I know. This brings us to another one of our most fundamental overlooked assumptions. This assumption is that we can and must use perception to become directly conscious of our true nature or the truth of existence. This is a false assumption.

THE ABSOLUTE AND BEYOND

When people contemplate, they will unthinkingly try to *perceive* the truth, and in whatever fashion they think it needs to be done. This sounds reasonable, but it can't work.

12:55   One problem we run into here is the idea that if we can't perceive it, we're left with merely imagining or conceptualizing what's true, and then forming a conclusion about it. This is a natural mistake, but a mistake nevertheless. First, grasp that we perceive the conceptual domain as well as the physical domain. We know these as different in nature, but that doesn't mean anything is excluded from the term "perception." So when searching for the "absolute existence," we need to acknowledge that our relationship to "reality" is to consider our perception of physical conditions as objective and real, and our perception of the mind's activities as subjective and just made up.

12:56   This is reasonable enough, since we respect objects as "true" and hold them to exist outside of what can easily be lied about, and outside the immediate domain of control we seem to have within our minds. Since objective reality is that in which we live and is unmoved by any of our beliefs or other mental gymnastics, we see it as the true reality. Our problem arises, however, in that our only access to objective reality is via perception, and perception is indirect. To be clear, our perception of our internal state is also indirect—that's the nature of perception. So no matter how hard we try to perceive whatever's true about existence, and no matter where we focus, perception will never be direct.

12:57   Direct-consciousness isn't brought about through indirect methods. Often when seriously committed people contemplate, attempting enlightenment, they will get past mind chatter, history, and distractions and begin to focus on the immediate experience of existing, and then set out to become conscious of the true nature of *this*. If their focus is on the self, then they locate this self in their experience—a necessary component—by directing attention toward the source of the perceiver. In other words, they try to locate the one who is seeing with the eyes, or listening between the ears, or feeling the body, etc. This tends to point to a location inside the head because the source of this perceiving then seems to be behind the eyes and between the ears. This is also the location of the assumed seat of thought, the brain. Other than sensation—a general whole-body sense—every perceptive faculty points to the source originating inside the head.

12:58 The overlooked assumption here is that your perceptions have something to do with the location of your true nature, or *you*. It is a reasonable conclusion that you are at the source of your perceptive faculties because you seem to be the one receiving the perceptive information. But because perception is indirect, any effort to perceive the location of the source of perception is doomed to failure. This perceptive effort is founded on the assumption that you *are* located. Such an assumption is inevitably made because perception requires something to be perceived. You assume that since an "object"—subjective or objective—is the subject of perception, the source of the perceiving must also be an object. So without even noticing, these assumptions will dominate your contemplation.

12:59 In order to become conscious of *you*, all you need to do is become conscious of *you*, directly and immediately. Being locked into perception isn't going to help. It turns out that *perceiving* is something of a red herring. You can't and don't need to perceive your absolute nature, but you can become directly conscious of *you*. I don't want you to hear this as a suggestion to avoid perceiving, or to avoid anything else for that matter. Contemplation is always open and organic. You have to do what you have to do in order to genuinely experience for yourself what's true.

12:60 But to be clear, I'm not saying that "experiencing for yourself" is the same as believing or concluding about what's true. That's not progress. Simply consider: the assumption that perception is needed or can be used to encounter your true nature is false. Perception is an illusion, an overlay or superimposition upon reality, and exists only as a function and figment of Mind. Challenge the assumption that you are located as the source "object" of perception, or that perception implies a location or located perceiver. These are big sticking points for everyone, but transcending them empowers the possibility of direct-consciousness. There is nowhere to *go* and nothing to *see*.

Get to the wall, intend, be open, and stay there.

The Siren of Experience

12:61 Our true nature is inevitably confused with self and experience. Besides the fact that self-survival is built into the organism that is the human body and brain, there is an existential reason our attention falls into an identity and clings to experience.

12:62 Given that what we are is an absolute, we are not located or to be found within or as an experience of any kind. To say it another way, our essence is absolutely Nothing. So, like the Sirens luring sailors to the rocks with their irresistible song, "attention" is drawn away from the absolute, which is inconceivable and not formed (nor separate from form, nor "elsewhere"), and toward what is formed and so *is* conceivable—which will arise for us as some form of experience. This is the only place mind can reside or attention can go. Even though mind is a very specific and limited aspect of Consciousness, it can only exist within the conceivable distinctions of experience. Mind creates. Consciousness *is*.

12:63 All this is a challenge to understand, I know, but when stated in any simpler way, it is too easy to miss because it's so far outside of what is accepted, assumed, and conceived. Mind, and self-mind, are forms of Consciousness. Yet they are limited forms of Consciousness that don't allow for the recognition of anything outside the context of Mind. It's something like the way a room might be called "a space," even though only the things that are apparent from wall to wall form the experience and perception of the space. Infinite space is inconceivable and the true nature of space is also unseen.

The most incomprehensible thing about the world is that it is at all comprehensible.
—Albert Einstein

12:64 Another analogy of the siren of experience might be to imagine your consciousness existing in a vacuum without objects, light, or space—where absolutely nothing exists. Now imagine that some object appeared reflecting light in space. Where would your attention go? It would have to go to the object because there is nothing else there, and nowhere else to put your attention. Just so, when Absolute Consciousness is formed into a self, the only place that attention and awareness *can* go is into the world of perception and experience, and this will be formed by the interpretations that are developed to manage self-survival.

12:65 Given that we're drawn to produce both a self and methods to deal with life, our cognition will exist within the limitations of the self-mind and the distinctions that can be made within this mind—creating what we call *experience*. But even if we could create some other form of experience, it would still fall short of the Truth, because experience must always be *formed* and the Absolute isn't limited to any form. We can hardly help but confuse the idea of infinity with "lots and lots" or "more than we can conceive of," but we can recognize that this limits *infinity* to the world of objects or numbers, and so the world of experience. Infinity isn't experienced and so shouldn't be limited to experience. Our inability to conceive of or perceive the matter in any real way forces us to relate to a symbolic representation. Infinity is actually the same as Nothing, and is also an absolute.

12:66 Notice that my talking about this now is likely to be held as a philosophy or a mystical belief system. If you believe in such things, or have some spiritual ideas of the cosmos it resonates with, then this may sound like it validates whatever you believe and you'll use it as a confirmation. If you don't have some belief system that concurs with this kind of chatter, you'll probably just glaze over or reject the communication as impractical and abstract. These reactions emphasize the point being made.

12:67 It is useless to believe or disbelieve, or to accept or reject this matter. Only becoming directly-conscious of what's true will make any difference. If this isn't true for you right now, then you can only use the argument for considering and contemplating in ways that you may have previously overlooked. If you've had some enlightenment experiences, this could help clear up some confusions that may have swirled in your mind while trying to sort out and reconcile the Truth that you've encountered with the perceived reality and ferocious mind that you experience.

12:68   The "siren of experience" dynamic is also why enlightenment will degrade into a form of "knowing." The mind cannot conceive of absolutes and so even such an encounter can only be represented in some way within mind. But the Truth is still the truth whether or not your brain can formulate it or hang onto it. Your true nature is whatever is actually true, not what anyone believes or has said, including me and you. Your job is to become conscious of the Truth for yourself, and sort out what's what. As you work to do that, don't take any of my assertions at face value or let them get in the way of a completely open investigation.

Whereof one cannot speak, thereof one must remain silent.
—Ludwig Wittgenstein

CHAPTER THIRTEEN

Approaching Absolutes

Absolute Mischief

13:1   There are many beliefs and systems of belief that appear as positive but which, in effect, are not beneficial to the human spirit they claim to serve. In our current open-minded culture, we are obliged to be tolerant, even deferential, toward all religions or spiritual practices on the grounds that each one ostensibly leads to the same universal truth. When reflecting on the millennia of evil done in the name of one religion or another, it's hard to disagree with the underlying ideal of peaceful coexistence. At the same time, this theological magnanimity obscures a few crucial facts regarding the nature of belief itself, foremost, that a belief is not the *truth*.

13:2   Considering what we've discussed so far regarding belief and the Absolute, it should be apparent that *no* religion is expressing the Truth, or is even true. This statement may rankle some readers, even when it's acknowledged that a fundamental principle common to virtually every religion is a call for faith. In fact "faith" is often used as another term for "religion." And why is faith needed? Because the foundation of most religions is not Truth, but belief. This dynamic isn't limited to formal religions; it occurs in all organized spiritual belief systems.

Approaching Absolutes

13:3   By definition, a belief is not a direct-experience or a consciousness of what's true. It is an *idea* that something is true. Granted, it might be a genuinely heartfelt idea, and have a hopeful and altruistic basis; it may even point knowingly in the direction of the "Unknowable," but a religion is still essentially a series of rites and customs organized around some claim or conclusion usually purported to be the "one truth."

God has no religion.
—Mahatma Gandhi

13:4   In reality, the Truth remains unknown for almost everyone. Grasping that fact is merely to acknowledge what's already so; holding onto it and abiding in a state of not-knowing is a useful starting point for any venture, be it spiritual, scientific, artistic, or otherwise. But religion in general holds that your capacity to become directly-conscious for yourself is invalid—not your beliefs, mind you, but your capability, and even your responsibility. It demands that you refrain from questioning and investigating, and be content to simply believe what you are told. Within the confines of religious dogma, when someone entertains doubts, it is not equated with "a state that precedes all insight" but is instead called something like a "crisis of faith." To the detriment of consciousness work, religion obliges followers to turn away from the universal fact of humanity's inherent ignorance regarding existence.

13:5   Accepting people regardless of their beliefs is not the same as validating whatever organized system they may follow. Certainly people can believe whatever they want—they tend to in any case—but that doesn't make the belief true. As a matter of fact, when it comes to absolutes, *no* belief can be true. It's possible to have a relatively valid belief in regard to some objective probability; in a conditional world, even a guess may turn out to be more or less correct. But absolutes are *absolute*, existing outside any context, and so they can't be represented by any kind of formulation. Remember that it is the job of religion to invite you to believe in some representation, an activity that moves you in the *opposite* direction of pursuing a direct-consciousness. This is not merely an opinion, but a fact based on the nature of what we refer to as "the Absolute." Because absolutes are neither conditional nor conceivable, it is not *possible* to have a belief that in any way matches or represents Absolute truth.

---

*By substituting faith for the truth,
we've abdicated our souls not saved them.*

13:6   It is the business of religions to peddle the notion that they possess knowledge of absolutes. Without this claim, all the dogma and traditions they disseminate would be seen for what they are: just made-up fantasies, superstitions, and rituals that certain people espouse for various reasons. They may have good reasons and produce some positive results in society, but the unnoticed cost is still too high. What creates the most mischief is that each religion lays claim to absolute knowledge, which is then used to add validity to its specific belief system, as well as credibility to its intercessors.

13:7   Taking a detached viewpoint, freed from the usual polite deference to the subject matter, tends to reveal that a large part of any religion is founded on the ritualization of superstitious nonsense. Fundamentalist zeal acted out in service of that nonsense can be a dangerous form of willful ignorance, precluding openness by promoting closed-mindedness. Organizations that adhere blindly to unquestioned beliefs are not only unnecessary, they are demeaning to the Truth and to anyone with the courage to pursue the Truth.

> *Truth does not hurt, rather, it is our resistance*
> *to its message that causes pain.*
> —Vernon Howard

13:8 Just like an individual self, religions are committed to their own organizational survival and are thus subject to the same unchallenged loops of mind that reinforce ignorance, assumptions, and dogma. As with people, any given organization can tend to be open-minded or closed, loving or hateful, inclusive or exclusive, and so on. But the underlying commitment of an organization will be to its own survival, not to the truth. If someone finds that adhering to certain beliefs or associating with a particular community empowers them or improves their lives, so be it. But claiming that absolute knowledge is somehow the foundation for these beliefs is a blatant disregard for the truth—which is that the Absolute remains unknown and can only be experienced directly. Encouraging people to simply believe without any personal validation or direct-experience is antithetical to consciousness of the Truth. Such "faith-based" thinking undermines reason, responsibility, a respect for fact, open-mindedness, and even common sense.

13:9 Beyond the good or bad of it, take a look at how people generally participate in religion. What is the main activity of Christianity, for example? Prayer. What are people doing when they pray? Asking for favors. If you visit a Buddhist temple or shrine, what do you find? All sorts of ways to give money through buying incense to burn at an altar, or paying for a piece of paper with a note on it to wrap ceremoniously onto a wall, or providing a place to toss coins, or a way to get your name on a stick, and so on. What is the purpose of these rituals? Again, asking for favors, which is clearly a self-serving activity—even asking for the benefit of another is self-serving. Is that what the Absolute is "for," to grant favors that advance our agendas?

A man's ethical behavior should be based effectually on sympathy, education, and social ties; no religious basis is necessary. Man would indeed be in a poor way if he had to be restrained by fear of punishment and hope of reward after death.
—Albert Einstein

13:10   Whatever the founders of these religions had to offer, it was most likely lost long ago in the inevitable decline into dogma, beliefs, and rituals. These "representations" evolve and persist because they serve the needs of both participants and organization. Not only are the founders' insights or consciousness lost but, in most doctrines, the doorway to openly considering the truth for oneself is closed, and the possibility of becoming directly-conscious is considered arrogance or heresy.

13:11   Because you find no perceptible evidence for god, merely considering this possibility requires some openness. Such a notion demands a mental leap, entertaining a possibility beyond normal experience and the observable world around you, which in itself leads to a healthy sense of wonder. In most religions, however, this kind of openness is immediately channeled into the demand to believe in some representation of this "unknown," and to accept a predetermined conclusion. The moment you're forced to choose a described scenario, the wonder is shut down. But why require that you choose a storyline when in fact *you don't know*? Creating the possibility for you to become conscious for yourself is a far more powerful position to take.

Honesty commands a declaration not of faith but of ignorance.
—Zia Haider Rahman

13:12   A few segments of religion call on people to participate in becoming more conscious of the truth for themselves, or transforming as a person. This is the only function such an organization should serve if it wants to be aligned with the Truth. Zen, for example, is a sect of Buddhism that requires its followers to contemplate and personally become "enlightened" for themselves. This spirit is useful no matter what form it may take. Unfortunately, as with almost all human endeavors, even this has become ritualized and systematized, degrading into beliefs, dogma, or fantasies that few manage to transcend in favor of the truth. Although it may be inevitable that confusion and misunderstandings occur within any such pursuit, care can be taken that the purpose and aim is repeatedly revisited and aligned with.

13:13   Moving toward a world that works for everyone—one that is loving, effective, harmonious, and healthy—is an intelligent and obvious course to take. No religious belief or sentiment is required before someone can aspire to such things. When observed from a distance, it should be clear that religions are often not performing that function and in many cases are resisting it. The more conscious one becomes, the clearer it becomes that a cooperative, effective, and inclusive world is the most appropriate course to pursue in life, but that doesn't make it the Truth. It is the best option for survival and persistence—for self, humanity, and the

THE ABSOLUTE AND BEYOND

planet. Yet make no mistake, this is still the domain of self and survival, just on a more inclusive and intelligent scale.

---

*Before Buddha or Jesus spoke, the nightingale sang,
and long after the words of Jesus and Buddha are gone into oblivion,
the nightingale still will sing.
Because it is neither preaching nor demanding nor urging.
It is just singing.*
—D. H. Lawrence

Challenges of Understanding the Absolute

13:14 People and cultures make many mistakes when attempting to comprehend the Absolute truth. This is understandable because, as I've said so many times, the Absolute truth is inconceivable and one of the very few aspects of reality that cannot be shared in any way between us. It has to be grasped personally, and directly. Anything so completely inaccessible to the mind is bound to be misunderstood.

13:15 People tend to imagine enlightenment as some sort of great new experience, perhaps filling the brain with light and the heart with love. This is not the Absolute. It is simply an idyllic imagined experience. Someone might imagine Absolute Consciousness as a sort of big Mind, or an ethereal formless understanding, or a super entity. It's not. No matter what can be imagined, it is incorrect. Whatever is thought or felt or experienced, it is not Absolute Consciousness. So again we are thrust up against our question: then how do we get there?

13:16 Predictably, our attention is pulled into finding a method we can use to solve this quandary. In the world of process, methods are developed to achieve some result and can be very useful. In the world of absolutes, however, there is no method that can guarantee results because direct-consciousness is neither a result nor a process. On the other hand, the human mind usually needs to focus on a method in order to proceed, even toward grasping the Absolute. So it seems inevitable that you will resort to using some method, but you must take care not to let the method use you. This can be difficult because you seem to be called upon to have "faith" in the method and so may become attached to it or "believe" in it. Neither faith nor belief should be the operating principle here. Don't confuse method with anything true. It must remain *only* a servant to the purpose for its adoption, which should always be kept in mind and at the forefront of your efforts. *You* are at the heart of the intent to grasp the Absolute, not any method you might use to help keep you on track.

13:17 I sympathize with the challenges involved in attempting to grasp the Truth. The paradoxes involved with absolutes can leave the mind whimpering in distress. For example, if someone says something like "Consciousness is *everything*," people usually think of this as being every "thing," and sometimes find their way to a state of mind that abides in such an experience. Not a bad state. But it isn't what's meant by "Consciousness *is* everything," because the focus is on the *experience* or the idea one has of every thing that exists or can be imagined to exist. This is still the domain of experience and mind. When it's said that Consciousness is "everything," what's true in this regard is that there's nothing there *and* there's no absence in any way, *nor* is there a separation from any "thing." This doesn't make sense and so boggles the mind. Grasping the real nature of self, objects, and experience helps bridge this paradox.

> *Appearances are a glimpse of the unseen.*
> —Anaxagoras

13:18   The mind "knowing" about Consciousness is itself a limited form of Consciousness, even when this is done directly. As I've said, after having an "enlightenment experience," most people confuse what becomes *known* with the increased consciousness that is the direct-experience. This consciousness affects the mind so that what is grasped or held within the domain of experience is a "knowingness" of what's true, but not the Truth itself. This relationship is missed by the majority of people who've had some initial form of enlightenment, or other direct-experience. The Consciousness that "sparks" this knowing in the mind is absolute and true and doesn't come or go, but the impact upon the mind is what is known, and thus what is perceivable and "relate-able." This knowingness is then confused with the enlightenment.

13:19   People keep trying to make sense of the Absolute without realizing that the mind can't make sense or conceive of absolutes. The "sense" that people make of any "real teaching" will invariably be a personal interpretation formulated within the context of their own mind-framework, not the Truth. Although overwhelmingly commonplace, trying to justify our ignorance and experience, or to convince ourselves that our opinions or conclusions are absolutely true, is a disservice to our contemplations. Taking these tendencies into account assists us in transcending them, and helps us more genuinely realize the direct-consciousness that we seek.

13:20   Ultimately the Truth is not something apart or elsewhere. It is the truth of absolutely everything. Therefore it can't be reduced to "an" experience, which is always a limitation. If you see life and death as a duality, you misunderstand. If you fear or reject death or life, you misunderstand. Don't idealize enlightenment or the Truth. Don't turn any teaching or communication, no matter how inspiring, into a belief system or a dogma. The moment this is done, the truth is lost, and the teaching is of no use.

Life and Death

13:21   Just as we have no experience of creating our own existence, we also have no genuine experience of what death is. We're left with an enormous unknown in our lives, a gaping hole in our consciousness that we might feel compelled to fill by adopting belief systems or religions claiming knowledge about such things. The truth is, however, that we *don't* know, and the search for Absolute Consciousness is not advanced by covering up that fact with comforting beliefs.

13:22   Earlier I brought up our inability to face death, mentioning that when people think they're confronting the reality of death, it is still only an imagined concept, and often of dying, not of death. The process of dying (the body falling apart and degrading) isn't the same as death. As far as we know, the body might go on forever, but it doesn't seem possible because we postulate that, since everything else does, the body will eventually disintegrate and cease to function. Without exception, this appears to be the case. Death is really just the flip side of birth.

13:23   It isn't hard to notice that we have no idea how we came to be. Somehow we became conscious of "existing," but prior to that we are completely blank—save for stories and concepts about how human life comes to pass, which do nothing to fill in the complete absence of a personal experience or consciousness in the matter. Just so, we have no idea about death either. How could we? Therefore, when we consider death, we are left with nothing but imagination.

13:24   What really marks death for us—and scares us to death—is that death is the absence of our selves. This is also only a concept since we've not experienced it, but due to our observation of many living things dying and the known fact that everyone dies, we have a reinforced and valid idea of the inevitability of death. Our very real experience of our own existence being finite is supported by the fact that we don't know how we came to exist, or to be alive. If we can "start," we can "stop." If we can be created, we can be destroyed. I also suspect that somewhere deep down, perhaps on a genetic level, we know that we will end.

13:25   The idea of dying brings dismay to the self since clearly it is the end to self-survival. Most of the time people just ignore it altogether, or fill the mind with alternative "religious" beliefs that counter this reality—which is actually just another form of ignoring the matter. Of course, an end to life is a failure of self to survive, so the "destiny" of our lifelong self-survival drive is inevitable failure. Unless we invent fantasies about life after death, or imagine that somehow the self persists and only the body dies, we are left with simply no more self.

13:26   What does remain is the Absolute, and it "remains" because it never lived or persisted as anything. Does that sound like the self? Does that sound like you? Of course not. So unless you can become conscious of the Nature that doesn't live or die, you will suffer death as an annihilation of your self. The implication that increased consciousness could result in a more "positive" possibility may sound like just more hopeful airy-fairy rhetoric, but keep in mind that this is the reason absolutes have so often been co-opted by belief systems in the first place. Your job is not to believe anything but to become conscious for yourself. In short, the observation here is that the self-mind can't comprehend either the Absolute truth or the death of the self.

13:27   If we're going to lose life, it might be useful to consider what it is we're losing. Of course we'll lose the story of our life, our history, and the drama that seems to be acting itself out, at least in our minds. We'll lose our social life and our connection to others, and so we'll lose interaction, touch, and any projects or endeavors we might be involved in. We'll lose the conceptual weave that constitutes most of what we experience and refer to as "life"—stories, internal chatter, fantasy, memory, dramas, society, culture, emotional turmoil, activities, and so on. The death of all this is significant. Even if we somehow survived in some form, without all that stuff our experience would certainly be transformed into something unrecognizable. But what else will we lose?

13:28   We'll lose the meaning of life and "existence." What our personal lives *mean,* and the *meaning* of life existentially, are ideas that appear to be very important to us, dominating our experience of existence. The domain where they arise is conceptual, but its foundation exists in what we experience as one of our more primal aspects of living. The meaning that we apply to anything and everything is what creates the impression that life has some inherent meaning. Actually—and you probably suspect this already by now—life has no more meaning than does a rock. What meaning does a rock have? None. It is only a rock, and it is only a rock to us. For itself, it is a lot more like nothing at all. What is the meaning of a toaster floating in space? For us this might be an amusing image but, without us, nada. This is life. The death of self is also the death of meaning. We create meaning. Mowing the lawn, taking a walk, fixing the shower, calling a friend. The only meaning these all have is what we give them via survival—social, physical, personal.

13:29 Given all this, what else is left of life that we would lose? Of course we'd lose the body and the whole realm of biological life. Although we are attached to the biological, and find our experience and perceptions residing in and as a function of the body, the body has no more inherent meaning than a rock. A sophisticated rock for sure, a complex system of individual life forms working collectively to produce what appears as an entity with which we then identify. Yet if you look closely, it all breaks down into elemental matter just like the rock. The fundamental distinction of life creates a context in which we make many distinctions in what's perceived, so it appears that the body is different in nature from a rock. Fundamentally the body doesn't create any more inherent meaning than any other object. Existence has no meaning. Meaning is a human invention. Existence just is.

13:30 Why bring all this up? There's nothing to do about it, except perhaps create a life worth living, and then, in the end, let it go. Yet we've seen there is a relationship between the principle that we call death and its role in transformation. There is also an inherent limitation in consciousness when we remain bound to objects and concepts. Remaining riveted to the illusion that you will somehow survive or that you have an inherent existential meaning only serves to block openness to the fact that neither of these are true. Confronting such anti-self realities is necessary to seriously contemplate the absolute nature of existence. Being able to consider what's true independent of self, and so independent of life and death, is a requirement for pursuing Absolute Consciousness.

13:31 Although we really don't care about the truth (we care about ourselves and our attachments) it is essential to grasp what we really are, our true nature, in order to create the possibility of de-identifying with the self-principle and survival—which, once again, *is* life. To pursue the truth, we also need to be conscious of what life actually is, as well as the nature of existence in any form or with no form at all. Here deepening enlightenment is necessary.

Reality is merely an illusion, albeit a very persistent one.
—Albert Einstein

Completing Enlightenment

13:32 Another avenue that may be a possibility for a total transformation is a complete immersion in contemplating the Absolute truth. In this way, a transformation of the "individual" could occur simply as a side effect of developing the clear consciousness that he or she is not "being" anything at all—a self, an identity, attachments, or any experience whatsoever—until the persistent presence of this consciousness finally dominates or replaces the domain of "experience."

13:33 With such immersion, one's experience would necessarily transform—it would be freed from any moorings and so the self would dissolve. The process of life would naturally continue as if of its own accord, but absent of a self-identity. Any human social activity would be a result of a consciously created form of invented "person," acting as a surrogate for your true nature.

How are you?
Perfect, thank you. I'm traveling incognito.
Oh? As what are you disguised?
I am disguised as myself.
Don't be silly. That's no disguise. That's what you are.
On the contrary, it must be a very good disguise,
for I see it has fooled you completely.
—Sufi Mullah Nasrudin

13:34　Yet, pursuing transformation in this manner is unrealistic as a practice because we rarely commit to such complete immersion. Even if someone tried, given that all attention would be on pursuing the Absolute truth and not at all on investigating the nature of self, that self is unlikely to be challenged much less transformed, shy of achieving complete enlightenment. I'm only guessing here, but it's an educated guess. Changes will occur after many deep enlightenments, but even those will probably still amount to less than a total transformation.

13:35　Even after the first enlightenments occur, the self is still the predominant source of experience and behavior, acting out whatever self-agenda remains and any newly created goals that are developed. Both experience and behavior are changed somewhat, depending on the depth and clarity of the enlightenment(s). Given the "knowledge" of one's true nature, a new perspective is created in relation to self and life. Although it may well alter the plan or course of one's life, this new perspective does not fundamentally or necessarily change the self. Understanding that you are not what you identify with doesn't shut down the act of identifying. It tends to continue in some form in order to relate to life. Changing this is the domain of transformation—either to free yourself from all identity, or to change what it is that you identify with.

13:36 Ultimately the self and life are limited forms of Absolute Consciousness—there is no difference between Consciousness, self, mind, or pizza. Turns out it's all Nothing, and the self *is* Being. It is all a manifestation of the very Consciousness that is realized in enlightenment. A self, however, is designed to live and die in complete ignorance of this Truth. But it doesn't have to stay that way.

CHAPTER FOURTEEN

Persisting and Maturing

14:1   We've already addressed the most important points and principles that contribute to any pursuit aimed at discovering the truth or attempting change. In wrapping up, I want to touch on a few additional principles and thoughts that may help with your ongoing practice. Developing a practice is one thing, continuing with it is another. Such continuation demands evolving and maturing if the practice is going to stay true to the increasing consciousness that will emerge from doing this work. The following will address a few matters that may not seem relevant to you now, but nevertheless should be available to you as you progress.

Responsibility and Balance

14:2   In taking up an ongoing practice toward increasing consciousness, transformation, or mastery, two principles that are useful to consider are responsibility and balance. One is essential for growth, the other for maturing.

Responsibility

14:3   When we hear the word "responsibility" we are likely to infer connotations of a burden, duty, blame, "being good," or some other association that has little to do with the principle of responsibility.

Responsibility—or this principle by any other name—is about personal accountability, you being at the source of your own growth and consciousness. If you don't put yourself in the driver's seat, so to speak, you can't make progress.

14:4   When it comes to contemplation, personal growth, transformation, and so on, if you aren't taking it on for yourself—putting your ass on the line, being in the middle of the questioning, the investigation, the change—it can't occur. If *you* don't become conscious, *you* won't become consciousness. This is obvious, and yet far too many people miss the fact that all of this work depends completely on them, including the initial stages of learning how to learn.

14:5   Over decades of teaching, I came to notice how many people assume that someone else—some other force, method, system, or body of knowledge—is needed for them to learn, grow, attain, or discover what's true. These people tend to accept as an aspect of reality that they personally lack the capacity to discover what's true for themselves and are dependent on outside help. People on the other end of the spectrum assume that they must do it all by themselves, and that whatever they figure out or believe is "their truth." Such people tend to hold their opinions, viewpoint, intuition, rationality, or some such as the final arbiter of truth. They often reject contributions, disdaining any assertions outside their beliefs as fraudulent nonsense. At one time or another, we've probably all exhibited a bit of each extreme, but neither of these dispositions is useful or appropriate to our work here.

14:6   Perhaps due to a childhood as an expatriate, during my own "edification" I was fortunate to have the perspective of being doggedly committed to my goals, determined to discover the truth or accomplish some undertaking with or without any help. I "learned how to learn" early on, largely through the spark of contemplative wonder that sometimes arises naturally in certain solitary children. Later on, this was complemented by learning to value feedback, most notably in the form of measurable results in my martial studies. I didn't depend on outside contributions, but I accepted any that offered honest assistance or facilitation. If there was a teaching or invention that could help me in my quest, I would dive into it, study obsessively, and use it to learn more.

14:7   Of course this meant having to discover firsthand what was and wasn't valid or true in each discipline offered. Although much of what was offered turned out to be mere beliefs, and many of the teachers were frauds (although not all were aware of it), I learned to distinguish true from false, which made the contributions of a few special teachers that much more valuable. To be clear, this awareness took a great deal of work because it was necessary to acquire some mastery before I allowed myself to make any critical assessment. Over time, I learned to better discern people's authenticity and whether they were coming from experience or simply belief, which saved me from pointless studies. In my efforts to save time by separating the genuine from the superficial, it also became clear that I myself was always available for investigation.

14:8   If there wasn't any help to be found, I would proceed anyway. If there was no method or exercise to help me progress, I invented one. If I didn't know how to advance after some existing system proved insufficient, I would investigate on my own, asking questions and contemplating until a way opened up. I didn't depend on anyone or anything, but I always sought out and appreciated any effective help that was offered. This is apparently not the norm, but it did elucidate that there was a principle involved, applicable to all manner of undertakings: To successfully achieve anything demands personally taking full responsibility for making it happen. Adhering to that principle, few conditions have the power to thwart one's efforts.

Balance

14:9 Another principle to consider is one of balance. Balance can be difficult to convey as a principle. One way we could approach it is to notice the tendency of youth to extremes. Their enthusiasm and passion may be laudable, but excessive belief in their own knowledge is limiting, which means that the big picture is often neglected and fails to be grasped. We might say that what's lacking here is balance—in this case, the balance between what is known and what is not known. Young people also might lack the balance between action and patience, between good ideas and the reality in which they must manifest, and the balance between valuing one's own perspective while still making room for that of other people.

14:10 Balance might also be seen as a formed cousin of paradox. Paradox is an essential aspect of the Absolute truth and so Absolute Consciousness. You can't grasp the Absolute without being inclusive of paradox.

> Paradox: from the ancient Greek *paradoxos*, "contrary to expectation"
> - a statement or proposition that, despite sound (or apparently sound) reasoning from acceptable premises, in reality expresses a truth or leads to a conclusion that seems senseless, logically unacceptable, or self-contradictory.
> - a seemingly absurd or self-contradictory statement or proposition that when investigated or explained may prove to be well-founded or true.

14:11 Balancing between reason and the Absolute truth that lies *beyond* reason can be tricky. The first requisite for such balance is to become directly-conscious of the Absolute truth. Reason seems to come more easily because it is often trapped within a self-invented rationality that's based on personal beliefs and assumptions, and masquerades as common sense. True reason, however, isn't so easy to come by, since it requires an unbiased and impartial search for the truth that is as honest as the powers and limitations of the mind allow. Open-minded reasoning can be useful, but it needs to be balanced with an openness beyond what's known or appears knowable.

14:12 We find balance as an aspect in the foundations of Buddhism. Remember, Gautama Buddha was a prince living in opulent pleasure. Leaving this life, he studied other available religions and practices and found them lacking. In despair, he chose the path of the ascetic, living in austerity and discomfort. His final contemplation attempt embraced neither comfort nor discomfort. Instead he chose balance in what he called "the middle path." Remaining committed to his purpose, he allowed no distractions or pleasures, but he didn't seek pain and also allowed himself to eat and be healthy. Of course, Gautama's idea of balance was much different than most of ours, and we might see his "middle" way as extremely austere. What he did was eliminate extraneous "methods," depriving himself of all pursuits other than that of the Truth.

14:13 Balance is better understood when you can grasp that any experience is only good *because* of bad, is only special *because* of mundane, is only exciting *because* of boredom, is pleasurable *because* of pain, and so on. There is no way to create the "sublime" without grasping that its very sublimity is based upon an experience of a reality that is generally devoid of it. When you understand this, it becomes increasingly possible to create experience by creating the context in which it's held. It also becomes more apparent that whatever experience you have is only that way in contrast to it *not* being that way. If you appreciate something fine or good or beautiful, you are also appreciating the coarse, bad, and ugly that provide these for you.

14:14   No inherent enjoyment exists within any action, outcome, or experience. Enjoyment is created by you and exists nowhere else. That doesn't make it unreal or inauthentic in any way; it simply makes it independent of circumstance. Enjoyment is exactly and only what it is, and knowing this empowers its creation. If a better life is your goal, then seeking balance and understanding the nature of good and bad would be useful undertakings.

14:15   Balance in life choices not only helps put things into perspective, it provides a healthier and more sustainable development and platform for growth. Contrasting whatever you perceive to be occurring with the concept of what is absent or preferred will "position" your current experience somewhere on a scale of better or worse. This means that your interpretation and relationship to whatever is perceived or experienced will be compared to your ideals to determine whether it is good or bad, and the degree to which it is either. Knowing this helps you develop an ability to keep a broader perspective and not get overly caught up in either the good or the bad. In other words, to not take it too seriously.

14:16   On the other hand, maintaining a constant sense of balance between what seems to be positive or negative will result in less reactivity because it allows a more sober and awake relation to whatever is experienced. From this perspective, the choices you make and the actions you take are likely to be more free of bias and ignorance, and so more stable and durable in the long run. To say it another way, life won't seem to turn around and bite you in the ass as often.

The most marvelous experience of life is to transform according to reality, not imagination.
—Vernon Howard

Balancing between Mind and Consciousness

14:17 In this kind of investigation, there needs to be a balance between the psychological and the existential. What I mean by that is, in order to make real progress, you shouldn't get bogged down in only working on your self-mind. Although it is essential to uncover unrecognized aspects of mind, you don't want to restrict your investigation by trapping your consciousness within a closed loop of psychology. You'll only be looking within your current experience as it is. Even if some aspect of this current experience is unrecognized, it is still a part of "as it is."

14:18 To get free of this domain of limited consciousness, you also have to consider what's true "existentially." You need to grasp, either experientially or directly, the real nature of the subject matter's *existence*. This provides the "space" to relate to that experience very differently. For example, discovering a bottom-line assumption may reveal something previously unrecognized about yourself. This can alter your perspective on related matters to some extent and give access to a deeper degree of honesty and integrity. Since such discovery reveals something new about the foundations of your self-framework, you could think this is the end of the story. You may fail to recognize that stopping here limits your investigation to the content of mind.

14:19   By contrast, if you keep going and proceed to grasp the *existential* nature of the bottom-line—or even the whole dynamic of mind that creates such assumptions—you will discover that what was formerly held as simply an inherent aspect of your self-nature is actually an activity you're *doing* rather than something you *are*. Your consciousness and so experience will be fundamentally changed because you will be in touch with how and where this self-aspect is created, thus allowing you to experience it as unreal and unnecessary. From here you are capable of eliminating the assumption rather than just recognizing it. This produces a completely new domain of change within your conscious experience.

14:20   Another example of a different kind can be found in your attachment to the body as an indispensable aspect of yourself. This is a reasonable and common self-identification because the mind is related to the brain, and perception appears to occur only through the body. But your body-identity comes with a lot of add-ons. Within the psychological, your experience of your body is tied up with a body-image, judgments about your body, level of attractiveness, assessed physical abilities, and other body-related issues. These will contribute to your self-image and identity.

14:21   Beyond the psychological relationship, there are distinctions made about the nature or substance of one's self-existence. Concurrent with body identification is a common assumption that one is not only (or not even) a body, but that one's self exists somewhere inside the body as an "object" without physical form. All these perspectives will strongly contribute to your self-experience, both psychologically and "existentially." These are just starting points, however, that direct attention to the already assumed experience of your self in regard to your body, and none of them is actually an existential insight.

14:22   If you were to become conscious of the true nature of the body, or even just contemplate the existence of bodily experience—something few would even think to do, since we're sure we already know what the body is—you might discover a very different reality than what's currently experienced and lived. I don't want to suggest what you might find because that would interfere with an open investigation on your part, but imagine seeing this *object* in a previously unimaginable light.

14:23   This would then open up a totally different relationship to the occurrence or activity that is your body, fundamentally changing your relationship to your self-idea. Your "psychology" relative to all things physical would be shifted to a new context, possibly eliminating many experiences and assumptions, problems and attachments in the process. Because it would be founded on an "objective" or existential consciousness, your new perspective would exist outside the domain of personal psychology or mind. This would free you from many lifelong beliefs, allowing a fresh look at your own self-experience. If, for example, you found out that existentially you aren't an object, or that objects aren't what you thought they were, everything associated with *being* an object would disappear, as would so many previous assumptions regarding the objective world and your place within it.

14:24   Yet, to concentrate solely on the existential carries the risk of falling into philosophical traps and remaining abstracted from the reality in which you live—the one you're *doing* and *being* as a self. When people aspire to grasp absolutes, they tend to focus on abstract notions or philosophical ideals. Here lies a real danger of remaining intellectual and thus lacking groundedness and depth in your investigations. Such efforts don't lead to really grasping absolutes but tend instead to keep you in denial of the experience you are "living." Until you can ground the *truth of existence* within your *experience of reality*, the two will remain separated in your consciousness, and the ultimate Truth will remain inaccessible.

14:25   In all matters of consciousness, the deeper you go, the more you need to balance your investigations with both the experiential *and* the existential. The experiential tells you what you are *doing*. The existential tells you what you *are*. In either case, becoming increasingly conscious of what is true allows for freedom from previously held assumptions, whether psychological or existential in nature.

14:26   The principle of balance can be beneficially applied to many different dynamics, subjects, experiences, and perspectives. As a principle, it is not limited to one way of using it or one way of thinking about it. If you investigate what this principle is, you might find something empowering. Balance and responsibility aren't the only principles to consider, however; there are many others—for one, joining.

The Principle of Joining

14:27   Within the field of effective interaction, whether physical or communicative, we find the principle of joining very useful. Joining has several components to it, one of which is accepting rather than resisting whatever is occurring. Another is to perceive and follow (stay conscious of and in sync with) whatever is happening. Once this connection is made, the third element is to contribute to what's occurring, adding what we will of our own energies. In a martial domain, this is done by blending with someone else's action and actively merging with what's happening; from there, we can choose to take over and redirect the action for our benefit.

14:28   Applying this same principle to our own internal activities or our challenges with personal growth, we find a similar effectiveness. Especially with difficult experiences, our first impulse is to move away or resist, which puts us at odds with our own experience. It's a natural and common reaction since the "job" of the experience—the emotional or mental state that arises as a reaction to what's encountered—is to press us into some disposition that is consistent with our self-survival. In the case of disagreeable experiences, this is usually to avoid or oppose them.

14:29   While the impulse to evade discomfort is the knee-jerk response of survival, when all is said and done, such opposition often leaves us in no better place with the experience or the circumstances to which we were reacting. All we manage to do is get through an unpleasant ordeal, whether minor or major. On the other hand, if instead of running away or resisting it, we consciously let the experience *be* and fully embrace its presence, we can then join with it.

14:30   We discussed this already in Chapter Eleven's "Learning to Enjoy Suffering," but it is worth revisiting from a slightly different perspective. By joining some reaction or experience, you become one with it, so to speak, and immediately stop resisting it. The power it had over you through your own resistance or evasion diminishes markedly, and the experience itself changes. It *has* to change because your previous reaction was a large contributor to your experience. This sounds almost too simple to be true, but once you embrace the experience, the mind is drawn to see it in a more positive light.

14:31   Since any reactivity or internal struggle is something you're doing, joining what you're already doing stops the conflict brought about by resisting it or trying to run from it. Instead of being engaged in two conflicting activities—experiencing a reaction plus struggling against it—you cease to struggle, and do only one activity. Once you move your consciousness to be in harmony with the experience, you can begin to take control, since you are now actively participating with its generation rather than battling with it. You can then steer it toward a more beneficial outcome. If you are conscious enough about what it is and why it exists, you can stop it altogether.

14:32 Let's look at an example. Say you're feeling depressed and moody— just about everyone has been there to some degree, so try to conjure up a realistic scenario. You wallow in a negative disposition that you feel is impossible to overcome. Your feeling of hopelessness is such that you hardly even care to continue with life— which, of course, you hate, and feel is all bullshit. Not only that, you feel like you are a piece of crap, inferior, incompetent, and not worth keeping alive. How's that? Is that a good enough bad experience for you?

14:33 So say this is your experience. You may want to get angry, or curl up in a ball on the floor, or fall into a mood of despair, or entertain some other negative and hopeless reaction. Perhaps you want to fight with it, or maybe you want to succumb and just let it overpower you. Another option, however, is to *join* the experience, letting it be and acknowledging its presence without resistance. Moving your feeling-attention as if to embrace whatever's there, without trying to change it in any way. In doing so, you begin to "join" the experience, not just intellectually or as a belief, but fully feeling and embracing it with no need for intellectual understanding at all.

14:34   When you join it completely, neither avoiding nor trying to alter it in any way, you put yourself in the same place as the activity. You fully *do it*, rather than resist or struggle with it, even slightly. This may seem counter-intuitive, as though it would only increase your suffering. Maybe you feel you'd be better off kicking and screaming against it. Still, you decide to go ahead and follow this illogical and stupid course recommended by some guy in a book. You move into the experience, fully feeling it, letting it be, and merging with it.

14:35   It's crucial that you don't confuse "joining" with acting out the negative experience, or overdramatizing it, or succumbing to it. Those activities occur in a different domain from what I'm recommending; they are all aspects of the usual reaction to difficult internal states. When joining what's there, you're not trying to maintain or keep the reaction the same as when it began, but neither are you suppressing it. You are simply moving all of your feeling-attention toward what seems to be the experience at hand. If it changes, fine, just keep moving in the direction of fully experiencing whatever seems to be there at the moment, as if it were an objective substance you could absorb or merge with.

14:36   Although you may initially experience it as bad, the experience will morph as you continue to join it. When it starts to become acceptable, maybe even satisfying in some unknown way, this means you're onto something. You become aware that it is indeed something that you want to do because you *are* doing it. Contrary to common sense, you might even enhance it, as if trying to *make* it happen on purpose. This puts you more and more in touch with the role you play in creating it. If you can enhance it, then you begin to experience that you're probably creating it in the first place. You may not find the source or "control switch" right away, but you get a sense that you are still somehow behind it. In this way, you are consciously doing it or creating it rather than holding it as if inflicted upon you. Your mind has joined with the experience and so you're in the driver's seat now.

14:37 Once you join with the depression—which you may not even call by that name anymore—you can choose to soak in it, or turn it around, or eliminate it. Your abilities here will depend on your level of consciousness in the matter. When you experience the real nature of whatever it is that you struggle with, you will discover that it's an activity you do with your own mind, an aspect of your self-survival. Your programmed unrecognized self-framework created this particular experience in order to manage life consistent with its own self-perspective. You may not know why you'd create such a thing or what it gets you, but your uncognized matrix of mind knows why, and so can you if you become conscious of what that is all about. But even shy of such a breakthrough, once you experience creating it, you can stop doing it.

14:38 Part of "managing" life is attempting to deal with a variety of what are interpreted as difficult circumstances. The goal may be to benefit your self in some way (which is not to say cause you pleasure), but that doesn't mean you're doing a good job of it. What your bottom-line mind decides you should do—as in the case of being depressed—isn't always effective or useful in any reasonable way. The foundation that generates the impulse doesn't exist in the domain of mind that you generally access, so the source of any particular reaction will likely elude you. Because it's rooted in assumptions within your uncognized matrix of mind, the reaction will still seem valid. This is territory we've covered, and you're already aware that contemplating the nature of your drives and emotions—becoming conscious of their bottom-line origins—makes a big difference in your ability to deal with them.

What you might not realize is that joining whatever comes up is an option that's available to you regardless of your current depth of understanding.

14:39 Don't underestimate the power of this simple principle. Joining with an internal state tends to reveal its conceptual nature, which moves you into a position of being *at the source* of the activity rather than merely at the effect of it. In other words, embracing the experience shifts your relationship to it such that you are empowered to change the experience itself. Instead of remaining stuck on the "receiving end" of some painful reaction, actively embracing it allows you to experience that you are, in fact, the one generating it. Taking charge of a reaction to any degree diminishes its power to dominate you, and no matter how far you get, a shift will occur. Check it out.

The Truth Transcends Negative and Positive

14:40 The word "harmony" is rooted in the Latin *harmonia*, which means "joining" or "concord." The Latin root of the word "concord" translates roughly as "together-heart." Simply considering the last two sentences, it's quite obvious how much we're affected by connotations of the terms we use. We watch always for the subtlest of signals, anything to indicate ups and downs, positives and negatives, in order to automatically position our "selves" to whatever is encountered.

14:41 When you perceive anything (an object, an animal, an idea), it is immediately placed in a positive or negative light. Think about it—what comes to mind when you imagine a rabbit? How about a vulture? These are simply animals and yet you probably have a very different "feel" and sense of each of these. So it is with everything. I've explained why this is so, and yet even the explanation itself is fed into the same system of assessment.

14:42   For example, we're naturally predisposed to being attracted to anything that suggests harmony and love, effectiveness and growth, cooperation and well-being, because through them our personal experience is enhanced. When we're touched by such principles, in fact, we tend to feel good about our experience of life and to imagine a better world. Each of these principles points to humanity's "better" instincts and seems to be arrived at through reason and free will, which also have quite positive associations. It's almost impossible not to hear these principles as good.

14:43   Just so, when I assert that our entire experience is founded upon self-survival, not only does it seem as though some element of choice is compromised, but even the word "survival" carries implications of threat, hardship, and struggle, all of which contribute to a sense of negativity about the whole matter. Declaring that no experience or belief is the Truth may also sound depressing or negative, while in reality it is neither. Becoming depressed about these unvarnished truths is inappropriate and is based on a misunderstanding.

14:44   These assertions sound negative because of the very fact that all our impulses and perceptions are dominated by self-survival. The principle itself makes its own name sound negative! The idea that life and self have such seemingly ignoble motives flies in the face of the preferred visions and fantasies that are consistent with self-significance. The truth about this domain, however, is that it contains a very broad spectrum of possibilities.

14:45 All of *life* is based upon the principle of survival, and people rarely hold the idea of *life* as a negative. Everything "good" comes out of this principle, yet wherever there is good, there must also be bad, so everything bad comes from it as well. Still, there is a vast difference in experience and effectiveness between actions that are based on the selfish motives of an unrecognized self-agenda and the conscientious pursuit of honest communication and cooperative effort. Both are in one's self-interest; one is just healthier and more enlivening than the other.

14:46 Remember, the fact that life is meaningless and that the truth has no value shouldn't be heard as something negative. It transcends negative and positive. The life we live is carried out with a sense of purpose and meaning, which can either be negative or positive. Meaning is *created,* so if you want a meaningful life, you need to create an empowering purpose. Even within self-survival, it is possible to detach from personal and cultural assumptions and programming that restrict your consciousness to the same old patterns of running on the wheel, and instead create a free and open experience that is genuine and enlivening. Just take care not to mistake any of it for the Truth!

When love and hate are both absent,
everything becomes clear and undisguised.
Make the smallest distinction, however,
and heaven and earth are set infinitely apart.
If you wish to see the truth then hold no opinion for or against.
The struggle of what one likes and what one dislikes
is the disease of the mind.
—Sengcan

Intense Contemplation and Life

14:47   If you are truly intent on becoming conscious of your true nature, at some point you will wind up alone with yourself, which is a good place to get serious. Even just physically removing your life distractions can be useful—disconnect the phone, set aside electronic devices, forget the TV, step away from your relationships, forget about work or recreational projects. Be alone with yourself—without all the usual distractions—for hours, or for days on end if you can. The aim here is to be *bored!* Without the distractions that you normally keep whirling around you, your mind will likely struggle with where to put its attention. This may be an uncomfortable process, but eventually your mind will calm down and you will begin to notice the present moment.

14:48   You may find it's more difficult than you thought. It may take quite some time for you to quiet your mind enough to settle in and be present. When your attention begins to be distracted by simple things that wouldn't normally register—maybe noticing a speck on the wall, or the appearance of a butterfly, or wondering about a meaningless noise—then you're getting there. Becoming more sensitive and present can be painfully mundane, but stay with it and resist the urge to seek out new distractions. Just be bored. You will be tempted to start daydreaming, or fantasizing, or going over memories, or acting out some drama in your mind. Don't. You need to let all that go, each and every time such distractions arise. Just return to being present and alone and with your self "as is" until you can't stand it.

14:49   Of course you *can* stand it, you're merely struggling with very strong habits of mind. Don't look elsewhere, or be distracted.

Simply be present. Now you can better ask the question, "Who am I?" Just focus on the fact of being aware, and ask, "Who is aware?" Don't try to fill in your awareness, just focus on trying to be conscious of the fact that you are aware. Grasp the source of being aware and stay there. Be still. Don't entertain yourself or have imaginings. Once you grasp who you are, then open up and intend to get the truth of your own existence in this moment.

I'm the one who has to die when it comes time for me to die.
—Jimi Hendrix

14:50 Over time, usually only after many days or weeks of unbroken, unrelenting contemplation, you will exhaust all available methods, everything you suppose might get you to the Absolute truth of you. This is good, because there is no method that can work—there is nowhere to go, no distance to cover, no process to engage. But don't try to bypass every effort to get there. You need to truly and experientially get this, trying everything you can to get what you really are—until there is nothing left for you to try. Eventually you will come up against a blank wall, so to speak, of true not-knowing, and can go no further. You don't know where to turn or what to do. The wall seems impenetrable. Stay there. Face the wall and stay. There is nowhere to go. You already are. The truth already is. Become directly conscious of what you are already. Stay pressed up against the wall of your ignorance until you get *you*—your true nature.

14:51 Beyond intense contemplations like this—which are invaluable and necessary to focus the mind and attention in ways not usually available in daily life—it isn't useful to hold such work as somehow separate from or different than the life you are living. As you work on consciousness, there will be a tendency to divide your experience into consciousness work, such as contemplation, being honest, introspection, and the like, and then "real life." You may contemplate profound truths, but then you go to lunch. When you enter into your "normal" life, there's a tendency to "put consciousness work on a shelf," as though it is a separate activity from the rest of life. This isn't a good idea. Take on the work everywhere and at all times.

14:52 This is not to say that you need to do formal contemplation in every moment, just don't separate them. Your so-called "real life" should be the very subject matter of consciousness and is definitely "the place" for transformation. When an artificial barrier is unconsciously put up between the two, holding them as somehow different and incompatible, a false relationship is likely to emerge regarding each. You'll tend to see normal life as a failure to measure up to your more "enlightened" moments, and consciousness work as artificially limited to its own time and place. It's best to break down this separation. Your solitary contemplations support your consciousness work in your daily life.

14:53 Consciousness and Truth are true and appropriate whether you are on vacation or sitting in a monastery. I'm not recommending a humorless approach to vacationing. On the contrary, I'd recommend fulfilling the purpose of the vacation by having fun and recreating, all with great humor and enjoyment. The question though is why is this activity separate in any way from the Truth or Consciousness? The idea is to know what it *is* no matter what you experience. What is humor, what is fun, why do they exist? What is enlightenment when you're on vacation? Does the Truth disappear because you took a break, or went to work, or someone died? No, not at all. Otherwise, it's not the Truth. So there's no benefit and much detriment to thinking and living as if these are different.

Questioning ourselves this way is quite unusual for most of us. We need to learn "where" to look, and then do so repeatedly and with honesty.

14:54   We've covered a great deal of useful material in this book, and grasping all of what's been communicated may appear to be a daunting task. You may be tempted to adopt a belief system as a cosmological overview in order to pin all this down. I don't recommend it—it will only act as a barrier between you and real Consciousness. I know it's next to impossible to avoid picturing some universal cosmology because your mind needs a way to hold all of these ideas and distinctions. Yet when you create a "picture" or belief system that seems consistent with the ideas you hear, this will become a kind of object-imagery. In other words, reality will be held as if it is separate objects—even if these "objects" are abstract or ethereal in nature—putting each in some "place" in the scheme of things and in relation to each other. This is simply the mind's "method" of trying to make sense of stuff generally inaccessible, and it won't be accurate or true. *It can't* be. But if you find it helpful at first to do this in order to keep things clear in your mind, remember to hold it as temporary and untrue, dropping it as soon as you can.

You may now return my camel.
—Abdul

Ask Consciousness

14:55 When students depart from a long workshop, or especially an apprenticeship, sometimes they panic at the prospect of a solitary pursuit of consciousness. Since finishing this book doesn't involve physically leaving a more monastic support structure, I don't suppose readers will get too worked up about coming to the last pages. At the same time, if you're serious about this work, there may be some sense that you're going to be on your own now. Whether or not that's the case, I want to send you off with one last tool that could prove useful as you push on ahead with this work.

14:56 As I've mentioned a few times already, most of the information I communicate, both in person and in books, comes from direct conscious experience. In workshop dialogues, people sometimes marvel at how difficult it seems to "stump" me, and I've heard comments about how I'm always "on" and able to tackle every aspect of these matters. While appearances may indicate that I know a lot, it isn't what it seems. It is also something you can gain access to for yourself.

14:57 Normally we learn through demonstration, explanation, and memorization, and sometimes through talking things out until we get clarity. When we say that we *know* something, we're referring to the ability to conceptually call up specifics from our collection of stored mental "objects." Because most of the "knowledge" that I share comes from direct-consciousness rather than a store of intellectual memory, it arises differently. For one thing, it is a relatively "silent" process, with no reaching into memory to clutch at verbiage, as I do with everyday matters. It is also more "effortless" in the sense that I don't have to "know" anything, I simply must "experience" it.

14:58   So although my communication regarding consciousness may be heard as "knowledge," something known, it's useful to recognize that the foundation of this knowledge appears less like a memory bank and much more like a state of not-knowing. It's actually Consciousness itself and, remember, the nature of Consciousness is *Nothing*—it has no "element" to it. Since absolutes can't be represented by any kind of "object"-distinction, the mind can't resort to its usual methods of knowing, i.e., creating an image, thought, feeling, or any other form. With no capacity for direct access, mind's rendition of Consciousness simply appears more like a heightened state of not-knowing.

14:59   When "tapped," this Consciousness can produce distinctions appropriate to whatever aspect of the human condition is being addressed. They're already present, so to speak, but in an unformed way. It's as if the question itself generates the distinctions, which then arise from Consciousness as a response in the form of "knowledge." Sort of like a hammer (question) hitting a bell (Consciousness) and creating a perceivable sound (knowledge). The "knowledge" only shows up when the bell is struck.

14:60   Even if direct-consciousness is currently just a vague notion for you, you can still access such knowledge in a similar way—both prior to and between major breakthroughs. While a state of not-knowing isn't the same as a personal connection to the Absolute, short of direct-consciousness it is the closest that we can get with the self-mind. Maintaining an open backdrop of not-knowing and wonder also appears to be an optimal foundation for contemplating this work. By now, you probably understand how to reach a state of not-knowing. From there, you can indirectly access a deeper consciousness by opening up and as if "asking" Consciousness what's true.

14:61   It's a bit tricky to convey what "asking Consciousness" is all about. To make it active, you'll have to create this function for yourselves. To make it effective, you must include: ruthless self-honesty, reason beyond your beliefs, a vigilance for hidden assumptions, and continually reaching toward a more genuine openness to complement your blank slate of not-knowing. This sounds complicated and unwieldy but, with experience, the practice becomes more familiar and straightforward. As a matter of fact, it's beyond simple—it's like nothing at all.

14:62   Not surprisingly, it was my students who helped me figure out how to ground this idea for others. I'd been told that when some of them ran into questions or challenges, they would ask themselves or each other: what would Ralston say? They found that simply framing the question with their teacher in mind would immediately help them know how to approach the issue at hand.

14:63   Of course this only works for those who've spent a good deal of time with me, largely because I'm the one actively facilitating their consciousness, honesty, and commitment to the truth. Because of this, over time they get a good sense of how I would direct them, and they can easily take on this function for themselves. In other words, they can access the same consciousness. All they need to do is look at the issue as if "from the outside," by using what their minds have created as this "Consciousness function" as represented by their teacher.

14:64 In a similar vein, you can "ask Consciousness" how to proceed with your transformation or enlightenment work, or your life, or even what questions to ask. Because Consciousness is wed to honesty—honesty is always seeking the truth—you know that it will demand integrity, be unbiased, and push you toward a perspective consistent with those qualities. Although Consciousness isn't at all limited to reason and is well beyond programming and beliefs, the open and intelligent application of rationality, along with a healthy dose of not-knowing, can help to point you in the right direction. You may have to wait a while for something to become clear, or it may be obvious immediately. Remain open and honest, and reach out. Some direction will arise in due course.

In Conclusion

14:65 Although this book was conceived for people familiar with my work, it's still difficult to predict how successful such an attempt at communication will be. The subject matter just doesn't easily lend itself to being understood within the context and assumptions that *are* our shared experience of reality. As always, I invite you to directly grasp what is ultimately true and settle the matter for yourself. Until that occurs for you, some of what I have said here will likely remain unintelligible. Since I can't foresee which parts might spark a breakthrough or help someone get free of an overlooked assumption or even an entire mind-set, all I can do is send it out and see what you do with it. I wish I could simply hand enlightenment to you but, as I found out early on, it just doesn't work that way.

14:66 We can see that the pursuits of Consciousness and transformation are complementary and this relationship is most beneficial when both objectives are undertaken with diligence and clarity. Using what's presented here to engage in fantasies about transformation or enlightenment can only obscure your understanding and sabotage your intentions, so keep an eye on yourself. This book contains a wealth of communication that I hope serves you in your efforts. Although I tried to be as clear as possible, the writing is dense at times. If the Truth matters to you, I know you'll meet me partway by taking the time to investigate what's presented until it becomes your own personal experience. I wish you all the best with your contemplations.

Free yourself. Know the Truth.
Be happy and enjoy whatever you experience.

ABOUT THE AUTHOR

Since having several enlightenment experiences in his early twenties, Peter Ralston has devoted his life to a relentless pursuit of the truth, investigating everything from the principles that govern movement and interaction to the true nature of self and reality.

As part of the San Francisco Bay Area consciousness movement in the 1970s, he founded Cheng Hsin *("true nature")*, a dogma-free approach to consciousness that assists people from all walks of life in exploring every aspect of their personal experience of *Being*, including enlightenment. He is also the creator of The Art of Effortless Power and in 1978 became the first non-Asian to win the World Championship full-contact martial arts tournament in China. He has students in more than thirty countries and travels the world teaching this work.

Ralston's other titles include *The Principles of Effortless Power, Zen Body-Being,* and *The Book of Not Knowing,* which *Spiritual Enlightenment* magazine voted the "Book of The Year" in 2010, calling it "a must-have book for the serious spiritual seeker." His books have been published in six languages.

For more information about the work of Peter Ralston, visit:
ChengHsin.com
or
PeterRalston.com

About North Atlantic Books

North Atlantic Books (NAB) is an independent, nonprofit publisher committed to a bold exploration of the relationships between mind, body, spirit, and nature. Founded in 1974, NAB aims to nurture a holistic view of the arts, sciences, humanities, and healing. To make a donation or to learn more about our books, authors, events, and newsletter, please visit www.northatlanticbooks.com.

North Atlantic Books is the publishing arm of the Society for the Study of Native Arts and Sciences, a 501(c)(3) nonprofit educational organization that promotes cross-cultural perspectives linking scientific, social, and artistic fields. To learn how you can support us, please visit our website.